# Popular Culture in Hong Kong After the National Security Law, 2020–2022

In this study, Ng examines the aftermath of the massive protests in 2019 and the implementation of the National Security Law in Hong Kong.

Despite 2 years of fluctuating COVID measures and social constraints, the city witnessed an unparalleled cultural resurgence after the enactment of the National Security Law in 2020. This book explores Hong Kong beyond the end of the Anti-Extradition Bill Movement in 2019, to examine what happened afterward, how society repaired itself, how the people of the city resumed their everyday life, and what this everyday life entails. Ng examines the social debates and conversations during these 2 years, analyzing a wide range of creative projects in the city, from television shows, popular music, and social media to literary writings. She describes the difficulties, emotional experiences, and also daily strategies to repair local life, recreate a self-identity, and reclaim the city's narrative against the pressures from China.

This book is a valuable resource for researchers, scholars, students, and general readers interested in popular culture and society, and the global uprisings of the first decades of the twenty-first century. The study, supported by detailed research, also makes this essential reading for those with a specialized interest in global studies, and China and Hong Kong studies.

**Janet Ng** is Professor at the Department of English at the City University of New York, USA.

## Routledge Contemporary Asia Series

**83. The Geopolitics of Health in South and Southeast Asia**
Perspectives from the Cold War to COVID-19
*Edited by Vivek Neelakantan*

**84. Knowledge Production and Epistemic Decolonization at the End of Pax Americana**
*Edited by Naoki Sakai, Jon Solomon, and Peter Button*

**85. Asia's Heritage Trend**
Examining Asia's Present through Its Past
*Edited by Jong-Il Kim and Minjae Zoh*

**86. Creationism in a South Korean Culture**
Science, Religion, and the Struggle against Evolution
*Hyung Wook Park*

**87. Asianization of Asia**
*Chang Kyung-Sup, Kim Taekyoon and Lee Joonkoo*

**88. Varieties of Civil Society Across Asia**
*Edited by Akihiro Ogawa and Anthony J. Spires*

**89. Indian Traces in Korean Culture**
The Legend and Beyond
*Renata Czekalska*

**90. Popular Culture in Hong Kong After the National Security Law, 2020–2022**
*Janet Ng*

For more information about this series, please visit: www.routledge.com/Routledge-Contemporary-Asia-Series/book-series/SE0794

# Popular Culture in Hong Kong After the National Security Law, 2020–2022

**Janet Ng**

Routledge
Taylor & Francis Group
LONDON AND NEW YORK

First published 2025
by Routledge
4 Park Square, Milton Park, Abingdon, Oxon OX14 4RN

and by Routledge
605 Third Avenue, New York, NY 10158

*Routledge is an imprint of the Taylor & Francis Group, an informa business*



*British Library Cataloguing-in-Publication Data*
A catalogue record for this book is available from the British Library

ISBN: 9781032860893 (hbk)
ISBN: 9781032860916 (pbk)
ISBN: 9781003521280 (ebk)

DOI: 10.4324/9781003521280

Typeset in Times New Roman
by Newgen Publishing UK

# Contents

# Acknowledgments

I am grateful to the PSC-CUNY Award for supporting the writing of this book. Also, I wish to acknowledge my colleagues and friends at the English Department of the College of Staten Island, and my friends beyond the college, who have offered much support, encouragement, and stimulating conversations over the years. I am especially grateful to those who have read parts of the project and have discussed with me the many issues in it. Rather than to give an accounting of my debts here, I prefer to offer my thanks in private. However, I do wish to take this opportunity to thank the reviewers of my manuscript. I have benefited tremendously from their thoughtful and helpful comments and criticisms. I also want to thank the wonderful team at Routledge, especially Clarissa Lim, whose encouragement, support, and good cheer made the process a pleasure.

# Introduction

In 2019, Hong Kong was rocked by a series of protests—the so-called "Anti-Legislation Movement" against the proposed "Fugitive Offenders and Mutual Legal Assistance in Criminal Matters Legislation (Amendment) Bill" that would allow the transfer of fugitives in Hong Kong, including political dissidents, to be tried in China. Critics of the law argued that it was a violation of Hong Kong's judicial sovereignty guaranteed under Hong Kong's Basic Law and the "One Country, Two Systems" arrangement with China. To many Hong Kong residents, this was another example of Beijing's increasing assertion of control over the city. A broad section of Hong Kong society, including many in the legal profession and even civil services, who were obligated by law to refrain from political activities, participated in demonstrations against the Bill. Many of the city's young people organized a series of protests against the Hong Kong government that got progressively more disruptive and violent. The normally bustling city was paralyzed for months. In response, China's central government imposed a new National Security Law (NSL) on the city by fiat. The NSL that came into effect on June 30, 2020, gave the Beijing-controlled Hong Kong government far-reaching authority, essentially outlawing any public expression of political dissent. Immediately after its implementation, a new police hotline for reporting suspected anti-national security activities was set up. Amnesty International pronounced a "human rights emergency" in Hong Kong.[1] The city's "global freedom score" measured by the political advocacy NGO, Freedom House, fell from 59/100 in 2017 to 42/100 in 2022.[2] Even by the neoliberal standards of the Fraser Institute and Cato Institute's "human freedom" index, Hong Kong lost its constant position at the top spot as the "freest" place in the world (second only to Switzerland in 2017), slipping down to the 34th place in 2022.[3] In the category of "personal freedom," Hong Kong went from 32nd in the world in 2018 to 62nd by 2022.[4] "The death of Hong Kong" was pronounced in headlines around the world on the day of the implementation of the NSL.[5] The COVID pandemic that raged from 2020 to 2022 further cast a pall over the city with the government attempting to control infection numbers through on-again–off-again regimes of lockdown, mandatory quarantine, and social restrictions. Together with the resultant serious economic downturn and mass emigration, the city's prospects could not have been gloomier.

DOI: 10.4324/9781003521280-1

This discourse of the city's death is both unhelpful and unfair to the Hong Kong people continuing to live in the city, who were and are diligently inventing ways to adapt to the new restrictive reality, to strive for normalcy, and even to find hope and happiness. This volume examines what happened in the 2 years after the protest, how many in Hong Kong experienced and responded to the new law, and how they found ways to recover and resume their everyday life despite their political disappointments and economic setbacks.

I examine these issues over these 2 years through an analysis of a wide range of popular phenomena, cultural activities, and creative projects, from television shows, popular music, social media, and literary writings. Against all odds, the city's popular culture experienced an unexpected efflorescence even as the new law served as a powerful vise on free expression. It is my goal in this study to provide a record of the city immediately after the NSL, finding in these creative works, strategies for living in Hong Kong's new reality.

The 2 years after the implementation of the NSL, from 2020 to 2022, was an exceptional period in Hong Kong. The city had to adjust to many changes brought about by the new law. Slogans, symbols, and objects associated with the protests were banned. Books on "sensitive topics," or by dissidents, oppositional politicians, and academics, were removed from public libraries and schools. Many pro-democracy teachers and professors were sacked from their teaching posts or had their contracts rescinded. Television programs that were critical or satirical of the Hong Kong government were canceled.[6] In the atmosphere of fear, several major oppositional news media organizations were terminated. Many student, professional, and labor unions disbanded. Grassroot community and advocacy groups shut down. International NGOs and news media organizations moved out of the city. Thousands of protest participants were arrested. Lawmakers from oppositional parties were excluded from the legislature or arrested. These upheavals and the aftermath of the protests and the NSL were then exacerbated by protracted Zero COVID policies. As more and more doctors and nurses emigrated, having lost faith in the Hong Kong government, the medical system buckled under the pressures during the pandemic when the city suffered from staggering infection and death rates. Many iconic businesses succumbed to the economic consequences of the stringent COVID regulations. Many Hong Kong residents lost relatives and friends to the disease. Many lost their employment. Many were separated from families and friends as tens of thousands emigrated from the city, unable or unwilling to live under the new political conditions, or not wanting to expose their children to the new patriotic educational agenda. For 2 years, the city seemed to be bombarded daily by bad news.

Political issues notwithstanding, these were years when Hong Kong turned intensely inward, by necessity and by choice. Because of the COVID pandemic and the draconian quarantine rules, few Hong Kong people traveled out of the city; even fewer tourists came to Hong Kong. In 2018, Hong Kong's population of 7.5 million residents hosted an overwhelming 65 million tourists, with the majority from mainland China. In 2020, in contrast, Hong Kong received only 605,000 visitors.[7] The routine streams of Hollywood movies and international performers—the J-drama

[Japanese-drama] stars, the K-pop [Korean-pop] groups, or American and British pop singers—also dried up. Trapped in their city, without distraction or competition for attention from outside in these 2 years, Hongkongers focused on their own society. They reclaimed their city. They re-assessed, re-built, and re-invented. The result was an extraordinary revival of community and creative production.

The creativity of this period is a result of various groups and individuals self-consciously rejecting the official narrative of inevitability and the fatalist assessment of some domestic and overseas commentators about the future of Hong Kong. Despite these merchants of gloom and the pressure of the NSL, many still attempted to find volition to produce an alternative "Hong Kong story." New things were created. Some were strategies against despair; others were strategies to live normal lives. These new things would be invisible without understanding their creators' rejection of determinism—that "there is no alternative."

## *Hou hou sangwut* 好好生活 Continue to Live Well

It is important to point out at the outset that this study is not about continued resistance in the political sphere. The major democracy movement in HK was defeated. The NSL functioned as a leash on dissent. For the most part, Hongkongers retreated into private lives to focus on adjusting to a new alien reality, seemingly yielding to their political fate. However, daily practices and decisions on how to live are not made in a vacuum. They are responses to the conditions of the real world. While acts of resistance in everyday life indeed do not bring about political or structural change and have variously been dismissed as mere "pragmatic resignation" or "practical acquiescence,"[8] as Michel De Certeau argues, resistance is in the act itself, as a response, and not necessarily the result or even the intent of the actors.[9] Power and resistance co-constitute each other.[10]

However, beyond the narrow understanding of resistance that assigns it solely to organized struggle, or the general assertion that living in of itself is resisting, there is another, more fine-grained way to understand it, as a force of "quiet encroachment."[11] These are strategies of living that can expose the everyday mechanisms of domination, and by so doing attenuate their power. A particular attitude toward living can destabilize power relationships; it can open up possibilities, and generate new positions, conditions, and spaces for making alternatives and choices. In this volume, I will discuss some of these efforts of "quiet encroachment" as many Hong Kong people continue to occupy the spaces of their everyday itinerary but traversing it with a renewed understanding of the effect of their everyday strategies.

In this understanding, most of the works I discuss are "resistant" texts only in so far as they demonstrate a desire to extend the limitations of daily lives, whether physical or mental, as well as create narrative possibilities for the city. The focus on the activities of ordinary people is to avoid overemphasis on the power of the state. Culture, as in the performance of reading, thinking, self-cultivation, etc., expands individual space. Moreover, the cultivation of different activities and diverse voices can foster strongly differing views without overt antagonism, even when democratic politics are forbidden. As Hongkongers constantly encouraged each other in these years with the phrase, "*hou hou sangwut* (continue to live well)," everyday life in the city was also about preserving agency and redrawing the social and political space.

The city is a "social fact," as Kristin Ross argues via Henri Lefebvre, a space inhabited, formed, and continually being transformed through its inhabitants' everyday use.[12] No matter what government is in charge, or what kind of political structures are imposed upon the people, its space will conform to the contour of the daily use of its inhabitants. The space of Hong Kong is continually evolving according to the dedication of the inhabitants to carry on their normal lives.

## *Hoenggongjan* 香港人 Hongkongers

As in any society, there are many stories and voices in Hong Kong. "Hong Kong people" are not a homogenous group, either ethnically or politically. Despite the surface calm under the NSL, Hong Kong people don't all share similar political goals or even ideological aspirations. Many are not necessarily anti-government, even if they are not pro-government.

Until the recent two decades, Hong Kong people's identity had been heavily inflected by their self-assumed responsibility of upholding the city's image as a neoliberal paradise. They lived in an environment designed for the smoothest transaction of goods and capital and were trained to be facilitators of these ventures. The continued stability that led to the prosperity of the city's development took precedence over individual will, freedom, and rights. The city's residents even once took pride in the orderliness of their political demonstrations as a sign of their civic sophistication. It was a city in which civic rectitude and aptitude replaced civil rights or democratic negotiations as the basis of governance, abiding by the guiding principle of "*onding faanwing* 安定繁榮 stability and prosperity."[13]

It was with their comparative affluence and more advanced urban organization that Hong Kong people distinguished themselves from the Chinese mainlanders in the past. In 1997, Hong Kong's GDP per capita at USD27,330 was over 35 times that of China at USD783. However, this distinction based on wealth became increasingly meaningless as China began its double-digit growth, while Hong Kong, suffering from the impact of major worldwide events and financial crises, had experienced a continuous decline since 2003.[14] In order to devise a new way to foster a Hong Kong Identity, to distinguish it from China, in 2004, there was an effort in the city to determine a set of so-called Hong Kong "core values."

These "*Hoenggong hatsam gaazik* 香港核心價值Hong Kong Core Values" were first presented by a group of 300 Hong Kong residents representing 42 different professions, from academics and lawyers to public intellectuals.[15] These values include freedom, democracy, respect for human rights, equality and justice, peace and humanity, trust and transparency, respect for diversity, individuality, and professionalism; rule of law; clean government; tolerance of different stances and views; respect for press freedom; and judicial independence. These values were subsequently co-opted by the government, as Dapiran explains, "to articulate

Hong Kong's competitive advantage over the rest of China, and indeed much of Asia."[16]

In 2013, the former Chief Executive of Hong Kong, Leung Chun-ying (2012–2017) affirmed their importance to the city in his policy address:

> I pledged to the Hong Kong people that I will safeguard the interests of the people, and uphold the core values of Hong Kong, including human rights, rule of law, clean government, freedom and democracy, tolerance of different stances and views, and respect for press freedom. Among them, judicial independence and the rule of law are not only our cherished core values but also the cornerstone of Hong Kong's success. The Government is steadfastly committed to upholding these core values.[17]

Although this litany of attributes evolved over the intervening years according to the different social and political concerns at the time, its key values remained unchanged. The identity of a Hongkonger is fundamentally connected to these liberal values. In 2014, the term, "HongKonger or Hong Kongese," meaning "a native or inhabitant of Hong Kong," was added to the Oxford English Dictionary. This inclusion was interpreted by mainly pro-democracy politicians and pundits in Hong Kong at the time as a sign of international recognition of the distinction between Hong Kong and China.[18]

During the fiery Anti-Extradition Legislation protests of 2019, Hong Kong's society was bitterly divided between the pro-democracy group, self-identified as the Yellow ribbons, and the pro-Beijing, pro-establishment as Blue ribbons. These distinctions were fuzzy at best. In reality, there were different strands within each group. The so-called "deep yellows," for example, tended to be more idealistic and activist. There were the "localists," such as the members of Civic Passion, or Youngspiration. Some of them held deeply xenophobic, especially anti-mainland immigrant sentiments, and socially conservative views. There were those who were not averse to using violent means, such as the "braves," who felt that rather than compromise, it would be better to all go down together in mutual immolation (*laam caau* 攬炒). They would rather see the Chinese-controlled government fail than see Hong Kong transformed into another Chinese city. There were those who had so-called "*zingzi gitpik* 政治潔癖 political mysophobia," who refused to have anything to do with mainland China even after the protests, seeing it as ceding even more to China's control. These different tribes were also at odds with each other. However, these remained a minority among the general "yellows." The "blues," in contrast, were simpler. While some were staunchly loyal to Beijing, most tended to be pro-business, supported free-market capitalism, and were against social disorder. They were willing to tolerate, even cooperate with Beijing, as long as there was money to be made and prosperity restored to the city.

Pro-Beijing politicians often cast all the "yellows" as just a small band of troublemakers, while the "silent majority" was hostage to their violence. Dapiran, however, argues that a 2019 midterm election of District Councilors in fact revealed the opposite:

> The election was seen as a referendum pitting the protest movement against Lam's government and Beijing. And speak the people did, although they did not say what Lam and Beijing had hoped they would. In a day that saw Hong Kong's highest ever election turnout—with 2.9 million people, representing seventy-one percent of eligible voters, casting a vote—the pan-democrats won in a landslide. Pan-democrat candidates won 385 seats; pro-Beijing ('establishment', pro-government) candidates won only fifty-nine seats; eight seats went to independents...Pan-democrats won control of seventeen of the eighteen district councils; previously, they had controlled none...The results were unequivocal: a clear majority of Hongkongers supported the protest movement and placed the blame for the ongoing chaos at the feet of Lam, her government, and the pro-Beijing politicians who support her.[19]

Everything became color-coded in the city. Businesses and public personalities, especially actors and performers, were constantly scrutinized for their political purity. Participation in certain events organized by the wrong parties, especially those seen to have relationship with mainland organizations, or even the Hong Kong government, would be enough to turn their "yellow" supporters against them. A performer who was popular among the "yellows" might be a target of trolling by the blues, and vice versa. Popularity among a majority of "yellows" could not protect a performer from attacks by the "deep yellows." For those advocating "mutual immolation," any success under the current government was a betrayal.

When it comes to the issue of "national identity," there might be more coherence among Hong Kong people. The majority of Hong Kong residents, even some pro-Beijing "blues," would not self-identify as a "Chinese" person. According to a poll from the Public Opinion Program of the University of Hong Kong, in 2019, the year of the protest, 52.9% of Hong Kong's residents self-identified as "Hongkongers."[20] By 2021, in another survey conducted by the university, it was discovered that "the number of people who regarded themselves as 'Hongkongers' in a broad sense grew from 69% to 72%, while those who identified themselves as 'Chinese' in a broad sense dropped from 29% to 26%." A large number of these 26% considered themselves as both "Chinese" and "Hongkongers."[21] This means only a very small group in Hong Kong would recognize themselves as a Chinese person. There is a caveat to this result. Conducted after the implementation of the NSL and during the emigration wave, those who felt most strongly against China would already have left the city. Also, some of the responses might have been influenced by the pressure of the NSL. In other words, the actual number of those who identified as "Hongkongers" could be even higher. Although it had been over two decades since Hong Kong's "return" to China, only a small minority of residents considered themselves "Chinese nationals."

Regardless of politics, the notion of a Hongkonger has long transcended a homogenous, ethnic-based definition. Hong Kong is one of the most diverse (though not necessarily inclusive) cities in East Asia, where 8.4% of the population is non-ethnic Han Chinese. Even among the ethnic Chinese, many are from different areas of the world. The Hong Kong writer, Dung Kai Cheung, cautioned against a narrow understanding of the Hong Kong identity based on a simplistic notion of race and blood. Instead, he argued that it should be one of active "becoming," through writing, narrating, or other activities on behalf of the city.[22] It is one's relationship with the city, rather than one's blood lineage that defines one's belonging. This notion of a Hong Kong person, and even the idea of the city, is necessarily fluid, uncontrollable, and as such, full of possibilities.

In this volume, I use the term, Hongkongers, to represent the large segment of Hong Kong resident-card holders, both local-born and immigrants, regardless of ethnic background and nationality, who self-identify as a Hong Kong person, and who continue to believe in the Hong Kong core values, and as such, generally sympathetic to the city's various struggles for democracy of the past decade, even if they never participated in political activities. Despite the many internal contradictions within this group, they could probably all agree on their antipathy toward further "mainlandization" of Hong Kong's governance, an enforced Chinese nationalistic agenda in the city, and the dilution of local Cantonese language culture and social practices, seeing these as contradictory to the Hong Kong core values.

Nine years after the pledge from former Chief Executive Officer, Leung Chun-ying, to uphold Hong Kong's core values, in 2022, the then Secretary for Education, Kevin Yeung, called for the teaching of a new set of values in schools, namely, correct national history and culture, law-abidingness, empathy, diligence, perseverance, respect for others, responsibility, national identity, commitment, integrity, and care for others.[23] The original list that included attributes such as clean government, respect for human rights, freedom and democracy, etc., focused on the behavior of the government, emphasizing governmental restraint and respect for individual rights. In the list proffered by the Secretary of Education, the focus shifted to the disciplining of individuals for the sake of the nation. Loyalty to Beijing now took precedence over the protection of individual and intellectual freedoms from the arbitrary powers of the state. This dramatic revision of the city's core values was seen as a further betrayal of the political and social contract between the government and the people of Hong Kong that had defined Hong Kong's culture and identity for decades.

With the destruction of Hong Kong's former core values, the comment that Hong Kong was dead was perhaps not surprising. Perhaps it is even true—a staid, old notion of the city as the neoliberal capital of the world and a free market paradise is perhaps dying.[24] Maybe the new generation of Hongkongers, politically strangulated, had other aspirations for the city. Maybe their vision of what they needed to fight for had changed. As Foucault argues, "Maybe the target nowadays is not to discover what we are, but to refuse what we are."[25] To refuse an identity prescribed for one is a process of self-creation. It is also a form of resistance.

## *Jinzanzou mouliu je* 認真做無聊嘢 Seriously Doing Silly Things

The refusal of one's designated identity was a direct legacy of the 2019 protest. One of the five major demands of the 2019 protestors was for the government to withdraw its characterization of the political movement and the participants as rioters.[26]

In order to delegitimize the movement, the government insistently designated the protests as riots, and the young protestors as *haak bou* 黑暴 (black rioters), black being the color of the protest. At the height of the movement in July 2019, 96.2% of the Anti-Legislation Movement participants surveyed rated the demand for the government "to retract its characterization of the June 12 protest as riot" as "very important."[27]

When the protest largely abated by the beginning of 2020, one of the most prominent young leaders of the pro-democracy movements, Agnes Chow, launched a YouTube Channel. Chow was a leader in various political movements in Hong Kong. She began her activism at 16 in the 2012 school children's protest against the implementation of "patriotic education" in the school curriculum. In 2014, she was one of the student leaders of the Umbrella Revolution against the restrictive electoral system imposed by China for the 2017 election of Hong Kong's Chief Executive. Chow also attempted to run for a seat in the Hong Kong Legislative Council. However, her candidacy was disqualified, and she was eventually jailed for her participation in the 2019 Anti-Extradition Legislation Movement. (She has been living in exile since 2023, after her release from prison.) For her courage and personal sacrifices, she was called, "Our Mulan," by many Hongkongers, or the "Real Mulan," in deliberate contrast to the Chinese actress, Liu Yifei, who played the fictional heroine in the 2020 Disney film. (Liu's public support for the Hong Kong police and their forceful suppression of the protests made her deeply unpopular in the city, resulting in a boycott of the film.)[28] Despite the martial association with Mulan, it was Chow's composure, intelligence, articulateness, as well as fluency in multiple languages—Cantonese, English, and Japanese—that made her one of the most important faces of Hong Kong's struggle for democracy.

From February 2020, after the last embers of the protest had been stamped out, until the start of her prison sentence that November, Chow posted various short videos on her YouTube channel, amassing over 330,000 subscribers within a very short period of time. This was on top of her over half a million followers on Twitter, mostly in Japan, since she tweeted in Japanese. Being such a political icon in Hong Kong, one might have expected to find discussions of serious political or social issues on her YouTube channel. Surprisingly, Chow used her social media platform, not as an extension of her activism, but for entertaining and connecting with her supporters and fans. Chow explained in her inaugural YouTube video that while most people knew her as a serious student activist, she wanted to demonstrate her other side to the world. Indeed, Chow was charming in her videos. She used the platform to talk about her everyday life. She demonstrated cooking, played games with her viewers, gave lively Japanese lessons, and answered fans' questions about herself. She talked about clothes, toys, and food, just like many young women of her age. She sometimes spoke in Cantonese, sometimes in Japanese. All her videos were supplied with subtitles in Japanese and standard Chinese for her audience in Hong Kong, Japan, and Taiwan. However, embedded in her lively banter was a vein of facetiousness. For example, knowing that she was under surveillance, she discussed issues of cyber security, ways to circumvent hacking or electronic monitoring, and how to keep personal data safe. She thanked her Japanese audience for their support, including the #freeAnges campaign that circulated widely in Japan when she was first arrested. She showed herself purchasing a new computer when her old devices were confiscated by the police.

Similarly, another very prominent public face of pro-democracy activism in Hong Kong, the Cantopop star, Denise Ho, hosted a lively weekly podcast and YouTube talk show with actress, Wong Wing Sze. Ho and Wong invited different guests to their show, from pop singers to actors and writers. They bantered on about things in their everyday life, from pets, to travel, astrology, and personal habits, constantly joking about their "low brow" program. In episode 36, released on November 6, 2020, one month before Agnes Chow was sentenced to prison, they had her on their program as their guest. Contrary to expectations, instead of focusing on Chow's impending court appearance, the topic of their discussion was, "How to be an *otaku* goddess." Chow, being very pretty and petite, was an idol to a lot of young men in Hong Kong. However, she laughed about the many messages on her social media in simplified Chinese (i.e., from trolls from mainland China) that demanded to know why a pretty young woman like her could not just be quiet and be more obedient.[29]

In a city still reeling from high emotions and deep trauma immediately after the protests and the implementation of the NSL, these icons of the democracy movement decided to engage in what might appear to be mindless entertainment. Rather than being disappointed, their supporters embraced these other sides of their heroes.

Like many young people, Chow was labeled a "rioter," legally branded a criminal and a threat to the Chinese state. However, in her videos, she revealed herself to be a young woman like any other of her age, who liked pretty things, was deeply immersed in the world of Japanese anime and youth culture, liked to eat fun foods, and was cheerful, smart, and confident. One can't help but question, after watching her videos, what led such an otherwise lively and likable young person in Hong Kong to butt against the powerful state machine at such great cost to her own life. One can't help but wonder about a government that labeled an intelligent, fun-loving, and sweet young woman a threat to the state.

Denise Ho was similarly accused of being a traitor when she called attention to the plight of the protestors at the United Nations Human Rights Council and her non-violent political activities were considered a threat to the state. She had been blacklisted in China, forbidden to perform there since her participation in the 2014 Umbrella Movement. Her music was removed from all platforms in China. In her YouTube videos, Ho revealed herself to be funny, self-deprecating, and someone who enjoyed the ordinariness of life. One can't help but wonder as well, what was wrong with a society that led a Cantopop diva, adored by legions, to sacrifice her career in order to challenge the state. Whether it was their intention or not, Chow and Ho's online activities disputed their official characterizations. Their insistence on continuing with normal lives, pursuing their interest, and ignoring the constant legal threats against them allowed them to reclaim control over their own stories and identity, as well as rectify the distorted images created by the dominant media about them. In many ways, Chow and Ho's experiences and strategies mirrored that of the city. Hongkongers were also eager to take back the narrative of their city, through creatively living their everyday lives, and telling their stories in their own ways.

## Why Popular Culture?

In 2019, Beijing released the blueprint for the development of a megalopolis. Hong Kong was to be officially incorporated into the so-called Greater Bay Area, which also includes Macao and nine cities in China's Guangdong province. China proclaimed that this Greater Bay Area would be the next world-class business and tech hub. Many Hongkongers, however, regarded the city's new geographical designation with suspicion and cynicism and viewed this as another process of "mainlandization" by Beijing to diminish, and even destroy Hong Kong's uniqueness.

The efforts to "mainlandize" Hong Kong were multivarious, from the inculcation of patriotism (through ceremonial performances, such as flag-raising and nightly broadcasting of the anthem), to requiring Hong Kong's Cantonese-speaking population to study and use Putonghua (China's official language), to allowing more and more mainland Chinese to visit or settle in Hong Kong, etc. Many Hong Kong people are fearful that the incursion of mainland culture in Hong Kong will eventually obliterate their own culture and destroy the city's values. A strong localist sentiment developed in response, especially among the younger people. This localism played a large part in the 2019 protests, but it also promoted a renewed attention to local customs and material and popular culture.

Popular culture in Hong Kong has always played an outsized role in constructing the local identity since the 1970s. In the 2020s, popular culture, for many young people, became a defense against the forces of "mainlandization." In many ways, Hong Kong is similar to South Korea where popular culture is also a focus of identity. John Lie argues that because of South Korea's complex political history, first as a Japanese colony, followed by a catastrophic fratricidal war, before an all-out adoption of American capitalism, there is very little sense of a tradition on which South Koreans can base their identity:

> In Korea, what has replaced tradition, with its function of providing a sense of continuity and coherence, is popular culture. The bonds of proverbial imagined community of South Koreans are to be found in television waves and cyberspace, where common cultural contents are disseminated and national discussion takes place.[30]

Hong Kong as a British colony played an important role as a Cold War stalwart against communism, receiving hundreds of thousands of refugees fleeing China after 1949. In its dedicated development as a free market bastion, the city had always identified itself against China. It was what China was not. With a population of about seven million packed into a small space, and lacking identification with a "traditional" culture, the idea of Hong Kong is generated through its popular culture. It is not possible to discuss Hong Kong's identity without consideration of its popular culture.

From the 1970s to the 1990s, it was Hong Kong's television dramas, especially from Hong Kong's predominant broadcaster, Television Broadcasts Ltd. (TVB), that accompanied families at their dinners.[31] At the same time, it was Hong Kong's Cantopop music that provided a common soundtrack to the major and minor events in the city, as well as individual lives. In the 1990s, many sang together in Karaoke clubs, the love songs or inspirational songs that were popular at the time. This music did not just give expression but also helped shape and define individuals' emotional responses to their social and political conditions. At the same time, Hong Kong's cinema articulated a distinct image and generated mythologies for the city. All the different strains of popular culture together created, not just the city's stories, but a local lexicon in which a collective narrative was formed, delineating a very particular cultural identity among Hong Kong's residents.[32]

Hong Kong's unique Cantonese language culture had, by the 1980s and 1990s, created one of the most vibrant entertainment industries` in the world, exerting an important cultural influence in Asia and the world through its films and Cantopop music. These industries, however, suffered from almost a decade and a half of serious contraction beginning in the early 2000s. The Closer Economic Partnership Arrangement (CEPA) between Hong Kong and China in 2003, to foster Hong Kong's economic integration with China, gave Hong Kong entertainment companies and performers access to China's vast market through co-productions. The major entertainment corporations, production companies, and established performers, indeed, almost all the biggest names in Cantopop and Hong Kong cinema moved their bases to China to focus on this market. Since then, these stars rarely appeared in local films, or issued new Cantopop songs, having switched to singing in Putonghua (Mandarin) for their mainland audience. Hong Kong's entertainment industry lost a whole generation of talent to the mainland market, from production technicians to performers.[33] During the 2019 protests, whether out of self-preservation or genuine patriotism, many of these actors and singers openly pledged support for the Beijing-controlled Hong Kong government and backed the police suppression of the protestors, earning the contempt of many Hongkongers. Since then, many of them have become unwelcome back in their home territory.

However, even if the creative industry in the city had declined, creativity itself certainly did not. This was on flamboyant display in all the political movements, especially beginning with the 2014 Umbrella Movement. The activists were keenly aware of the visual impact of their actions in the media. Political demonstrations were no longer just marching with individual signs with witty slogans. They were about large public spectacles and sounds.[34] If the explosiveness of the 2019 Anti-Legislation protests put Hong Kong's decade-long struggle for democracy on the international stage, it was the visual impact from the extensive use of popular culture, such as graphic art, performances, film, and music, often professionally and beautifully produced, sometimes on a monumental scale, that garnered worldwide interest, as well as captured hearts and minds at home and abroad. One of the most spectacular images of the 2019 movement was a 30-mile-long glowing human chain called the Hong Kong Way, formed by tens of thousands of participants holding hands and flashing their cell phone lights. The chain stretched from Hong Kong Island to Kowloon, to the New Territories, picking out the iconic outline of Lion Rock Hill. The protest anthem, "Glory to Hong Kong," topped all Hong Kong's music charts in 2019. The MV, professionally produced and artfully designed, depicts a "Blorchestra (Black Orchestra)"—musicians in black clothes, yellow hard hats, and gasmasks (the uniform of the protest) performing in billowing smoke to represent both the "white terror" and tear gas enveloping the city. The producers and members of the orchestra also released different versions of the anthem sung in different languages that attracted international media as well as millions of views worldwide. "Glory to Hong Kong" became so closely associated with Hong Kong that a search for "Hong Kong national anthem" on Google a few years after the movement consistently yielded this song in the top results, much to the chagrin of the Hong Kong government. This protest song was broadcast erroneously as Hong Kong's national anthem during several international sporting events, causing great embarrassment to the Hong Kong government. The song was banned and removed from different media platforms, including YouTube, in 2024.

The high emotions of the Anti-Extradition Legislation Movement of 2019 unleashed tremendous creativity. The end of the movement might have meant the halting of all kinds of overt political expression. However, what came afterward in Hong Kong's popular culture was in many ways a continuation of this creative energy, re-directed and re-defined.

## *Ce joeng ngomun jyulok zi se* 且讓我們娛樂至死 Let Us Amuse Ourselves to Death

In the new NSL era, when they felt their identity was under threat, Hongkongers once again looked to the city's popular culture and rallied behind it. It was in the city's darkest moments in 2020 that Hong Kong's popular culture began an unexpected and brilliant resurgence. Replacing much of the old order, the monopolies, and the dominance of established and bankable mega stars, the industry in Hong Kong was now also driven by newer companies, collectives, and independent industry workers and artists. There was more flexibility and tolerance for innovation and change. New actors and directors brought new vigor and freshness to films, television programs, and other innovative visual media projects. The new generation of young performers had not merely revived interest in Cantopop but had whipped up so much fervor that they had veritably transformed the whole cultural landscape of the city. Also unprecedented was the spirit of collaboration and openness among these artists from across genres and styles, which resulted in a reinvigoration of music. Indirectly, they also brought attention to many other forms of popular culture, from dance to animation and illustration, to stage drama, and even to different kinds of sports.

Without a doubt, Hong Kong's new entertainment industry offered the public much escape and enjoyment, especially in the grim reality of the city. However, being entertained alone was no longer enough. The new audience saw themselves as playing roles that were more than just passive consumers. They believed they had a part to play in supporting and championing this local cultural revival.

In 2016, the Chinese translation of Neil Postman's 1985 book, *Amusing Ourselves to Death*, was reissued for the 20th anniversary of its publication, attracting a new generation of readers. Despite the fact that Postman's book was already over 30 years old, for obvious reasons, after the implementation of the NSL, it became one of the most talked-about books in Hong Kong, together with George Orwell's *1984* and Aldous Huxley's *Brave New World*. In 2020, the still independent public broadcaster, Radio Television Hong Kong (RTHK), aired a discussion of these books in the episode, "*Ce joeng ngomun jyulok zisei* 且讓我們娛樂至死 (Let us amuse ourselves to death)," in the popular philosophy talk show series, "Z*it hok jau gai king*哲學有偈傾 (There's much to talk about in philosophy)."[35]

In his work, Postman argues it is not merely Orwell's dystopic totalitarian world of mass surveillance that one should worry about. One should also be concerned about the scenario described in Huxley's *Brave New World*, in which people are so enraptured by mass entertainment they no longer read or think critically, becoming manipulable and acquiescent. In addition, the information we receive through mass media is often distorted. The presenters or actors, eager to hold our attention, design their delivery of information through manipulations of images, behavior, tone of voice, and general performance, in order to condition our reception of it. The scenario that Postman presents is a frightening one of mass distraction and manipulation.[36]

The attention Postman's book received reflected an anxiety among some Hongkongers in 2020 that despite the political idealism of the previous decades, the society would now fall into political complacence and social indifference under the enthrallment of mass entertainment. Considering the blatantly pro-establishment track record of major media corporations in recent years, the distrust of mass media was understandable. However, this worry about the effect of mass entertainment underestimates the power of pop culture as well as the agency and ingenuity of the consumers of entertainment. Postman and many in Hong Kong could not have foreseen the complexity and multidimensionality of recent fan culture. Fan activities in Hong Kong, especially surrounding the super group, MIRROR, which rose to popularity in 2021, defy the simplistic notion of the consumption of entertainment as exploitation and manipulation. In fact, these consumers of pop entertainment wield enormous cultural power in Hong Kong as will be obvious in the discussions in this volume.

The phenomenon of audiences of popular culture taking an active role in shaping the city's cultural and social conditions was not limited to music lovers but was also extended to film and television audiences. The public's active support for individual actors or production teams was often critical for the success of a production. In response, actors and directors of a movie often personally appeared in cinemas where their film was shown, to literally, thank the audience for buying tickets to their film, in a now routine practice of "*ze piu* 謝票 (Thanking the audience for buying tickets)." In these events, audience members felt the personal effect of their act of consumption that they were contributing directly to the survival and health of the industry. By the same token, many performers were no longer satisfied with just entertaining a mass audience. The artists who had chosen to remain in Hong Kong, usually younger and newer to the business, were eager to introduce new musical and artistic styles and content to distinguish their music from older Cantopop. They felt a deep sense of commitment to Hong Kong society and their audiences, not just to entertain but also to comfort, encourage, and give expression to their listener's concerns, especially in the difficult post-protest and COVID years. Sandy Ip of the pop duo, Per Se, explains:

> Because everyone has gone through very similar experiences, as we sing, we feel we are keeping our audience company, and the audience is keeping us company...We never had this sense of community before. Our songs were purely about how we feel about the world. It was from the time of [our album], "*character/character* (2021)," on that we started having fans telling us how our songs affected them or helped them through difficult times. We were going through similar experiences together with them.[37]

## ***Baak faa cai fong*** 百花齊放 **Let a Hundred Flowers Bloom**

The revival of Cantopop in 2021 is one of the most interesting developments in Hong Kong culture. What differentiates Cantopop from other kinds of popular music, such as K-pop [Korean pop], J-pop [Japanese pop], American and British pop, and even Mando-pop [Mandarin pop] that dominated Hong Kong's entertainment before 2019, is its emphasis on lyrics. Some might even argue that in Cantopop, the lyrics are more important than the music (*ci dai gwo kuk* 詞大過曲). Cantopop lyrics are arguably one of Hong Kong's most distinct cultural forms. Because they are widely transmitted through popular music, it is a literary form that touches most people in the city. One of Hong Kong's veteran lyricists, Poon Yuen Leung 潘源良, calls Cantopop lyrics Hong Kong's "secret garden."[38] A successful lyricist is able to capture and give expression to the sentiments and thoughts of a particular moment in society, create a sense of collective belonging, and sometimes even inspire and give hope. In this sense, Cantopop is the city's common language, and it has been especially significant in the NSL and COVID years, pulling people together amid differences, separations, social isolation, and general feelings of alienation. The lyricist, Siu Hak小克, explains:

> Perhaps, subconsciously, there is a feeling that Hong Kong people are all bound together. I think because there are a lot of things we can no longer say directly, we are now getting used to saying them in a circuitous way. There are no longer songs that are a hundred-percent love songs. All songs are connected with the emotions of the society...Till now, it is an artistic format that still retains its independence and has not yet been pressed into political service. Also, the scale of a song's production is much smaller than films, and a song has more mass appeal than literature or drama. It is as if every Cantopop song is telling everyone, "Hong Kong is still here."[39]

When most Hong Kong people stopped listening to Cantopop for almost 20 years, what that meant was not only the decline of local music but also a serious threat to a unique cultural form. Listening to Cantopop was more than indulging in entertainment. This was why when Cantopop made a comeback in 2021, many Hongkongers felt a keen sense of duty to keep it alive, to keep nurturing and supporting it. Invested in the new Cantopop and the young singers was a whole host of complex feelings and aspirations, as well as hope for Hong Kong's future.

The vibrance of the city's popular culture revealed a spirit of perseverance despite everything. Through their creative endeavors, artists, writers, and performers attempted to spin new tales for the city, and in doing so, design the city's future. Even "if it turns out that the world is not as [they] had expected," to quote Charmaine Fong's 2019 popular song, "*Gaasi saigaai jyunloi bat zoeng nei jyukei* 假使世界原來不像你預期,"[40] Hongkongers tried to adapt the new reality into one in which they could not just live a normal life, but "continue to live well," as a common post-2019 greeting exhorted. Stephen Mok, the other half of the duo, Per Se, commented,

> There are a lot of unknowns. We don't know what the future holds. At least what we have learned here is to *adapt*. Once you get used to it, you will still be able to do what you like. We should value this.[41]

## Language Subterfuge

The Hong Kong government was determined to manage the city's narrative after years of unrest. New ordinances and rules were implemented. Unacceptable ideas were censored. The use of some words had suddenly become a crime. Certain symbols and images could land one in jail. Political slogans and graffiti around the city had all been wiped away. Pieces of protest art that expressed public sentiments were taken down. The "Lennon Walls" that recorded the public's political aspirations were destroyed. There were no more critical commentaries or alternative views in the media. In general, there were no longer oppositional voices in the city. In essence, the Chinese state and the Hong Kong government had shut down the "textual public space" in the city, monopolized narratives, and declared war against civil discourse.[42]

Opposition to state power, to a large extent, is about loosening this grip over language and meaning.[43] On the day the new NSL came into effect, a protest banner was unfurled across a pedestrian bridge, emblazoned with the first line of the Chinese national anthem: "Arise ye who refuse to be slaves!" At the same time, a Maoist slogan, "Those who suppress student movements will not come to a good end," went viral on social media. Most Hongkongers recognized the irony and humor behind such appropriation of the slogans of the Chinese Communist Party. They not only highlighted Hongkongers' new state of subjugation but also reflected the hypocrisy of the Chinese state in its betrayal of its own early revolutionary ideals. Despite this blatant challenge to the Chinese Communist Party, even the most faithful pro-Beijing official would be hard-pressed to find an issue with these sayings.

When certain slogans such as "Liberate Hong Kong; Revolution of our Times" were outlawed, protesters resorted to an oblique representation—3, 2, 1, 9, 0, 2, 4, 6—a series of numbers that are the same in rhythm and tone to the forbidden phrase when read out loud in Cantonese. "Liberate Hong Kong" became "Seize back the banana," using "*hoengziu* banana" as a close homophone to "*Hoenggong* Hong Kong." These puns and wordplays were neither subtle nor opaque. However, the Hong Kong government could hardly begin to outlaw numbers or the mention of a common fruit. This use of language subterfuge in the face of state censorship and effort to direct conversations in the city, though playful and irreverent, seemed to have little practical function or actual effect on reality. These small impertinences, nevertheless, made a mockery of and demonstrate the futility of the attempt to control meaning.

Hong Kong Cantonese is known for its wildly colorful expressions, gallows humor, and swear words. Each chapter in this volume is centered on a few popular or particularly representative slang phrases or viral sayings of these years—the so-called *ciujyu* 潮語. These phrases were widely circulated and used in both everyday conversations and social media and were particularly representative of the city in the 2 years in this study. This means most people in Hong Kong would immediately understand the complex reality behind these concise and often humorous usages. These expressions were evocative at a time when words had become more and more politicized, and speech more hazardous. In each chapter, I explain how these phrases were used or came about and describe the specific contexts of their usages in order to reveal the world of emotions and ideological issues embedded in them. Sometimes, they were spirited reactions to the political situation or certain social phenomena. Sometimes, they represented the social attitudes and expectations of individuals. Often, they captured the collective moods and emotions in the city. Each chapter is then an analysis of the conditions, context, and issues behind these sayings.

There was a lot of anger, anxiety, and fear in Hong Kong under the NSL. However, faced with threats to their history, values, and identity, many Hongkongers decided to forge ahead anyway, to shape their reality, push back against a monolithic state-imposed narrative, and, as much as possible, take charge of their own future. The popular culture from Hong Kong in the 2 years after the implementation of the NSL reflects immense creativity and vivaciousness, producing a new narrative that is multifarious, heterogeneous, and diverse. The phrase most popular in these couple of years to celebrate and to affirm this vibrant creativity in the city was originally from Mao Zedong during the notorious, short-lived free-speech campaign in China from 1956 to 1957: "*baak faa cai fong* 百花齊放 (Let a hundred flowers bloom)." Whereas the Maoist campaign ended in betrayals and repression, Hongkongers demonstrated how it could be done.

Finally, a note on proper names: All the transcriptions of Chinese titles and terms in this volume are based on Cantonese, the *lingua franca* of Hong Kong and the mother tongue of close to 90% of the population. *Pinyin* is used when referencing non-Cantonese speakers, such as mainland Chinese officials, e.g., the Chinese premier, Xi Jinping. I have used the *Jyutping* system in the transcription of Cantonese into English, save for common words and names, such as Kowloon rather than *Gaulung*. In general, I use the preferred spelling of individuals' names where known, except for aliases or monikers. Consistent with common practice, surnames come first in East Asian names, and last in European names, for example, Leung Ka Yan 梁嘉蒽, where Leung is the surname, and Agnus Chow, where Chow is the surname. All translations are mine unless otherwise specified.

## Notes

1 "Hong Kong: National Security Law has created a human rights emergency," *Amnesty International*, June 30, 2021, www.amnesty.org/en/latest/news/2021/06/hong-kong-national-security-law-has-created-a-human-rights-emergency-2/.

2 "Freedom in the world, 2022," https://freedomhouse.org/report/freedom-world.

3 The ranking include measuring the heaviness of tax burden in the territory, openness of borders, ease of doing business, as well as civil liberty, right to association, free expression, as well as items such as number of terrorist fatalities and female genital mutilations, etc. See Quinn Slobodian, *Crack-Up Capitalism: Market Radicals and the Dream of a World Without Democracy* (New York: Metropolitan Books, 2003), 33–35.

4 Ian Vasquez and Tanja Porčnik, "The Human Freedom Index," 2018. www.fraserinstitute.org/sites/default/files/human-freedom-index-2018.pdf. Ian Vasquez, et al., "The Human Freedom Index: A Global Measurement of Personal, Civil and Economic Freedoms," 2022. www.fraserinstitute.org/sites/default/files/human-freedom-index-2022.pdf.

5 "Who lost Hong Kong on June 30?" *The Japan Times*, June 30, 2020, www.japantimes.co.jp/opinion/2020/07/06/commentary/japan-commentary/lost-hong-kong-june-30/. Benedict Rogers and Johnny Patterson, "The death of Hong Kong," *The Spectator*, July 1, 2020, www.spectator.co.uk/article/the-death-of-hong-kong/. William Yang, "National security law is Beijing's death knell for HK," *Deutsche Welle*, June 29, 2020, www.dw.com/en/jimmy-lai-national-security-law-is-beijings-death-knell-for-hong-kong/a-53981830. Eryk Bagshaw, "The end of the Hong Kong the world knew," *The Sydney Morning Herald*, June 30, 2020, www.smh.com.au/world/asia/the-end-of-the-hong-kong-we-knew-20200630-p557ma.html.

6 For example, the popular show, 頭條新聞 (Headliner), that often made fun of politicians or satirized current affairs, ran from 1989 till it was withdrawn in 2020. Its existence had often been regarded as a symbol of Hong Kong's press freedom and political tolerance.

7 "Facts and Statistics," Hong Kong Tourism Commission, www.tourism.gov.hk/en/tourism-statistics.php.

8 The former term is used by Gutmann in critique of Scott's notion of resistance, and the latter from Scott's defense. Matthew C. Gutmann, "Rituals of resistance: A critique of the theory of everyday forms of resistance," *Latin American Perspectives* 20, no. 2 (1993): 74–92, https://doi.org/:10.1177/0094582X9302000206. James C. Scott, "Rituals of resistance: A critique of the theory of everyday forms of resistance: Reply," *Latin American Perspectives* 20, no. 2 (1993): 93–94, www.jstor.org/stable/2633595.

9 Michel de Certeau, *The Practice of Everyday Life* (Berkeley: University of California Press, 1984). Claire Colebrook, "The Politics and Potential of Everyday Life," *New Literary History* 33, no. 4 (2002): 687–706, http://doi.org:10.1353/NLH.2002.0036.

10 Mikael Baaz, et al., "Defining and analyzing "Resistance": Possible entrances to the study of subversive practices," *Alternatives: Global, Local, Political* 41, no. 3 (2017): 137–153: 139, https://doi.org/10.1177/0304375417700170.

11 Asef Bayat, "From 'Dangerous Classes' to 'Quiet Rebels': Politics of urban subaltern in the Global South," *International Sociology* 15, no. 3 (2000): 533–557, doi:10.1177/026858000015003005.

12 Kristin Ross, *The Emergence of Social Space: Rimbaud and the Paris Commune* (Minneapolis: University of Minnesota Press, 1988), 8.

13 Janet Ng, *Paradigm, City: Space, Culture and Capitalism in Hong Kong* (New York, SUNY, 2009), 11.

14 Antony Dapiran, "Hong Kong's Reckoning," Golley, Jaivin, Hillman & Strange edits., *China Dreams* (Canberra, Australian National University Press, 2020), 54, accessed December 12, 2022, www.jstor.org/stable/j.ctv12sdxmk.9. Also, Hung Ho-Fung, *City on the Edge: Hong Kong Under Chinese Rule* (UK, Cambridge University Press, 2022).

15 Yew Chiew Ping and Kwong Kin-ming, "Hong Kong Identity on the Rise," *Asian Survey* 54, no. 6 (2014): 1088–1112: 1102–3, https://doi.org/:10.1525/as.2014.54.6.1088.

16 Antony Dapiran, 54.

17 Leung Chun-ying, "Policy Address," 2013, www.policyaddress.gov.hk/2013/eng/.

18 Jeffie Lam, "Hongkonger' makes it to world stage with place in the Oxford English Dictionary," *South China Morning Post*, March 19, 2014, www.scmp.com/news/hong-kong/article/1451929/finally-hongkonger-arrives-world-stage.

19 Antony Dapiran, 50–67: 66.

20 Niall McCarthy, "Fewer people in Hong Kong tend to identify as Chinese," *Statista*, September 9, 2019, www.statista.com/chart/19186/would-you-identify-yourself-as-a-hongkonger-or-chinese/.

21 Yang Zhenfei, "Survey: More Hong Kong people feel they are both 'Hongkongers' and 'Chinese'," *TYR*, June 22, 2021, https://tyr-jour.hkbu.edu.hk/2021/06/22/survey-more-hong-kong-people-feel-they-are-both-hongkongers-and-chinese/.

22 Dung Kai-Cheung, *在世界中寫作, 為世界而 寫 (Writing in the World, Writing for the World)* (Taipei, Lianjing chuban shiyegongsi), 2011.

23 "Hong Kong students must 'love motherland' under new values curriculum," *South China Morning Post*, November 30, 2021, www.scmp.com/yp/discover/news/hong-kong/article/3157978/hong-kong-students-must-love-motherland-under-new-values.

24 Stephen Roach, "It pains me to say Hong Kong is over," *Financial Times*, February 12, 2024, www.ft.com/stream/b8e1a08c-1c66-3235-b074-a90d8a482f71.

25 Quoted in Brent L. Pickett, "Foucault and the politics of resistance," *Polity* 28, no. 4 (1996): 445–466: 464.

26 The others include complete withdrawal of the extradition bill, exoneration of arrested protesters, an independent investigation into police conduct, and universal suffrage.

27 Olivier Krischer, "Thinking of art as informal life politics in Hong Kong," in Morris-Suzuki and Eun, edits., *New Worlds from Below: Informal Life Politics and Grassroots Action in Twenty-First-Century Northeast Asia* (Canberra, Australian National University Press, 2017), https://doi.org/10.22459/nwfb.03.2017.08.

28 "Mulan: Why Disney's latest reboot is facing boycott calls," *BBC* online, September 4, 2020, www.bbc.com/news/newsbeat-54024810.

29 Denise Ho, "如何成為宅男女神 (How to become an Otaku goddess)?" 菇武門*Gumoumun*, Ep. 39, September 6, 2020, Podcast, 120.0, www.youtube.com/watch?v=tIGFlNopFYU). All of Agnus Chow's YouTube films from before her jail sentence have been removed.

30 John Lie, *K-Pop: Popular Music, Cultural Amnesia, and Economic Innovation in South Korea* (California, University of California Press, 2014), 158.
31 Eric Kit-wai Ma and Ma and Chieh-Wei, *Culture, Politics, and Television in Hong Kong* (UK, Routledge, 1999).
32 Janet Ng, chapter 6.
33 Stephen Yiu-wai Chu, "Before and after the Fall: Mapping Hong Kong Cantopop in the Global Era," Hong Kong: LEWI Working Paper Series 63 (2007), https://scholars.hkbu.edu.hk/ws/portalfiles/portal/55416356/RO_lewi_wp-10.pdf. See also Chu's discussion of the effect of CEPA and the "Mainlandization" of Hong Kong films, television, and Cantopop. *Lost in Translation: Hong Kong Culture in the Age of China* (SUNY Press, 2013).
34 Sebastian Veg, "Creating a textual public space: Slogans and texts from Hong Kong's Umbrella Movement," *The Journal of Asian Studies* 75, no. 3 (2016): 673–702: 699, https://doi.org/10.1017/S0021911816000565.
35 "且讓我們娛樂至死 (Let us amuse ourselves to death)," 哲學有偈傾 (There's much to talk about in philosophy), RTHK, November 9, 2020, video, 52.05, www.archive.org/details/philosophynight2020. Corrupt the Youth, November 28, 2020, YouTube, www.youtube.com/watch?v=sTaITDkai1I.
36 Neil Postman, *Amusing ourselves to Death* (USA, Viking Penguin, 1985).
37 Wong zing mei zi zi黃靜美智子, "在廢托邦築樂園: Per Se十年的變與不變. 願音樂可上太空：沒有想過放棄Per Se, (Building a paradise in dystopia: The change and non-change of Per Se in the last ten years. Hoping their music could go to space. Never thought of giving up), *Ming Pao Weekly*, August 12, 2022, www.mpweekly.com/culture/%E8%97%9D%E6%96%87/per-se-per-se-%E6%96%B0%E6%AD%8C-%E7%AB%8A%E7%AB%8A%E8%A9%A9-209418, www.mpweekly.com/culture.
38 Quoted from Zeng Jau-zing, 鄭又禎, "潘源良x鍾永豐：香港粵語與台灣客語，如何用「自己的語言」寫流行歌？(Poon Yuen Leung x Chung Yung Fang: Hong Kong Cantonese and Taiwan Hakka. How to use 'one's own language' to write popular songs?)," *The Initium*, August 14, 2022, https://theinitium.com/article/20220814-culture-poon-and-chung-dialogue-pop-music-lyrics.
39 Wong Zing Mei Zi Zi 黃靜美智子.
40 Charmaine Fong, "假使世界原來不像你預期 (If it turns out that the world is not as you had expected)," music and lyrics by Charmaine Fong, Strawberry Fields, 2019, www.youtube.com/watch?v=4sg-K53kODE.
41 WongZing MeiZiZi黃靜美智子.
42 Sebastian Veg, "Creating a textual public space: Slogans and texts from Hong Kong's Umbrella Movement," *The Journal of Asian Studies* 75, no. 3 (2016): 673–702: 699, https://doi.org/10.1017/S0021911816000565.
43 Michel Foucault most notably studies how dominance is asserted through creation of particular discourses and institutions that have the power to define, for example, madness, sexual deviation, or criminality. To diffuse or disassemble these definitions is a way to destabilize such power.

## References

Baaz, Mikael, Mona Lilja, Michael Schulz, and Stellan Vinthagen. "Defining and analyzing 'Resistance': Possible entrances to the study of subversive practices." *Alternatives: Global, Local, Political* 41, no. 3 (2016): 137–153: 139, https://doi.org/10.1177/0304375417700170.

Bayat, Asef. "From 'Dangerous Classes' to 'Quiet Rebels': Politics of urban subaltern in the Global South." *International Sociology* 15, no. 3 (2000): 533–557. doi:10.1177/026858000015003005.

Chow, Vivienne. "The rise and fall of Canto-pop and, with it, Hong Kong's cultural identity." *South China Morning Post*, January 5, 2018. www.scmp.com/comment/insight-opinion/article/2126956/rise-and-fall-canto-pop-and-it-hong-kongs-cultural-identity.

Chu, Stephen Yiu-wai. *Before and after the Fall: Mapping Hong Kong Cantopop in the Global Era*. Hong Kong: LEWI Working Paper Series 63 (2007). https://scholars.hkbu.edu.hk/ws/portalfiles/portal/55416356/RO_lewi_wp-10.pdf.

Chu, Stephen Yiu-wai. *Lost in Translation: Hong Kong Culture in the Age of China*. New York: SUNY Press, 2013.

Colebrook, Claire. "The politics and potential of everyday life." *New Literary History* 33, no. 4 (2002): 687–706. http://doi.org:10.1353/NLH.2002.0036.

Dapiran, Antony. "Hong Kong's Reckoning." Golley, Jaivin, Hillman & Strange Edits., *China Dreams*, Canberra: Australian National University Press, 2020. Accessed December 12, 2022. www.jstor.org/stable/j.ctv12sdxmk.9.

De Certeau, Michel. *The Practice of Everyday Life*. Berkeley: University of California Press, 1984.

Dung Kai-Cheung, *在世界中寫作, 為世界而 寫 (Writing in the World, Writing for the World*). Taipei: Lianjing chuban shiyegongsi, 2011.

Fong, Charmaine. "假使世界原來不像你預期 (If it turns out that the world is not as you had expected)." Music and lyrics by Charmaine Fong. Strawberry Fields, 2019. www.youtube.com/watch?v=4sg-K53kODE.

"Freedom in the world, 2022." https://freedomhouse.org/report/freedom-world.

Gutmann, Matthew C. "Rituals of resistance: A critique of the theory of everyday forms of resistance," *Latin American Perspectives* 20, no. 2 (1993): 74–92. https://doi.org/:10.1177/0094582X9302000206.

Ho, Denise. "如何成為宅男女神 (How to become an Otaku goddess)?" 菇武門*Gumoumun*, Episode 39. September 6, 2020. Podcast, 120.0. www.youtube.com/watch?v=tIGFlNopFYU).

"Hong Kong: National Security Law has created a human rights emergency." *Amnesty International*, June 30, 2021. www.amnesty.org/en/latest/news/2021/06/hong-kong-national-security-law-has-created-a-human-rights-emergency-2/.

"Hong Kong students must 'love motherland' under new values curriculum." *South China Morning Post*, November 30, 2021. www.scmp.com/yp/discover/news/hong-kong/article/3157978/hong-kong-students-must-love-motherland-under-new-values.

Hong Kong Tourism Commission. *Facts and Statistics*. www.tourism.gov.hk/en/tourism-statistics.php.

Hung Ho-Fung. *City on the Edge: Hong Kong Under Chinese Rule*. UK: Cambridge University Press, 2022.

Krischer, Olivier. "Thinking of art as informal life politics in Hong Kong." Tessa Morris-Suzuki and Eun Jeong Soh Edits., *New Worlds from Below: Informal Life Politics and Grassroots Action in Twenty-First-Century Northeast Asia*. Canberra: Australian National University Press, 2017. https://doi.org/10.22459/nwfb.03.2017.08.

Lam, Jeffie. "Hongkonger' makes it to world stage with place in the Oxford English Dictionary." *South China Morning Post*, March 19, 2014. www.scmp.com/news/hong-kong/article/1451929/finally-hongkonger-arrives-world-stage.

Leung Chun-ying. *Policy Address*, 2013. www.policyaddress.gov.hk/2013/eng/.

Lie, John. *K-Pop: Popular Music, Cultural Amnesia, and Economic Innovation in South Korea*. California: University of California Press, 2014.

Ma, Eric Kit-wai and Ma and Chieh-Wei. *Culture, Politics, and Television in Hong Kong*. UK: Routledge, 1999.

Masse, Kaper. "Popular culture, 'Resistance,' 'Cultural Radicalism,' and 'Self-Formation'. Comments on the development of a theory: Subjects, representations, contexts." Martin Butler, Paul Mecheril and Lea Brenningmeyer Edits., *Resistance*. Transcript Verlag, 2017. http://DOI:10.14361/9783839431498-004.

McCarthy, Niall. "Fewer people in Hong Kong tend to identify as Chinese." *Statista*, September 9, 2019. www.statista.com/chart/19186/would-you-identify-yourself-as-a-hongkonger-or-chinese/.

"Mulan: Why Disney's latest reboot is facing boycott calls." *BBC* online, September 4, 2020. www.bbc.com/news/newsbeat-54024810.

Ng, Janet. *Paradigm City: Space, Culture and Capitalism in Hong Kong*. New York: SUNY, 2009.

Per Se, featuring Serrini. "粉碎糖果屋 (Hansel and Gretel)." Music by Per Se, lyrics by Serrini, Frenzi Music Limited, 2020, www.youtube.com/watch?v=FjS50ATT1v0.

Pickett, Brent L. "Foucault and the politics of resistance." *Polity* 28, no. 4 (1996): 445–466: 464.

Postman, Neil. *Amusing Ourselves to Death.* USA: Viking Penguin, 1985.

Roach, Stephen. "It pains me to say Hong Kong is over." *Financial Times*, February 12, 2024. www.ft.com/stream/b8e1a08c-1c66-3235-b074-a90d8a482f71.

Ross, Kristin. *The Emergence of Social Space: Rimbaud and the Paris Commune*. Minneapolis: University of Minnesota Press, 1988.

Scott, James C. "Rituals of resistance: A critique of the theory of everyday forms of resistance: Reply." *Latin American Perspectives* 20, no. 2 (1993): 93–94. www.jstor.org/stable/2633595.

Slobodian, Quinn. *Crack-Up Capitalism: Market Radicals and the Dream of a World Without Democracy*. New York: Metropolitan Books, 2003.

Vasquez, Ian and Tanja Porčnik. *The Human Freedom Index*, 2018. www.fraserinstitute.org/sites/default/files/human-freedom-index-2018.pdf.

Vasquez, Ian, et al. *The Human Freedom Index: A Global Measurement of Personal, Civil and Economic Freedoms,* 2022. www.fraserinstitute.org/sites/default/files/human-freedom-index-2022.pdf.

Veg, Sebastian. "Creating a textual public space: Slogans and texts from Hong Kong's Umbrella Movement." *The Journal of Asian Studies* 75, no. 3 (2016): 673–702: 699. https://doi.org/10.1017/S0021911816000565.

Wongzing meizizi黃靜美智子. "在廢托邦築樂園: Per Se十年的變與不變. 願音樂可上太空：沒有想過放棄Per Se, (Building a paradise in dystopia: The change and non-change of Per Se in the last ten years. Hoping their music could go to space. Never thought of giving up)." *Ming Pao Weekly*, August 12, 2022. www.mpweekly.com/culture.

Yang Zhenfei, "Survey: More Hong Kong people feel they are both 'Hongkongers' and 'Chinese'." *TYR*, June 22, 2021. https://tyr-jour.hkbu.edu.hk/2021/06/22/survey-more-hong-kong-people-feel-they-are-both-hongkongers-and-chinese/.

Yew Chiew Ping and Kwong Kin-ming. "Hong Kong identity on the rise." *Asian Survey* 54, no. 6 (2014): 1088–1112: 1102–3. https://doi.org/:10.1525/as.2014.54.6.1088.

Zeng Jau-zing, 鄭又禎. "潘源良x鍾永豐：香港粵語與台灣客語，如何用「自己的語言」寫流行歌？(Poon Yuen Leung x Chung Yung Fang: Hong Kong Cantonese and Taiwan Hakka. How to use 'one's own language' to write popular songs?)." *The Initium*, August 14, 2022. https://theinitium.com/article/20220814-culture-poon-and-chung-dialogue-pop-music-lyrics.

"且讓我們娛樂至死 (Let us amuse ourselves to death)." 哲學有偈傾 (There's much to talk about in philosophy). RTHK. November 9, 2020. Video, 52.05. www.archive.org/details/philosophynight2020.

# 1 New Reality, New Communities, New Identities

## *Wailou Ceoinyun* 圍爐取暖 Huddling Together Around a Stove for Warmth

The 2 years after the implementation of the National Security Law (NSL) on June 30, 2020, were long and dreary by any definition. As they came to the end of their dreams for democracy, Hongkongers had to learn anew their relationship to the city and how to live a normal, if not happy, life in the suddenly altered reality. The saying, "*wailou ceoinyun* 圍爐取暖 (to huddle together around a stove for warmth)," entered the popular lexicon and became a catchphrase in conversations. Originally used negatively to describe small, exclusive circles for mutual political or financial benefit, it had come to be redesignated as a kind of positive communitarianism. In a society torn apart by political differences, when overt criticism of the government or support for alternative political causes could bring the National Security police to one's door, and when neighbors and family members were encouraged to report on each other's political improprieties, understandably, many people tried to find refuge among the like-minded. As many of the old institutions that had defined the everyday life and values of the city succumbed under the new law, there was a need to find new ways to restore a sensc of civil society and social belonging. The notion of "huddling together," reflects this effort to create closeness and revive communal spaces in the midst of recriminations and loss.

Even though many traditional media and groups had shut down because of the NSL, new kinds of communities were also formed. Many different social media groups were created where large numbers of individuals could gather virtually instead of at physical meeting places. Several YouTube channels quickly gained prominence and functioned to sustain the intellectual and collective space of the city. A couple of reality shows from ViuTV, a new television platform, managed to capture the zeitgeist of the period and by fulfilling certain social needs, generated an immense response and conversation in Hong Kong. The synergy created by the many different groups and organizations sparked the beginning of 2 years of cultural innovation and regeneration.

DOI: 10.4324/9781003521280-2

### The Losses

Government figures showed that by January 2021, 10,277 persons had been arrested for their participation in the 2019 protests. Among them, 2820 had been charged and 1158 had been indicted. The longest sentence for the convicted was 12 years. By February 2022, 166 persons had been arrested for violating the NSL. A hundred of them had been charged.[1] At the same time, the Census and Statistics Department recorded a net outflow of 75,300 persons from mid-2020 to mid-2021. In 2022, 60,000 more emigrated from the city. Hong Kong's total population shrank from about 7.5 million in 2019 to 7.19 million by the end of 2022.[2]

In 2021, close to 60 large and small civic, political, and community associations, professional and student unions, and international and local NGOs were pressured to disband or move out of the city. These included the Amnesty International's Hong Kong office; Wall-Fare, a local prisoners' rights organization; the Hong Kong Confederation of Trade Unions; and the Hong Kong Alliance in Support of Patriotic Democratic Movements of China, a pro-democracy advocacy group initially founded to support the students of the 1989 June Fourth student democracy movement in China, and later known for organizing annual commemorations in Hong Kong of the Tiananmen massacre; etc. Numerous grassroots political and community organizations that sprang up in Hong Kong's two-decade-long democracy struggle also broke up. They had once been places for not just political discussions and organizing but also community mutual aid and social gatherings. The loss of these groups spelled the end of civic activities in Hong Kong.

The implementation of the NSL also resulted in dozens of opposition politicians being jailed or disqualified from public office. Many judges were cleared off the bench. Many retired; others were reassigned. Pro-democracy teachers and professors lost their teaching contracts. Books with "sensitive" contents or written by pro-democracy activists and politicians were removed from public library shelves and schools. Even though there was not an overt ban, many books on taboo topics or penned by "problematic" writers were no longer available for purchase in the major bookstores.

News media considered critical of the government shutdown one after another. Several editors and journalists were arrested and prosecuted, charged under the new NSL for collusion with foreign powers, promoting secession, or fanning hatred of the government. However, long before the implementation of the NSL, Hong Kong's flamboyant media had already been reigned in. Mainland interests had started to take over Hong Kong's major media soon after the "Return" of Hong Kong to China in 1997:

> Chinese businessman Wang Jing became the largest shareholder in Asia Television in 2000, Ku Zhouheng bought up the daily paper *Sing Pao* in 2014, media tycoon Li Ruigang took over the majority of shares of the dominant broadcaster Television Broadcasting (TVB) in 2015 and Jack Ma, CEO of e-commerce giant Alibaba, bought up the largest English-language daily paper in

> Hong Kong, the *South China Morning Post* in 2015, among other high profile cases...
>
> The actual owners of the media company, including TVB (Hong Kong's primary television station), 星島日報Singdao Daily, and the Hong Kong Economic Journal (信報Xin Bao), are now all members of the local or national Chinese People's Political Consultative Conference. Beijing saw to increase Chinese investment in Hong Kong's media. By the end of 2017, about 40% of Hong Kong's primary media was controlled by the Chinese government or Chinese stockholders. [3]

In other words, "Media ownership in Hong Kong is largely concentrated into the hands of a group of businesspeople sharing the same basic interests of pleasing or at least not provoking China."[4] Hong Kong's media had been rendered toothless, even becoming mouthpieces of the ruling power.[5] The disappearance of Hong Kong's famously boisterous print and media culture had significant implications for the continued flourishing, not just of civil society but also of local culture, as Baat-Maau 八貓 points out,

> Hong Kong's media had for a long time, carried out a "*surrogate democracy function*" in place of the city's lack. They provided a venue for the discussion of politics and current affairs, transmitting public opinion, and acted as government watchdogs. After Hong Kong's Return, China immediately began to tame Hong Kong's media.[6] (Original in English in italics.)

The closing of *Apple Daily* 蘋果日報 *Pingguo jatbou*, one of the last remaining and the most prominent oppositional voices in the city, on June 24, 2021, was deeply mourned by the Hong Kong public because it signaled the beginning of a new level of intolerance and repression. On the last night of the newspaper, a large crowd congregated outside its headquarters, shining their cell phone lights at the offices, shouting their goodbyes and gratitude to the staff inside. Long queues of people waited patiently in front of newsstands around the city for the delivery of the last edition of the newspaper early the next morning. By 8:30 AM, all one million copies printed were sold out. *Apple Daily* was the first media platform to fold as a result of the NSL. As one of the most-read news media in Hong Kong, *Apple Daily*, also known for its exhaustive coverage of local entertainment and pop culture, had an important place in the city's daily conversations and stories. By the time *Stand News* 立場新聞 *Lapcoeng Sanman* decided to shut down in December of the same year, people were saddened, but no longer shocked. When *Citizen News* 眾新聞*Zong sanman* also announced its termination a couple of weeks later, they were numb, understanding this continuously narrowing civic space had become the new reality.

At the same time, the once beloved Radio Television HK (RTHK) was "restructured." The public broadcaster, established in 1970, was known for thoroughness and objectivity in its current affairs and news programs, their effectiveness as a government watchdog, as well as for the high quality of their educational and cultural programs. The RTHK's flagship program, the news and current affairs show, *Hong Kong Connection* 鏗鏘集 *Hungcoeng zap*, which began broadcasting in 1978, underwent major revamping. Not only were a large number of the editorial staff and journalists purged from the station, but all the episodes of the program prior to 2021 were scrubbed from RTHK's online archive and from its YouTube channel. This multiple award-winning program had been reduced to reporting on innocuous issues, such as government tree-planting schemes, recycling, or other government-sponsored social and cultural programs, many produced by sub-contractors. The loss of these media platforms meant diminished space for rational discussions of social and political issues.

It is not surprising that news analysis, current affairs programs, and political satires would be considered sensitive in the new Hong Kong. However, even certain cultural and educational programs were deemed unacceptable. A series of programs called *RTHK Talk Show* that hosted nightly discussions by academics and public intellectuals on subjects like Philosophy, Literature, History, Society, and Science and Technology were terminated without explanation, and apparently without forewarning the presenters. Despite the academic nature of the discussions, these late-night shows were surprisingly popular. They were all canceled as if intellectualism was an affront to the new political regime.

## *Wailou zeong zisik* 圍爐長知識 Huddling Around a Stove, Cultivating One's Knowledge

For a brief period of time, before its own demise, *Stand News* attempted to fill in the cultural and social, if not psychological, lacuna created by the shutdown of *Apple Daily*. It launched a podcast and YouTube series that offered a variety of content, from political and social analysis to discussions of popular culture. Called *Wailou zoeng zi sik* 圍爐長知識 (huddling around a stove, cultivating one's knowledge), the program demonstrated another crucial dimension to the new kind of communitarianism, which was to extend the public sphere and to encourage *zoeng zisik* 長知識 (cultivation of knowledge).

Just before its closure, *Stand News* started to broadcast a series of three short documentaries on its YouTube channel: *Farewell to 2021*, that recorded the experience of Hong Kong people in the first year after the enactment of the NSL. The first of the series, "2021 *Gaaitai: Neimun waan hou ma* 解體: 你們還好嗎 (Dissolutions: Are you still alright?)," interviews the organizers of several grassroot community groups, humanitarian organizations, and professional unions that disbanded in the year. The second film, "2021 *Gamjyu zi nin* 禁語之年 (The Year of the Forbidden Words)," on censorship enumerates the books, movies, and the different kinds of media and cultural productions taken off public circulation, and tallies the words and phrases that could no longer be uttered in public in the city. The final film, "2021 *Syu dong* 樹洞 (Tree Hollow),"[7] is a reading of letters from readers sent anonymously via secure social media, describing their experiences and emotions during the difficult year. These documentaries, together with *Stand News*' YouTube channel and website, were all wiped from the internet when it terminated operation after the editor, assistant editor, and a number of the trustees (including the pop singer mentioned in the Introduction, Denise Ho) were arrested.

As the major news and media platforms disappeared, many less formal, grassroots *gwan zyu zou* 關注組 (interest or concern groups) sprang up in their places. However, most of these were resolutely apolitical. These groups were organized through social media, through which members connected with each other, sharing information and opinions, allowing those with similar interests to *wailou*, even as COVID rules made actual social gathering impossible. A Facebook group on the topic of picnicking unexpectedly exploded in popularity as the use of the government contact-tracing app, "Leave Home Safe," became mandatory in the city. Through almost 3 years of COVID control in the city, this app doubled as a vaccine pass required for using the public transportation system or entering stores, restaurants, and all public or large facilities, such as markets and shopping malls. Where large parts of the city are connected by arcades, malls, and interior walkways, this essentially meant movement around the city required official permission and submission to constant surveillance.

The picnic Facebook group was originally organized by a few friends who resisted the use of the government app. Instead of going into the malls or to restaurants, the group advocated dining al fresco. Members of the group exchanged information about the best picnic spots around the city, made recommendations for socially responsible take-out businesses (*loengsam siu dim* 良心小店 small businesses with a conscience), and introduced picnic paraphernalia and know-how.

Many other Facebook groups popped up one after another on many different aspects of life in the city. There were a few evaluating "Two-dish meals"[8] from different takeout places, especially after sit-down meals in restaurants were banned. Some were organized around a single food item, the best *shumai* in the city, for example. Organizers of these social media groups often took care to explain that their aim was simply to *wailou* with people with similar interests and concerns. These groups might seem silly. However, in the midst of collective despair as Hongkongers witnessed, not only the defeat of their political aspirations but also the rapid erosion of their way of life under COVID, they provided an important sense of community and social, if not emotional, support.

A popular philosophy study group, Corrupt the Youth 好青年荼毒室 *Houcingnin touduk sat* (a reference to Athenians' charge against Socrates), quickly gained prominence, taking over an important intellectual space left vacant after the cancellation of RTHK's talk shows. The group was established in 2016 by 13 graduate students and academics in Philosophy. On their Facebook, they explained, "The founding aim of the group is to 'to huddle around a stove for warmth,' and to spark a sense of existence among ourselves."

Corrupt the Youth started posting talks and lectures on YouTube in 2017. However, it was not till 2020 that they started to actively expand their online activities. By 2021, their YouTube channel had accrued over 90,000 subscribers. The group's activities were multifarious. Aside from public lectures, on their YouTube channel, they offered a variety of programs, from formal discussions and presentations to interviews, live shows, games, and even dramatic skits. They posted lectures and discussions on podcasts; they presented essays on their website; they published their writings in several volumes of *Corrupt the Youth Reader*. (The *Corrupt the Youth Reader* Vol. 3, which includes chapters on artificial intelligence, nationality, democracy, and political struggle published in 2020, was removed from public library shelves in November 2021.) They offered online courses and hosted intellectual and cultural events around the city. They had several sold-out live shows and even participated in a dance performance. Gradually, the group also branched into discussing different aspects of the city's popular culture. They provided analysis of films and dramas, interviewed pop singers, lyricists, actors, and directors of current popular TV shows and films, etc. The members also often collaborated with other Hong Kong-based YouTube channels, even those with content totally different from theirs.

Sei-go四哥, a member of the group, spoke of their desire to create community through their different endeavors: "I have always hoped that Corrupt the Youth is more than just the ten or so of us, and that [the audience members] would hang out with each other, go paint pictures or sing and form a real community."[9] Another member, Gam-zai甘仔, pointed out that after the protests, "[t]he social bonds that we built are fundamentally disintegrating." Groups like theirs functioned to assuage the feelings of powerlessness, because "the feeling of powerlessness comes from the feeling of aloneness."[10]

Indeed, one of Corrupt the Youth's most popular programs was their Friday night live-streams, which often lasted for 4–5 hours each time, during which, members, sometimes special guests, would sit together to discuss anything that struck their fancy, ranging from the silly to the profound. There was usually much drinking, heated arguments, joking, laughing, and swearing. Tens of thousands tuned in every Friday night to join in, laugh along, and occasionally learn new things or be inspired by the conversations. The journalist, Leung Jyut梁越, explains the importance of these programs:

> [Many Hongkongers] do not want to feel alone anymore. They are also looking for truth...In Corrupt the Youth's live streams, the members would go off on anything. Sometimes they would seriously discuss philosophy. They'd talk and drink. When they get drunk, they might get angry or cry, revealing their true personalities. Many audience members have shared with them how much their discussions resonate with them. Corrupt the Youth has filled the emptiness in their souls.[11]

By March 2022, Corrupt the Youth had become so popular that they were referred to as the boyband of philosophy.

After the devastating protests and changes under the NSL, Sei-go believes the entire cultural terrain of the city was facing collapse. As far as communities are based on these cultural and historical foundations, he said, "We are forced to save ourselves," through the reinvention of a new culture, new stories, and new identity.[12]

## *Zeoi mung* 追夢 Chasing Dreams: Self Re-creation

Singing or talent contests are stories of self-invention. To the contestants, these are opportunities to *zeoi mung*, to chase his or her dream, to become someone. The audiences feel as if they are witnessing and are even a part of the birth of something significant—a new star. In this context, one of the most talked-about television reality shows in these years was ViuTV's flagship program, the *King Maker* 全民造星 *Cyunman zou sing*, an annual talent competition show first aired in 2018.

ViuTV was the most significant new presence in Hong Kong's entertainment landscape in the last years of the 2010s because it was the biggest in scale. Established in 2016, it was part of a large streaming media corporation that provides (OTT) streaming services in Asia and the Middle East. However, the local ViuTV, a free broadcast station in the city, produces programs specifically for the Hong Kong audience. This new station has broken up years of near monopoly of the city's entertainment industry by Television Broadcasts Limited (TVB). Unlike TVB, which has been diligently cultivating the mainland audiences since CEPA in 2003 (see Introduction), ViuTV professed no ambition to expand into the Chinese market and had no obvious political affiliation or leaning. Its youthful image, local-centric productions, use of diverse and new talent, and simply being an alternative to the much more established and now, Chinese-owned, TVB, made it an appealing contender for the city's viewing audience, especially younger Hongkongers.

Hong Kong has a history of talent shows. In fact, some of Asia's top artists, especially from the 1980s and 1990s, came from Hong Kong's talent contests. In these early contest shows, usually only the finals would be broadcast. Recent contest shows, however, have been produced in the format of a reality show in which the audience witnesses and experiences vicariously the transformation of ordinary individuals into stars. The competitions of the earlier generations were about uncovering "real talent." These programs operated under the assumption that the truly gifted would be "discovered," in a fair system in which everyone was judged equally and rewarded accordingly. This kind of story had no appeal to the new generation of viewers in Hong Kong, who had discovered that society could be fundamentally unjust. (These issues will be further explored in Chapter 3.) The producers and judges on the *King Maker* selected those with potential through open auditions and then winnowed the contestants down through rounds of competition while offering them some instruction and training along the way. Sometimes, the "injustices" of the process were deliberately revealed. The best singer might be eliminated; the mediocre performer might get through. Producers could resurrect a contestant they favored, overriding the judges, etc. The show was often more about the "authentic" personalities of the competitors, together with their backstories or personal struggles.

What gripped the audience of *King Maker* was not necessarily the performances, but the narrative of "becoming," especially through the competitors' perseverance through all the discouraging moments and obstacles. Many of the contestants gave up stable jobs to participate in the show even though the odds of winning were low.

Others endured grueling schedules as they tried to accommodate practice and performance while working, often low-paying jobs, to sustain their livelihood.

Much of the show also focused on the backstage drama that revealed the "honest" emotions and "genuine" personalities of the participants. The contestants worked together in teams to plan their performances and learn new songs or dance routines. They had to help and support each other because winning as a team allowed them to advance to the next level of the contest. However, ultimately the contestants had to compete against each other. Many would be eliminated in the advance toward the finals. There could only be one champion. The program often showed how the contestants were torn between the desire to win and loyalty to their teammates. The most emotional moments were when some managed to advance to another level while others were eliminated..

As the viewers followed the participants' long journeys in the 60 episodes of the first season, they became more and more emotionally invested in them. This was manifested in increasingly heated nightly commentaries and discussions on the show's social media throughout the broadcast. By showing what many young people were willing to do and sacrifice to achieve their dreams, the program also helped change social attitudes toward them. It was not uncommon, at the beginning of the program, to hear criticisms of the contestants as vain or out of touch with reality, dreaming of being famous instead of seriously earning a living. However, whether successful or not, the contestants gradually gained respect from the viewing audience by their sheer persistence.

At the end of the first season of *King Maker*, ViuTV absorbed a number of the contestants as their own in-house artists. In 2019, ViuTV introduced to the Hong Kong audience two male performance groups, the 12-member idol group, MIRROR, and the four-member, ERROR, all selected from the contestants in the show, including many of the finalists. Many young people found these young men inspiring because they fought hard against immense odds and made real sacrifices for their dreams.[13] In a survey conducted in 2022 among young people of an average age of 21.7, it was found that even though over 80% of those surveyed said they were not MIRROR or ERROR fans, 84.5% of them said they admired how the members of these groups actively pursued their dreams. Of these, 49.8% agreed that their stories, "encourage me not to give up my own dreams."[14]

When MIRROR and ERROR were first introduced to the general public, however, they were much maligned. No one expected the groups to last, let alone become significant cultural forces in the city 2 years later. The members' transition from amateur contestants to professional performers began with appearances in yet more reality shows, in which they were asked to play games and perform tasks that were sometimes humiliating, sometimes repulsive, or even terrifying, from walking around in embarrassing clothes to eating unsavory foods like insects or worms, for comic effect. It appeared as if their management was expending as much money and effort in destroying idols as in creating them. In unguarded moments during these games or other exercises, the unedited reactions and facial expressions of the young men in the groups broke through their otherwise constant camera-ready images. In effect, what these shows destroyed was the old Hong

Kong notion of idols—two-dimensional perfections with flawless looks, impeccable behavior, and coached to always make appropriate, if innocuous, statements and responses in interviews. The new idols had real personalities. They had likes and dislikes. They made mistakes, said the wrong things, could feel hurt, or be ill-tempered. They sometimes showed impatience or distraction or looked tired. Audiences felt that they were "real" flesh and blood, troubled by the same hurts, navigating the same difficulties, and trying to survive in the same social and political conditions. According to a report on the effect of MIRROR on young people in Hong Kong:

> [Reality] shows like *Tiu gaau nei MIRROR調教你MIRROR* (Educating MIRROR) also let people see the more personal side of the MIRROR members, including their inner struggles, allowing audiences to understand more how they seek to continue to improve themselves. These all become a connection between MIRROR and their supporters.[15]

In a reality where truth was in short supply, these young men laid bare their true selves to the world, and in return, they received fierce devotion and support from their growing fan base.

## The Social and Economic Effects of MIRROR Fans

By the end of 2020, MIRROR fever gripped the city. Consumer products that the MIRROR members endorsed or magazines in which their images appeared sold out instantly. Advertisements with their images dominated the city's public spaces. Their ability to sell products led commentators to marvel at the MIRROR economic miracle in the midst of Hong Kong's COVID-induced economic recession. Others worried about their fans being taken advantage of.

Unlike the fans of previous generations who collected paraphernalia, participated in the occasional meet-and-greets with their idols organized by the artists' management, or who waited patiently outside their stars' performance venues for signatures, the new fans that emerged in Hong Kong, facilitated by social media, took an active role in cultivating their idols. They used their power in numbers to advocate for them.

Indeed, MIRROR fans played an enormous part in the group's success. They were indulgent in their stars even when some of them were still struggling to perfect their skills. They tolerated flaws while pushing them toward continued growth and innovation. They supported them by buying the goods the group members endorsed, so brands would continue to hire them to promote their products. They rented huge outdoor advertisements, electronic boards, signs on bus stop shelters, and any public surface available for hire, to publicize the group's work. In this way, Galbraith argues, "this is not to say that consumers and fans are duped or exploited, which assumes passivity and weakness. On the contrary...fans are active and empowered in their support for idols." Fans comprise a "collective force" or a "collective force of desire," which can be both economic and political.[16]

While this kind of fan culture is common in the world of Korean pop, it was relatively new and was particularly poignant in post-NSL Hong Kong. Even though it seems that the fan's free economic labor was being taken advantage of by corporations, Galbraith argues that the convergence of the market interests of corporations and the fans' emotional interests was mutually beneficial. He calls this a "labor of love:"

> [The fans] labor doing what they love and labor for love. Corporations act as apparatuses to capture some of the value generated by fans, who labor for love in relation to idols; idols, fans, and their relations are supported by corporations, which they in turn support.[17]

This labor of love cannot be separated from issues of the city's identity. The fans understood that Hong Kong was a very small market with a population of less than 7.5 million. In order to have a viable career many performers had no other options but to cultivate the Chinese market. However, these fans wanted to prove that Hong Kong people could afford to have their own stars. The economic effect of the fans' activities was so significant that it created what was called a MIRROR *gingzai hyun* 經濟圈(MIRROR economic circle).

By embarking on what might be called "affective activism," the fans' activities turned pop culture from an economic activity to a form of social conversation and transformation.[18] MIRROR and ERROR fan clubs organized events to support their idols, but there were also continuous exchanges on social media among the fan members themselves, discussing topics sometimes beyond their fandom, and supporting each other in their daily difficulties. The performers too often interacted with the fans directly on social media. The relationships were more immediate and more intimate than those between the older generations of artists and their fans. The MIRROR and ERROR fan clubs became important spaces for a much-needed sense of community in a society fragmented by distrust and political recriminations. They offered opportunities to not only gather together but also, to *coei nyun*, to spread warmth and nurture among each other. According to Chan Zi Wan 陳子雲,

> Following idols offer the fans emotional connection with each other. The crowds reappropriated public space in the name of entertainment to preserve and continue Hong Kong's unique entertainment culture (including MIRROR's particular position in Hong Kong at the present). Although not every fan is cognizant of this, their collective activities allow each broken and weary soul a new place of reprieve.[19]

In a sense, the new idol culture was a form of *wailou* on a societal level.

These fan clubs opened a new kind of civil space in Hong Kong. Ze Hoi Jan謝愷忻points out, "these large-scale fans activities attempt to blur the boundaries of reality, allowing fans to connect with society. They are no longer marginalized and invisible. Their activities allow them entry into public sight, to be part of the public culture."[20] Organized through social media, MIRROR fans engaged in charity work and public services in the name of individual MIRROR members they supported, extending the relevance of their organizations to the greater society. For example, they organized clean-up campaigns in the country parks and beaches, arranged for food delivery to shut-ins during COVID, and volunteered at animal shelters. To celebrate their idols' birthdays, they organized festive activities, purchased free rides for the public on various forms of public transportation, and raised money for different charities in the city. Ze describes how the fans extended their influence on the cultural and social life of the city.

> [T]he fans attempt to turn social media expression into actual social experiences. At the same time, in the process, they insist on explaining the creation of their organization, asserting their right to criticize and construct cultural ideals, and to participate in influencing social culture.[21]

Through fan activities many became re-engaged in the city, suggesting that these idols not only offered comfort and company through their songs and performances but motivated their fans to become again, full-fledged citizens, not just through their economic participation but also their intervention in the life of the city. Fan activities became a form of social power.

The birthdays of popular idols became alternative, city-wide celebrations, more eagerly anticipated by their fans than any public holiday. Each of the large fan clubs took turns to celebrate their idols' birthday around the calendar in different areas of the city. The bigger the star, the bigger the festivities. On April 30, 2022, tens of thousands gathered in Causeway Bay, jokingly renamed Keung To Bay, after the idol who lived there, to celebrate his birthday. Buses, trams, billboards, digital boards, and every available public surface were emblazoned with Keung To's image. Coinciding with the easing of COVID restrictions after a couple of months of lockdown caused by a particularly virulent wave of infections, ecstatic crowds packed the streets, joined the carnival, enjoyed free rides on the "Keung To" trams, took photos, and reveled in the general festivities. It was a happy family day that lasted into the night. Images of the huge crowds that packed the streets in Causeway Bay were reminiscent of the once familiar scenes of the now-forbidden annual July 1 demonstrations that also used to be held there. Jenkins et al. point out that this kind of "participatory audience" is a form of grassroots mobilization.[22] These birthday celebrations had become an alternative civic participation.

In contrast, during the celebration of the 25th anniversary of "The Return" of Hong Kong to China two and a half months later, on July 1, the police closed off long stretches of roads, even whole districts, to the public. Thousands were stuck for hours in traffic jams all over the city amid road closings, roadblocks, and re-routings, with thousands more pressed into overcrowded subway trains, trying to make their way home before the stations were shut down for the day. Social media was filled with angry comments from infuriated commuters. This was all to secure the city in preparation for the arrival of the Chinese premier, Xi Jinping, for the official ceremonies.

MIRROR might not be the best performers in the city, but they were elected by many to be their stars. While Hong Kong people may have been politically disenfranchised, they were able to vote for their favorite performers on *King Maker*. They were of course keenly aware of this irony. The success of the group as new home-grown performers was personal for many Hongkongers, having invested in them symbolic significance far beyond that of any other performers. They felt proud every time the group or the members achieved any kind of international attention. As Hong Kong's status as an international city and its cultural and political relevance in the world began to shrink under China's increasing control, external recognition made many feel the city had not yet completely disappeared. More and more, the new Cantopop audiences in Hong Kong refused the role of mere passive consumers of entertainment content. Even as some commentators had decided that Hong Kong music and cinema were in irrevocable decline, many believed that if they could be resurrected, the city might survive the forces of "mainlandization." The more Hong Kong was able to resuscitate its pop culture, the less likely its culture and identity would be lost. It was also ultimately about rebuilding and remaking a new Cantopop culture that belonged specifically to the city, one that was not created solely by large multinational entertainment corporations, but to a large extent, pushed into prominence by the general public. Large fan clubs boisterously cheered on the new Cantopop performers and groups. Rallying around MIRROR, in particular, had become an important collective project in these years.

In return, MIRROR was steadfastly committed to its audience in Hong Kong and to expanding the local Cantopop scene. They often collaborated with different Hong Kong-based independent musicians and artists, promoting new sounds for the new generation. MIRROR and ERROR represented a new cultural force in the city, leading the way to a broader recovery of Hong Kong's culture. Because they were products of ViuTV, the TVB alternative, they were embraced as local heroes, if not local hope. (See Chapter 4 for further discussion of MIRROR's music.)

Without a doubt, popular songs as commercial products are often created for mass entertainment and consumption. The performers or the cultural industries might not have any particular intention or meaning in their products other than to appeal to their market. A performer's decision to cultivate the Chinese market is often purely based on strategic consideration of where his or her fanbase might be. However, as Maase points out,

> [though] popular culture is not produced or controlled by 'the people,' but rather by the culture industries; yet the consumers of such culture have considerable room of action in their individual and collective appropriation as in the actual attribution of cultural value to such goods.[23]

The different political tribes engaged in bewildering interpretive battles and semiotic wars, each side rallying behind or promoting their chosen idols and stars while denigrating those from the other side.

**Piloting ERROR**

While MIRROR is unambiguously an idol group, ERROR is more difficult to define. ERROR was made up of a group of four men, also from among the *King Maker* contestants in 2018. However, except for one or two of them, they were not particularly good at dancing or singing, nor were they all conventionally good-looking. However, they were beloved for their personalities, attitude, wit, lack of inhibition, and comic abilities, all fully on display in their reality shows. They sprinkled slang, suggestive inferences, sexual innuendos, and crass jokes in their conversations, and scandalized the self-appointed moral guardians of society. They mostly made fun of themselves but didn't shy away from disparaging anyone they deemed undeserving of their respect—usually figures of authority or influence who were critical of them. In the world of idol culture, they did seem like an error. They were the obverse of MIRROR, an identity they happily embraced. Their first song was the same as MIRROR's but with different lyrics. MIRROR's song was called, "*Jatmiu gaan*一秒間ASAP"; ERROR's was called "404." While poking fun at themselves, ERROR parodied MIRROR's "perfection," and even the whole idea of idols.

ERROR's explosion in popularity in 2021 can largely be attributed to the reality show, *ERROR Selfish Projects ERROR* 自肥企画*zifei keiwaak*, produced and directed by the same team responsible for the 2018 *King Maker*, the self-styled Infinite OT Production Battlegroup 無制限OT編集団*mouzaihaan OT pinzaaptyun*, a ViuTV production unit helmed by director, Mike Lau (Lau Lok Hang 劉諾衡), and the screen writer, Mak Ho Fai 麥可暉. *ERROR Selfish Projects* brought much-needed hilarity. However, in all its apparent silliness, the show raised some fundamental issues, not just of the strangeness of ERROR's existence in the world of idols, but how their existence itself reflected the absurdist condition of the city itself. The show created a stir in Hong Kong when it was broadcast in June 2021.

*ERROR Selfish Projects* opens with a direct reference to the iconic Japanese *anime*, *Neon Genesis Evangelion*, a series about a teenage boy charged with piloting a "bio-machine," the "Eva," to fight against the "Angels," an alien force that is trying to destroy the Earth. The *ERROR* members open the show dressed in the costumes of the *anime's* characters. In a direct quote of the *anime*, *ERROR* member, Ah Dee, is asked to pilot a bio-machine, the "Error," to save the world. (Because of the lack of fricatives in Japanese pronunciation, "Eva" often becomes "e-wa." Cantonese does not have labialized "r." As a result, "ERROR" in Cantonese pronunciation often also becomes "e-wa," a pun of "Eva" in Japanese.) However, Ah Dee resists this mission. Leaving this storyline hanging, the show switches abruptly to a more familiar vein—a game show, in which the ERROR members are to compete against each other for prizes. In the disordered and upside-down world that ERROR inhabits, the distinction between winning and losing in the games is ambiguous at best. Winning and receiving prizes could sometimes feel more like a punishment. (In one of the games Ah Dee received a literal ton of canned beer for winning, which was then filmed being delivered to and overwhelming his family's tiny apartment.) The greatest enticement for them to continue participating in the games in the show, other than avoiding penalties, was the promise that they would be given resources and assistance to complete a project of their choice, whether it was to make a short film, a short documentary, a music video (MV), or to learn a new skill—things not available to them in their career trajectories.

The games to which the members of ERROR were subjected had preposterous premises and blatantly unfair rules. They responded by trying to outsmart the production team by flagrantly cheating and flouting the rules, which meant their behavior in the show was often unscripted, disruptive, and chaotic. It also means the production team often lost control of the situation to the delight of the show's writer, Mak Ho Fai. Why wouldn't one rebel, he asked, if the rules were meaningless and unfair? He continued,

> Think about it. Your opponent is the designer of the game. The referee is also the designer of the game. The natural positioning of the game is one that is tilted against the player. You would be a bit foolish if you play by the rules honestly. Breaking the rules is one thing. Being wrong is another. These are two different things. However, there are people who always link them together. It's a weapon they frequently wield. Whereas, ours is the spirit of 'ERROR x *mouzaihaan*無制限 (Infinite [possibilities]).'"[24]

While the ERROR members' strategies to thwart the rules were often more quixotic than effective, they created endless comic catharsis for their viewers. If their uncompromising but impotent antics (as futile, for example, as giving the corporate ViuTV mascot, a man in a bear suit, a swift kick) are painfully funny to watch, it is because they provoke in many, a recognition of their own impotence when confronted with the banal absurdities and injustices of everyday life.

The games that form the bulk of *ERROR Selfish Project* accentuate the uneasy balance between hilarity and discomfort. In their previous shows, the *ERROR* members either worked as a team or took turns tackling difficult or unpleasant tasks with the others cheering them on. In *ERROR Selfish Projects*, they are required to compete against each other. The members try to best each other, not because they want to win, since winning could bring its own headaches, but losing means punishment. The show also constantly tried to sow dissonance among the ERROR members. In one game, they are asked to pick each other out from groups of heavily disguised people as a test of their "true friendship" with each other. While it is a ridiculous premise, when one member fails to identify his teammate, the camera catches the irritation on his teammate's face. Even the name of the show, *zifei*自肥 (for selfish gains), suggests that it is on some level about negating camaraderie. This show forces the ERROR members to be competitive, devious, and even selfish, situating them in an environment where "truth" is not always true, rules are capricious, and rewards and punishments are not commensurate with effort. The ERROR members' banter back and forth, their self-mockeries and taunts of each other, and the punishments and prizes they receive, while uproariously funny, also leave the viewers unsettled. If MIRROR's glittery and beautiful world is a fantasy and brings pleasure and relief to the daily grind, ERROR's world feels very real. It is the viciously competitive reality and the poisonous politics of the city writ small.

In the last episode of *ERROR Selfish Projects*, the show returns to the opening storyline left hanging in episode one, when Ah Dee was asked to pilot the "bio-machine," "Error." Back in their *anime* costume, surrounded by his teammates, Fatboy, Poki, and 193, Ah Dee is in a surreal, liminal space between the completion of the entertainment in the program, and the end of the broadcast. Ah Dee asks his teammates, "Why do we have to make the program and pilot 'Error?'"

| | |
|---|---|
| *Fatboy:* | The point of entertainment is purely to entertain—to amuse. It is to provide companionship and comfort. |
| *Poki:* | These are difficult times. |
| *Fatboy:* | ERROR is a sign that there aren't many constraints in the world after all. |
| *Ah Dee:* | But there *are* lots of constraints. |
| *Fatboy:* | ERROR is a sign that there isn't much pain after all. |
| *Dee:* | But there *is* actually so much pain that one feels one could die from it! |
| *193:* | Even in the most painful moment, we can still laugh joyously and deliriously. This is what ERROR projects to the world. This is an ability that everyone needs now. |
| *Poki:* | It is also an ability you need to have; you are a part of everyone. |

The *Infinite OT Battlegroup* has addressed Ah Dee's question in different ways in different shows with different cast members—*Mountain Girl* 美女郊遊遊 *Mei Neoi Gao Jau Jau* (2020), and *Let's Sea* 大海男兒 *Dai Hoi Naam Ji* (2020). Why do something foolhardy, such as trying to generate joy in a bleak reality, or find meaning within absurdities? Why persist in doing something even when the obstacles seem insurmountable and moving forward seem so impossible? Or as in the case of *King Maker*—why insist on one's dream when the conditions are so hopeless?

Like the ERROR members, the participants of all the other *Infinite OT Production Battlegroup's* shows are made to undertake tasks that challenge their self-presumed physical and mental limitations, from abseiling down sheer mountain cliffs to free-diving into the ocean, to eating things that are normally considered inedible. The actors from these shows now all show up to help Ah Dee in his moment of crisis:

| | |
|---|---|
| *Shirley Sham (*from *Mountain Girl):* | Don't run away from what you see. No matter how powerless you feel, you must keep going, keeping your eyes open. |
| *Ah Dee:* | Mountain Girl? |
| *Shirley Chan (*from *Mountain Girl):* | Do not allow yourself to be constrained by the so-called conventions of the battle. Better yourself every day; you will find strength in the end. Wait peacefully and patiently. |

| | |
|---|---|
| *Marco (*from *Let's Sea):* | To overcome absurdities, you must first accept that absurdities are inevitable. |
| *George (*from *Let's Sea):* | Light and reason will always win! This is our belief. |
| *Ah Dee:* | *Let's Sea*? |
| *Phoebus (*from *Let's Sea):* | Believe in something, because we are the ones who determine the value of things. |
| *Ah Dee:* | More and more people I don't know have shown up! |
| *Fatboy:* | None of them is just sitting around waiting for doom. |
| *Poki:* | Even if you are imperfect… |
| *Marco:* | Even if there are people who despise you... |
| *Ah Dee:* | Don't run away! |
| *Phoebus:* | Even if nothing goes your way, you must remember what you have to offer. Don't negate what you have always believed in. |
| *Ah Dee:* | Don't run away! |
| *Shirley Sham:* | When you have doubts, ask yourself, why I am here, and what I can do here. |
| *Shirley Chan:* | If you still don't have an answer, try again. Never stop trying. |
| *Ah Dee:* | Don't run away! I get it now! |

Finally, Ah Dee realizes:

> ERROR are not the only ones fighting in this battle. As long as one remains in this place, one must use one's own method to fight from within one's position. One won't succeed by oneself. But if everyone does his or her best…

This segment ends with everyone applauding and cheering, while Ah Dee makes an affirmation of collectivity by exclaiming, "*Min-na* (Japanese for 'everyone')!"

This show, especially this last segment, resonated powerfully among its viewers. Immediately after its broadcast, the various social media platforms in Hong Kong were filled with tens of thousands of comments and discussions. *Stand News*, still operating at the time, published the entire last part of the script, verbatim. Many young people loved ERROR because of their improbable existence in a world that valued conformity at the expense of individuality. Moreover, many identified with ERROR because, like them, they too had been designated as aberrations by the authorities in the city, to be disciplined and punished (see Chapter 3).

The *Infinite OT Production Battlegroup* often strove to tell an alternative narrative, especially about the young people in the city, through their programs, whether it was in *King Maker* or *ERROR Selfish Projects*. These programs celebrate their determination and hard work, countering the established view of them as spoilt, useless, and self-indulgent. They asserted that individual effort, supported by the collective, could eventually bring about great things. After the experience of 2019, the message held enormous consolation to those trapped in hopelessness.

The two performance groups, MIRROR and ERROR, rose to prominence for many reasons, but without a doubt, the popularity of their music and TV shows reflected a longing for connectedness in Hong Kong. The song that MIRROR released at the end of 2020, "We are one and all," for the second anniversary of their formation extoled community, ending with the words: "Whatever tomorrow brings, in this place, I am not alone. I have never been alone."[25] ERROR also pledged in their song, "I Promise" (2021), to give hope, companionship, and love in a broken world:

> *Oh Oh baby, for all my love, I promise*...In this still bustling city but now besieged, who will make mischief with who? In this now voiceless and besieged city, who will make vows with who? Who will keep company with who in this tumultuous dusty world? In this prosperous, but besieged city, who will be decadent with who? In this wordless and besieged city, who will make vows with you? Loving forever, kissing you, kissing forever…[26] (Words originally in English in Italics.)

The song's promise of permanence offered comfort in a year of separations and loss when everything might at any moment disappear. Would this new boisterous pop culture be considered unacceptable and be disciplined one day? Would all the social media groups and programs on YouTube and other online platforms that have offered so much wisdom, encouragement, and companionship in these years be shut down because they threaten the new *status quo*? This uncertainty was expressed by Yau Hawk-Sau 游學修, one of the founders of the influential YouTube channel, Trial and Error (more on this group in Chapter 2). Responding to the news that Trial and Error was the most viewed YouTube channel with creative content in Hong Kong in 2021, Yao wrote on his social media,

> We are first this year, but we might not even be on the list next year. We might disappear; we might go out of business. I don't know how far we can go, but I will do my best before the world comes to an end. *Prepare for the worst and hope for the Best!* (Last sentence originally in English).[27]

It was partly this sense of the fragileness of what had collectively been created that led to, not only intense support and fandom for the various groups in entertainment but also a general rallying around Hong Kong's newly re-made popular culture, especially Cantopop, as we will see in the following chapters. It was this collective mission to nurture and protect what was deemed valuable and vulnerable that contributed to a new sense of community in the city.

The disappearance of grassroot groups, labor and professional unions, and rights groups under the new NSL was deeply mourned. However, individuals found new ways to *wailou*, finding warmth and strength among each other. These new networks helped resist the corrosive social fragmentation and sense of hopelessness permeating the city in the years after the protests.

## Notes

1 Jip Gaa Jeon葉家潤, "撕裂與鬱結: 從「林鄭語錄」看特首5年任期歸家路 (Tearing apart and causing despair: a look at where the last of the five years of the Chief Executive led through 'The Recorded Words of Carrie Lam')," *The Initium*, April 8, 2022, https://theinitium.com/article/20220409-hongkong-carrie-lam-five-year-term.

2 William Yu, "Hong Kong's population drops for third straight year while city posts net outflow of 60,000 residents in 2022," *South China Morning Post*, February 16, 2023, www.scmp.com/news/hong-kong/society/article/3210429/hong-kong-emigration-wave-net-outflow-60000-residents-2022-marking-09-cent-population-drop-3rd. "Mid-Year Population for 2022," The Government of Hong Kong Special Administrative Region Press Releases, August 11, 2022, www.info.gov.hk/gia/general/202208/11/P2022081100393.htm.

3 Baat-maau八貓, "扎進清零漩渦的港府: 香港抗疫治理矛盾, 從「中港」到「央地」的模式轉變 (Falling into the vortex of Hong Kong government's Covid Zero: Contradictions in Hong Kong's pandemic policy—the changing mode from 'Chinese Hong Kong' to 'a place controlled by Central)," *The Initium*, February 16, 2022, https://theinitium.com/article/20220216-opinion-hk-govern-covid-tension-bj?inviteToken=uyHfHoYgdu.

4 Quoted in Macabe Keliher, "Mass protests and the structure of power in contemporary Hong Kong," *China Review International* no. 1/2 (2019): 1–37, http://doi.org: 10.1353/cri.2019.0000.

5 Joseph Chan and Francis Lee, "The primacy of local interests and press freedom in Hong Kong: A survey study of professional journalists," *Journalism* 12, no. 1 (2011): 89–105, https://doi.org/10.1177/1464884910385189.

6 Baat-maau八貓.

7 *Syu dong*樹洞 (tree hollow) is a popular usage to represent a secure receptacle for one's secrets or an a trusted person in whom one could confide.

8 *Loeng sung faan*兩餸飯 (two-dish rice) was a culinary phenomenon that appeared in Hong Kong during the pandemic when eat-in service in restaurants was suspended. These are economical prix fixe take-out dinners that allows one to choose two from a range of ready-to-serve meat or vegetables dishes to go with rice.

9 梁越Leung Jyut, "專訪好青年荼毒室: 沉默的一年, 哲學還有甚麼用? (Interview with *Corrupt the Youth*: The silent year; Is there still any use for philosophy?)," *The Initium*, February 9, 2022, https://theinitium.com/article/20220209-hongkong-corrupttheyouth.

10 Ibid.

11 Ibid.

12 Ibid.

13 "八成半受訪青少年欣賞MIRROR ERROR追夢 從男團追夢經歷中產生「共悟感」增強追夢熱誠 (85% of interviewed youths admire MIRROR, ERROR chasing dreams. 'Empathy' toward the boybands' process of chasing dream, led to increase in passion for chasing dreams)," Breakthrough.org, July 5, 2023, www.breakthrough.org.hk/en/press/八成半受訪青少年欣賞mirror-error追夢-從男團追夢經歷中/.

14 Ibid.

15 Ibid.

16 Patrick W. Galbraith, "Labor of love, on the convergence of fan and corporate interests in contemporary idol culture in Japan," in Galbraith and Karlin, *Media Convergence in Japan*, (Kinema Club, 2016) 232–264: 253. Galbraith also quotes Marshalls' argument that celebrities embody audiences and social power, work at an affective level,

and represent "the potential for societal transformation." Galbraith argues that although, "[t]here are structural limitations and seldom 'a clear social movement,' but Marshall is prescient in connecting the social power of celebrities with politics. One might take this in the direction of a politics of moving bodies, supporting life, and forming new collectivities." Galbraith, 252–253. See also P. David Marshall, *Celebrity and Power: Fame in Contemporary Culture*, (Minneapolis, MN: University of Minnesota Press, 2014).

17 Galbraith, 234.

18 Anne Allison, "The cool brand, affective activism and Japanese youth," *Theory Culture & Society* 26, no. 2–3 (2009): 89–111, https://doi.org/10.1177/0263276409103118.

19 Can Zi Wan陳子雲, "2021年的香港人怎樣笑: MIRROR 同 ERROR, 緣何在崩壞時代迷狂全港? (How did Hong Kong people manage to laugh in 2021: MIRROR and ERROR: how did they captivate the entire city in an era when everything has collapsed?)," *The Initium*, https://theinitium.com/article/20210527-culture-mirror-and-error-hk-new-entertainment.

20 謝愷忻Ze Hoi Jan, "'姜濤灣'及應援活動: 淺記香港公共空間下的粉絲文化 ('Keung To Bay' and fans activities: brief record of Hong Kong public space under fans culture)," *P-articles*, May 30, 2022, https://p-articles.com/critics/2936.html.

21 Ibid.

22 Jenkins, Sam Ford, and Joshua Green, *Spreadable Media: Creating Value and Meaning in a Networked Culture* (New York: New York University Press, 2013).

23 Kaspar Maase, "Popular Culture, 'Resistance,' 'Cultural Radicalism,' and 'Self-Formation' Comments on the Development of a Theory," in Butler, Mecheril and Brenningmeyer, edits., *Resistance: Subjects, Representations, Contexts,* (Bielefeld, Germany: 2017), 46–7, accessed June 28, 2024, www.jstor.org/stable/j.ctv1xxrtf.6.

24 Quoted in "無制限OT編集団「理性軍師」28歲麥可暉：如果你還老老實實地玩，未免有點笨實 (Infinite OT Production Battlegroup's rational strategist—28 year-old Mak Ho Fai: If you are still playing the game honestly, you are a bit stupid)," *Next Magazine*, May 18, 2021, archived in https://web.archive.org/web/20210519111725/https://hk.nextmgz.com/article/2_786791_0?utm_campaign=hknext_social_nextmagazinefansclub&utm_medium=social&utm_source=facebook&utm_content=link_post&$web_only=true&_branch_match_id=916679296855033148&fbclid=IwAR2ECb78HreKR65AcZYylPX-TPFRWX6TjWmCPrGOJqW75XQ-_9I9izMLwR4.

25 MIRROR, "One and all," music by Ng Lam Fung, lyrics by T-Rexx, Music Nation, 2020.

26 ERROR, "I Promise," music by Kenneth Tse, lyrics by Chow Yiu-Fai, Music Nation, 2021.

27 Trial and Error, "Channel 得個吉 *dak go gat* (The channel got zilch)," December 13, 2021, YouTube video, www.youtube.com/watch?v=xq6ifbX4p10.

## References

Allison, Anne. "The cool brand, affective activism and Japanese youth." *Theory Culture & Society,* 26, no. 2–3 (2009): 89–111. https://doi.org/10.1177/0263276409103118.

Baat-maau八貓. "扎進清零漩渦的港府: 香港抗疫治理矛盾, 從「中港」到「央地」的模式轉變 (Falling into the vortex of Hong Kong government's Covid Zero: Contradictions in Hong Kong's pandemic policy—the changing mode from 'Chinese Hong Kong' to 'a place controlled by Central')." *The Initium*, February 16, 2022. https://theinitium.com/article/20220216-opinion-hk-govern-covid-tension-bj?inviteToken=uyHfHoYgdu.

Can Zi Wan陳子雲. "2021年的香港人怎樣笑: MIRROR 同 ERROR, 緣何在崩壞時代迷狂全港? (How did Hong Kong people manage to laugh in 2021: MIRROR and

ERROR: how did they captivate the entire city in an era when everything has collapsed?).” *The Initium*, May 27, 2021. https://theinitium.com/article/20210527-culture-mirror-and-error-hk-new-entertainment.

Chan, Joseph and Francis Lee. “The primacy of local interests and press freedom in Hong Kong: a survey study of professional journalists.” *Journalism* 12, no. 1 (2011): 89–105. https://doi.org/10.1177/1464884910385189.

ERROR. “I Promise.” Music by Kenneth Tse, lyrics by Chow Yiu-Fai. Music Nation, 2021.

Galbraith, Patrick W. “Labor of love, on the convergence of fan and corporate interests in contemporary idol culture in Japan.” In Patrick W. Galbraith and Jason G. Karlin Edits., *Media Convergence in Japan*. Kinema Club, 2016.

Jenkins, Henry, Sam Ford, and Joshua Green. *Spreadable Media: Creating Value and Meaning in a Networked Culture*. New York: New York University Press, 2013.

Jip Gaa Jeon葉家潤. “撕裂與鬱結: 從「林鄭語錄」看特首5年任期歸家路 (Tearing apart and causing despair: a look at where the last of the five years of the Chief Executive led through ‘The Recorded Words of Carrie Lam’).” *The Initium*, April 8, 2022. https://theinitium.com/article/20220409-hongkong-carrie-lam-five-year-term.

Leung Jyut梁越. “專訪好青年荼毒室: 沉默的一年, 哲學還有甚麼用? (Interview with *Corrupt the Youth*: the silent year; Is there still any use for philosophy?).” *The Initium*, February 9, 2022. https://theinitium.com/article/20220209-hongkong-corrupttheyouth.

Maase, Kaspar. “Popular culture, ‘Resistance,’ ‘Cultural Radicalism,’ and ‘Self-Formation’ comments on the development of a theory.” Martin Butler, Paul Mecheril and Lea Brenningmeyer, Edits., *Resistance: Subjects, Representations, Contexts*. Germany: Bielefeld, 2017. Accessed June 28, 2024. www.jstor.org/stable/j.ctv1xxrtf.6.

Macabe, Keliher. “Mass protests and the structure of power in contemporary Hong Kong.” *China Review International* no. 1/2 (2019): 1–37, http://doi.org:10.1353/cri.2019.0000.

Marshall, David. *Celebrity and Power: Fame in Contemporary Culture*. Minneapolis, MN: University of Minnesota Press, 2014.

“Mid-Year Population for 2022.” The Government of Hong Kong Special Administrative Region Press Releases, August 11, 2022. www.info.gov.hk/gia/general/202208/11/P2022081100393.htm.

MIRROR. “One and all.” Music by Ng Lam Fung, lyrics by T-Rexx. Music Nation, 2020.

Trial and Error. “Channel 得個吉 *dak go gat* (The channel got zilch).” December 13, 2021. YouTube Video, www.youtube.com/watch?v=xq6ifbX4p10.

Yu, William. “Hong Kong’s population drops for third straight year while city posts net outflow of 60,000 residents in 2022.” *South China Morning Post*, February 16, 2023. www.scmp.com/news/hong-kong/society/article/3210429/hong-kong-emigration-wave-net-outflow-60000-residents-2022-marking-09-cent-population-drop-3rd.

Ze Hoi Jan謝愷忻. “‘姜濤灣’及應援活動: 淺記香港公共空間下的粉絲文化 (‘Keung To Bay’ and fans activities: brief record of Hong Kong public space under fans culture).” *P-articles*, May 30, 2022. https://p-articles.com/critics/2936.html.

“八成半受訪青少年欣賞MIRROR ERROR追夢 從男團追夢經歷中產生「共悟感」增強追夢熱誠 (85% of interviewed youths admire MIRROR, ERROR chasing dreams. ‘Empathy’ toward the boybands’ process of chasing dream, led to increase in passion for chasing dreams).” Breakthrough.org, July 5, 2023. www.breakthrough.org.hk/en/press/八成半受訪青少年欣賞mirror-error追夢-從男團追夢經歷中/.

“無制限OT編集団「理性軍師」28歲麥可暉：如果你還老老實實地玩，未免有點笨實 (Infinite OT Production Battlegroup’s rational strategist—28 year-old Mak Ho Fai: if you are still playing the game honestly, you are a bit stupid).” *Next Magazine*, May 18,

2021. https://web.archive.org/web/20210519111725/https://hk.nextmgz.com/article/2_786791_0?utm_campaign=hknext_social_nextmagazinefansclub&utm_medium=social&utm_source=facebook&utm_content=link_post&$web_only=true&_branch_match_id=916679296855033148&fbclid=IwAR2ECb78HreKR65AcZYylPX-TPFRWX6TjWmCPrGOJqW75XQ-_9I9izMLwR4.

# 2 Caring for the Self, Expanding the Intellectual Space

Drink water seemed to be one of the most proffered solutions to everything that ailed one in Hong Kong in 2021. The phrase, "*gin zi jam seoi*見字飲水 (see words drink water)," became a common greeting. Given the general focus on health during the COVID pandemic, it is not too surprising that the counsel to drink water would become a popular shorthand for expressing concern for others. Behind this exhortation to take care of oneself in 2021, however, was a more nuanced concern for wellbeing, not just of the body but also of one's mental state. The instruction to drink more water was often followed by the advice to read more books. "Drink more water and read more books" became a strategy of life in the city. If to drink more water was to maintain one's life and wellbeing, to read more books was to preserve one's intellectual integrity amidst the challenges to Hong Kong's core values. Continuing from the previous chapter, I examine some of the intellectual, educational, and informational social media groups and YouTube channels that proliferated during this time. Following the evolution of the phrase "drink water," I discuss this idea of self-cultivation as a strategy to create individual freedom in a continually narrowing political space.

## *Jam do di seoi* 飲多啲水 Drink More Water

The phrase, "*gin zi jam seoi* 見字飲水," originated from a popular Facebook group, the "Drink Water Association." The phrase literally means, "drink water when you see these words." Innocently enough, the group was started by a young man who was prone to kidney stones caused by his work conditions and a generally unhealthy diet and lifestyle. At his doctor's advice, he changed his habits and his health improved. He founded the "Drink Water Association" as a joke, but he also earnestly wanted to raise awareness of the ill effects of bad habits. He posted different memes on his Facebook page to remind readers to literally drink water when they viewed his posts. The phrase caught the imagination of the general public, went viral, and became a common greeting. When messaging or emailing a friend, one might end with the phrase, "see words drink water," as a way to remind the other person to take care of himself or herself. The fact that this phrase appealed to so many reflected the toll of the tremendous daily pressures of living in the city,

DOI: 10.4324/9781003521280-3

mental and physical. The COVID pandemic only increased its pertinence. (This phrase fell out of public favor in 2022 when it was reported that the "Drink Water Association" copyrighted it.)

A couple of years before "see words drink water" became a popular maxim, the admonishment to drink more water famously came from Serrini, a popular independent Cantopop singer, during her 2018 concert. By that time, Hong Kong had already been through a decade and a half of major political activism that had failed to bring about changes. In 2003, half a million demonstrators marched to protest against the proposed implementation of a Hong Kong National Security Ordinance, "Article 23." Before the NSL, there was at least one large-scale demonstration in the city every year over various political and social issues surrounding concerns over local rights, political freedoms, and universal suffrage. The year 2009–2010 saw a protest against the construction of a high-speed rail to connect the city with mainland cities. The construction project, at a huge cost to the city, was believed to bring little benefit to Hong Kong while destroying a 40-year-old farming village, *Coi jyun cyun* 菜園村, in its path. In 2011, Hongkongers joined the worldwide Occupy Movement to protest against economic inequality in the city. Hong Kong's Gini coefficient that year was 0.537, among the highest in the world. In 2012, middle school children and their supporters protested against the imposition of a national education curriculum.[1] In 2014 and 2015, Hong Kong experienced the 79-day Umbrella Revolution and Occupy Central Movement to protest against Beijing's rescinding of its promise of universal suffrage in the then-upcoming 2017 election of the city's Chief Executive Officer. In 2016, Hong Kong people protested against the abduction of several independent publishers of oppositional books by Chinese operatives in Hong Kong, violating Hong Kong's administrative and legal sovereignty guaranteed in the Basic Law. The "Fishball Revolution," the first violent confrontation between protestors and police since 1967 also happened earlier that year. It was sparked off by anger over the arrests of hawkers selling fishballs and other street snacks during Chinese New Year by officers of the Food and Environmental Hygiene Department. These hawkers were considered part of Hong Kong's street culture, and the clearing of hawkers was perceived as a part of a process of gentrification. Thuggish counter-protesters rushed onto the scene to beat up the activists, while police stood by, leading to a conflagration of violence.

In 2018, another Chief Executive, Carrie Lam, was installed without democratic participation. Years of seemingly continuous but fruitless political struggle had led to fatigue and hopelessness among many. Serrini's exhortation to drink water was made in this context. In the midst of her performance of the song, "Let us go then, you and I," which she composed and for which she wrote the lyrics, she rallied her audience: "Read more books; drink more water; eat healthy food; don't eat too much candy. Children, we are going to be the pillar of society one day."[2]

Serrini's "drink more water" was a counsel to take care of oneself. In her words lies the comforting message that no matter how bad things look now, the situation will change. When young people grow up it will be their turn to be in charge. Those in power now will recede into irrelevance. Meanwhile, one should prepare oneself, expand one's learning, strengthen one's resolve, and take care of one's physical health, so one will live to see that day. It was an attitude of defiance in the face of continuous defeat. Her song ends with the lines,

> Get rid of all the dross from our minds. Write a new line for our lives. Let's overcome our trials today and run toward brightness. Whether forward or backward, go in peace.
> Even if nothing is right, even if everything is lost,
> We have learned from all our trials. We will not be broken.
> Keep going forward. Push back the disappointments and fatigue.
> Be grateful to all those who bravely charged ahead yesterday.
> Even if the sky has suddenly become so dark that shadows will not recede, continue forward. Go without worry.
> Forge your new order.
> Go without worry, for I too will go forth.

In an interview in early 2019, Serrini explained that she believed that real changes took time and persistent effort, and that one needed to be patient and have perseverance:

> Perhaps when one is young, one feels there are many things beyond one's capabilities. My feeling is, do what you can. It is like playing video games; you would not give up the moment you start a game even if you are unable to immediately kill the big monster. You might go study game strategy. Or you might realize this game is not for you. Then find another one. To live, you need to continue to enjoy life. I believe this is also a very good way of rebelling.[3]

Serrini could not have known that the battle with the "big monster" would occur just a few months after the publication of her interview. The scale of the 2019 Anti-Legislation demonstrations, the government's intolerant response, and the anger and desperation of the protestors knowing they were engaged in yet another hopeless struggle resulted in a fury on a scale not seen before in the city. There was little time to consider whether one was fit to play the game or not, let alone study "game strategy."

While the advice to "drink more water" continued to resonate during the protests, the meaning of this phrase changed according to the evolving situation. Instead of counseling care of oneself, it became a plea to young people to just stay alive. This was reflected in the song, "*Zeoi hau dik seonjoeng* 最後信仰 (The Last Belief)," composed by singer-songwriter, Pong Nan藍奕邦, with lyrics by one of Hong Kong's most respected Cantopop lyricist, Lam Zik林夕:

> The light may be broken, my heart may rend; it's hard to disembody love. Ice might scald; sugar turn bitter. I couldn't be bothered to figure out these perversions. In this reality, no matter how much one stomps, one can't change the direction of the world's spin. Understand that flesh and blood will decay, but integrity cannot be buried.

> Before one fights monsters, one must first learn to be human. First, I want to wish you joy in your heart.
>
> When I raise my head, the sky is still above; it cannot be shattered. When I look inside myself, I still have wisdom and thoughts that others can't steal from me. Weakness and powerlessness are proof of my perseverance. There is a belief in my soul; they cannot take that away from me. These kinds of bandits are perhaps even more afraid of you. If you want to preserve the purity of your being, you must continue to live well (*hou hou gwo haa heoi*好好過下去).
>
> I can be defeated but I cannot be bought. I believe I can fail, but I have never believed that I could escape evil by sacrificing my honor.
>
> We are going to see who lives longer; we will keep going out to the streets. If the monster comes, don't be alarmed. Even if the railroads are destroyed, our direction will not be burried. Our broken dreams might turn to nothing, but there is still the idea, a belief that in the end, goodness will remain in the world.
>
> When I raise my head, the sky is still above; it cannot be shattered. When I look inside myself, I still have wisdom and thoughts that cannot be stolen from me. I regret I am powerless. But there's nothing wrong with that. We only need to stay alive. We must drink water when we cry. Believe in the future. As long as we stay alive, there will still be meaning in the fight ....[4]

The song was released in September 2019, at the height of the Anti-Extradition Legislation movement. The social atmosphere at the time had turned dark. Several young people who saw no way out of the situation and were under pressure from their unsympathetic families committed suicide. These deaths sent shockwaves through society. Lam Zik's words aimed to provide assurance and encouragement. Most of all, it was a plea to young people to stay alive. The reference to "drink water" in the song is more than to take care of one's health or restore one's strength. "Drink water" in this context is literally about sustaining life. There is hope only if one remains alive.

As the scale and violence of the 2019 protests escalated, the city was filled with tear gas and detritus, as police armored vehicles rolled down the streets. These images, rendered as scenes of an apocalypse or war destruction, appeared in many popular songs in the years immediately following the protest. The band, Yusobeit's "*Soeng jung maan soei* 雙擁萬歲 (Hugging each other forever)," released in February 2021, describes a young couple's fear and despair in the midst of a battle. The song's MV is an animation by Tommy Ng. It depicts a story set sometime in the future when the Earth is beset by alien invaders. The young couple, armed with primitive, ineffectual weapons, are part of a resistance that tries to fend off the invading force with its massive artillery power. Reminiscent of the protesters in 2019, the characters in the MV wear gas masks while running from a noxious gas released by the enemy. The young lovers are separated in the chaos and can only send messages to each other through their feeble communication devices. Among their exchanges is the counsel to drink water. In the end, they are both killed. In the last scene, they are depicted in each other's embrace while drifting into the dark expanse of space. The lyrics are from the perspective of the young man as he tries to reach his lover:

> ... Where are you? Even if you are in the war zone, drink more warm water. Even if your tears fall, let's promise to keep safe with our comrades. The two of us in this broken world--we don't need special gas to make our tears fall--lovers in the land of death.
>
> I am here. If I find your body in the rubble, I'll cry but, even if we die, we'll go on holding hands. In this broken world, there are the two of us. Love erases the terror of the battle. We will embrace each other forever.
>
> I am here, holding your body tight in the midst of artillery fire. We will be together again. Even if we die, we'd go on holding hands.
>
> In this broken world, there are the two of us. Love erases the terror of the battle.
>
> We are together with our comrades. We kiss each other. Let's cheer to that.[5]

Though such scenarios of destruction and violence are common in Japanese animation and video games popular among young people in Hong Kong, they were virtually non-existent in the Cantopop repertoire up to that point.

The song, "*Do hot seoi* 多喝水 (Drink more water)," released in January 2021, sung by Stephanie Cheng 鄭融, approaches the battle from another angle. Equally defeated, this time, however, it is in a war of love.[6] It was one of the biggest Cantopop hits of the year. In the MV of the song, the singer, as her song's character, bathes herself in a stream of water under the shower. The lyrics are written by another of Hong Kong's primary Cantopop lyricists, Wyman Wong. "Drink more water" is ostensibly a torch song, but Wong's lyrics are famous for their multiple layers of meaning:

> Let it pour. Sweat and tears are mostly just water. You are human, that's why you feel such surging love and hate--fully overwhelming, yet not moving enough.
>
> Even having given your body and soul, you ultimately still lost to him. Hold your head up; pretend to receive your misfortune with maturity. You can turn this misguided love into nutrients for yourself. If you can, kiss your enemy goodbye. Drink a glass of water; replenish with fresh blood. Then give them a good kiss.
>
> Your loved one is gone; the world looks like a pile of ruins. Take a break; drink some water before you gather your strength to set out again. There's use for what remains of your sweat and blood. You've been brave; now pull back. There will still be all kinds of struggle later on in life. It's not time yet. Set out again tomorrow...
>
> You have to be strong in order to get past this. If you feel weak, first, strengthen your backbone. There is no point using a ladle of tears to cultivate even more tears. It is a sin to indulge in self-pity.

> You have to live a long life to get through this. Those who want to pursue their dreams should drink more water. If you still have dreams, you will not grow tired. You won't be forced out of Eden without being able to return.

To drink more water is about taking care of oneself—to rest, to restore, and to keep well till the right time comes to set out again. As a break-up song, the lyrics of "Drink more water" are unusually bellicose. There are images of physical struggle, mentions of the flow of sweat and blood, and strengthening of one's backbone that one might not normally expect in a song about a bad romance. Most of its intended audience in Hong Kong in 2021 would associate this song with another kind of heartbreak, not from love in vain, but from a political battle lost.

"Drink more water" was no longer a casual greeting as its significance continued to evolve. Musing on how the meaning of the phrase, "drink water," shifted over time, historian Wu Yi-Jui wrote in 2021,

> Hong Kong's young people use the phrase to remind themselves in the year when evil reigns that they still have to love and protect themselves. They must *hou hou wut zoek* (continue to live well). In the beginning, this was just a trendy saying that got shared around on Facebook, but it unexpectedly became this year's New Year's greeting. The Facebook page owner [of "See Words, Drink Water"] probably never expected this. Originally, he had only wanted to warn people about kidney stones.[7]

Unchanged through all the permutations of the phrase was the deep sense of loss and powerlessness reflected in it. The commentator, Jan-kei 殷琦 points out,

> Everybody is fearful and anxious. "See words drink water," seems to also contain the sense of "What else can we do? All we can do is 'see words drink water.'" In this moment, all one can do is to love oneself, to *hou hou wut zoek* (continue to live well)—after all, this is all one can do at this moment. That's right. We can't reach our distant dreams; what we can hold onto, is just the glass of water in front of us.[8]

## *Hou hou sang wut* 好好生活 Continue to Live Well

To drink more water is to *hou hou sang wut*—another common exhortation in Hong Kong after the protests. To "live well" is not about living the good life in the normal sense. It is a deliberate effort and determination to take care of oneself and to live as normal a life as one can in a broken world. To live well is about a certain attitude rather than one's material condition. Many Hongkongers faced serious legal and other consequences for their political activism in the previous years. It is estimated that by January 2020, one in three adults suffered from posttraumatic stress disorder (PTSD) from the protests and the political aftermath, a level comparable to those living in conflict zones.[9] To be able to carry on and live well requires courage and fortitude.

To take care of oneself, in this sense, might seem to retreat and yield one's claim to the public sphere. State power was broadly felt on an individual level in Hong Kong, especially during COVID when one's movements around and in and out of the city were restricted. There was enforced testing, masking, and scanning everywhere one went. This kind of state intrusion in individual life, exercised in one's physical practices and inscribed in one's daily habits, was often internalized. The way to evade this control was to withdraw from the site of power. Many in Hong Kong chose to emigrate. Those who couldn't or wouldn't, as Jan Kei counseled, could only "continue to live well." However, this does not mean to retreat in submission. On the contrary, Foucault argued, to care for oneself allows one to become aware of all the internalized rules and procedures that govern one's behavior and determine one's identity in society. This awareness ultimately gives one the ability to recreate and liberate oneself.[10] In this sense, self-care is self-creation.

In Alan Po's song, "*Dai jatjik ci saibaau fanlit* 第一億次細胞分裂 (The first billionth time the cells divide)," with lyrics by Chan Wing Him陳詠謙, caring for oneself is neither defeatist nor passive, but a powerful act of self-creation and defiance. [11] The song describes how the process of healing and self-regeneration leads to a joyous release of energy:

> What can we do? Darkness is in all four corners. But you are glowing. Wearing your injured hair and skin, you battle on even when disadvantaged. Your body starts to become different.
>
> Let's imagine, tens of billions of cells are screaming with life. They have dodged the knife's edge; blood is flowing along a new path. The whole organization will regrow. We'll see who will outlive who (*dau coeng meng*) …
>
> Even if we lose oxygen, we must have courage. We'll put ourselves forth to challenge the world even if takes more than half a century. This side laughs at you; that side wants you dead. But you will act. I do not worry that you will lose your arm; I am just afraid that you will lose your will. Your cells will explode with energy, overrun heaven and earth. They will unceasingly regenerate and turn things around. *It's another day*![12] (Words originally in English in Italics.)

As Po sings, "Your cells will explode with energy, overrun heaven and earth. They will unceasingly regenerate and turn things around," many Hong Kong people might recognize this as a description of "*baau* 爆*seed* (literally, a seed exploding)," an explosion of individual power. It is a reference to the Japanese *anime*, *Gundam Seed*. In the *anime* series, when pushed to the edge in an urgent and dangerous situation, the protagonists would see an image of an explosion of a seedlike object before them, signifying a blast of inner resource and energy, which would then enable them to defeat their enemy.

Self-care brings about regenerative power. White argues that "when the subject becomes aware of the power relations that surround and threaten her, she also becomes aware of her own possibilities of action and response."[13] In this sense, caring for the self is to expand self-agency.

### *Kung zak duk sin kei san* 窮則獨善其身 When One Comes to the End of the Road, One Cultivates Oneself Instead

"Drink more water" was only part of the equation in "living well" in Hong Kong's new reality. The second part of Serrini's counsel to her audience in 2018, after "drink more water," was "read more books." In one of the popular multi-hour live-streams on their YouTube channel in February 2021, members of the popular philosophy study group, Corrupt the Youth好青年荼毒室*Hou cing nin tou duk sat*, mentioned in the previous chapter, emphasized the importance of retreat and self-cultivation. They discussed the famous phrase from the third-century BC Confucian follower, Mencius: "*kung zak duk sin kei san* 窮則獨善其身 (When one comes to the end of the road, one cultivates or takes care of oneself)." This segment of the live-stream was excerpted and posted separately and was viewed about 70,000 times by October 2022.[14]

In Confucian thought, as illustrated by this phrase, retreat is for the sake of self-improvement. Rather than a self-focused endeavor, the Confucian notion of self-cultivation is ultimately about public good. It is not only to ensure that one's behavior does not impinge on others, but that one's behavior has the capacity to exert moral influence over others. Through constant self-examination and cultivation, one makes sure one does not veer from the good, that is, the moral, path. When one holds the correct values, one can also transform others by example. Eventually in a ripple effect, individual goodness will lead to the moral transformation of the whole society. Therefore, when the conditions to move forward are not favorable, retreating to focus on one's self-improvement has a public and moral function.

Corrupt the Youth provided a vital service at the time, introducing discussions of different philosophical works and offering different ways to help their audience navigate the new reality. Not only did they help their viewers understand the external manipulations to which one could be subjected but also how to recognize one's own ideological intransigence and blind spots. For example, early on during the COVID pandemic, many Hongkongers supported the city's medics who threatened to strike in order to pressure the government to close the border with China, especially after it was known that COVID originated and was transmitted from China. They discussed this issue on their YouTube channel, in the series, "What 7 I say?" ("7" is a homonym of a Cantonese swear word. The phrase loosely means, "what the fuck did I say?"). Rather than reflexively siding with popular sentiment, members of Corrupt the Youth analyzed the ethical implications of closing the city's border. On another occasion, they discussed the topic of "*heimong* 希望 (hope)," at a time when it seemed to many there was none. These programs aimed to give their audience some critical tools to help them analyze their reality, and by doing so, enable them to respond to it rationally, rather than being trapped in a self-defeating emotional state. The general premise of their work is articulated in the promotional material for their book, *Daaisidoi dik zithok* 大時代的哲學 (*Philosophy for the Times*), posted on August 7, 2020:

> When the times are quiet, we wouldn't ask what day it is. We go to work, get off work, eat, sleep. Then we grow old and die. However, when there is turmoil, even if we don't question the times, the times will raise issues at us. Race, democracy, environment, technology, love—everything becomes an issue. *The philosophy of the times*--the times raise questions. We also question.[15]

As part of their questioning of the times, in the second half of 2020, immediately after the implementation of the NSL, Corrupt the Youth produced a series of discussions under "What 7 I say," to explore topics that were foremost in most people's minds at the time. In August 2020, they issued a video called, "*1984* vs 2020 *dik saamgo taisi* 的三個提示 (The three lessons of 1984 vs 2020)." Till October 2022, it had been viewed 142,000 times. In an equally popular post in September 2020, they questioned if, "*Faatzi ji sei* 法治已死? (Is the rule of law dead?)" discussing the work of Ronald Dworkin. In these videos, Corrupt the Youth did not just propound on things their audience wanted to hear. They challenged their audience to question their own assumptions. In September 2020, in another video titled, "為何有言論自由？追求言論自由是為了甚麼？ *Waiho jau jinleon zijau? Zeoi kau jinleon zijau si wai liu sammo?* (Why is there freedom of speech? Why do we pursue freedom of speech?)," the group asked,

> Today, we are all trying to defend freedom of speech. However, the history of free speech does not go back that far. How did it come about? What is the difference between free speech in the past and today? What do we want to achieve in seeking free speech...?[16]

Free speech was obviously a burning issue in the NSL reality. However, rather than simply accepting its natural givenness, they explored the assumptions behind it.

The aim of Corrupt the Youth was less about supporting a particular stance than encouraging a re-examination of all values, including ones that were assumed natural, universal, and correct. When the public broadcaster, RTHK (Radio Television Hong Kong), terminated a series of popular talk shows on different intellectual subjects, including one on philosophy hosted by some of the members of Corrupt the Youth, Jim-suk 鹽叔, one of the founders (who has since left the group), lamented the loss of an important intellectual platform: "… [RTHK was] a very important public resource. It promoted intellectual exploration in society which was especially important in Hong Kong because it presented a different perspective from the same old Hong Kong pragmatism."[17]

In 2021, Corrupt the Youth decided to recreate the philosophy talk show on their own YouTube channel, calling it, "*Zithok hai gam king*哲學係咁傾 (*Keep talking about philosophy* or *This is how one talks about philosophy*. The Cantonese phrase can be and is intended to be read both ways)." This is a play on the name of the original RTHK program, "*Zithok jau gai king*哲學有偈傾 (*There's much to talk about in philosophy*)." Corrupt the Youth replicated the format of the old show, even creating a set similar to the original. Jim-suk said,

> It is very important for Hong Kong society to preserve this space. Even though the government no longer gives us the resources to make this program, we feel that if it is meaningful enough to people, we can rely on the power of our own community to reopen the space.[18]

To fund the production, Corrupt the Youth decided to raise HKD600,000 (about USD75,000) through crowdfunding. The enthusiasm for this proposed show was such that the target amount was reached within twelve hours.

The first episode of the show was broadcasted on the Corrupt the Youth YouTube channel on January 31, 2022. By the end of March, this episode had already accumulated over 180,000 views. These hour-long programs routinely accrued tens of thousands of views within the week they were posted. The appeal of the group, beyond the personalities of the individual members, reflected a yearning for moral certainty in an ethically ambiguous world. Jim-suk pointed out, "Sometimes we feel a bit anxious, a bit uncertain. That's when we need to carefully examine what we ought to believe in. This makes our lives meaningful."[19] Through its many different programs, Corrupt the Youth, aimed, not to define what was right or wrong, but to nurture critical thinking, and to introduce methods of seeing and assessing truth. In a reality that had been greatly transformed, perhaps the strategy was not to resist change, but to cultivate and re-invent oneself.

In their 2020 book, *Daai bun zithoksyu soeng gaai heoi 帶本哲學書上街去* (*Going to the streets with a philosophy book*), a volume that explores the issues of the 2019 protests, Corrupt the Youth argues for the importance of self-reflection, pointing out that to live a conscious life is essential to one's sense of self as a human:

> Socrates might have said, "an unexamined life is not worth living"...Socrates' emphasis is perhaps not on "life" itself, but on the act of examination. Animals' lives are precious even though they do not engage in self-examination. However, this kind of life is not suitable for humans...Naturally, one can live like a dumb and happy pig. However, this is a human living the life of pigs. No matter how happy one is, is this really the life humans should live? Is this not burying our nature as humans? If we are to live as humans, with human dignity, shouldn't we choose to live as clearheaded humans, even if it means living a painful life?

They end this discussion with a quote from John Stuart Mill, "It is better to be a human being dissatisfied than a pig satisfied; better to be Socrates dissatisfied than a fool satisfied."[20]

In the same way, the literary organization, *Hoenggong manhok gun*香港文學館The House of Hong Kong Literature, an organization established for the promotion of local literature that publishes the online literary magazine, *P-articles*, as well as organizes different literary and cultural events in Hong Kong, attempted to continue the conversation of the literature segment of the also defunct RTHK Talk Show, *Manhok jau gai king*文學有偈傾 (*There's much to talk about in literature*). Their YouTube channel was created in 2018, with over 27,000 subscribers by 2022. In their short films, they presented discussions of different kinds of literature, from manga to graphic novels, to nature and science writings, inviting authors, celebrities, and academics to lead discussions. They also held live-streams of different books and literary events in the city. Their program was casual, light-hearted, and humorous. Their discussions were often topical, responding to the current events in the city. During the height of the pandemic in 2020, for example, the group produced a couple of videos on Gabriel Garcia Marquez's *Love in the Times of Cholera*, and Albert Camus' *The Plague.*

Encouraging intellectual endeavors, Corrupt the Youth and The House of Hong Kong Literature helped equip their audiences with the ability to overcome the different challenges in the city. In this way, they facilitated independent thinking so as to extend personal freedom within the narrowing public sphere.

## Expanding the Intellectual Space

To many Hongkongers after the NSL, cultivating one's mind was an act of self-preservation, to safeguard one's intellectual autonomy. As an independent bookstore owner wrote on his social media, "reading [is] a kind of resistance. The bookstore is thus a base for revolution."[21] This is not an exaggeration considering that the Chinese state had, in the past decade, begun to interfere in Hong Kong's reading choices. The abduction and imprisonment of several Hong Kong independent booksellers and publishers by agents of the Chinese state was only a more dramatic part of the effort to control knowledge. Since 2015, through a series of holding companies, the Chinese state acquired Hong Kong's largest book publisher/distributer/wholesaler, Sino United Publishing, which controlled 70% of Hong Kong's book market. The corporation was, in effect, overseen by the Hong Kong Liaison Office of the Central People's Government. Since 2021, Sino United has operated 14 of the 25 largest bookstores in the city.[22] According to Louise Law, the director of the Hong Kong Chinese language literary magazine, *Zifaa* 字花 *Fleurs de Lettres*,

> They can flood their own bookshops with their own publications and decide what not to display. Not only does this greatly affect what Hong Kong people read, it also allows books on politically sensitive topics such as the Tiananmen Square protest, Tibetan identity and culture, the Nobel Peace Prize winner Liu Xiaobo, as well as the Umbrella Movement, to be banned from the shelves. Even though many independent bookshops can still display and sell these books, the reach of these books is greatly reduced. Therefore, even without censoring a book before it is published, any books deemed undesirable by the authorities can be easily silenced in the logistic web before they reach their readers.[23]

In other words, Sino United Publishing had been interfering in Hong Kong people's reading habits and taste for years, indirectly censoring works with undesirable content through its clout in the industry.

In fact, the intrusion into the intellectual life of the city began as early as 2004. Under pressure from Beijing, the Hong Kong government developed strategies to instill Chinese nationalist sentiment among the city's youth, which the culture chief of the Chinese Liaison Office in Hong Kong, Hap Tiechuan, baldly called, "necessary brainwashing (*bitjiu dik sainou*必要的洗腦)."[24] In 2012, the Hong Kong government introduced a proposal to include national education in the school curriculum, triggering a mass protest, which caused the government to retract the proposal at the time. However, after the suppression of the Anti-Extradition Legislation protest in 2019 and the implementation of the NSL, this issue was once again brought to the fore (see discussion in Chapter 3). In March 2022, the then Hong Kong Secretary for Education, Kevin Yeung, announced that all schools would be given a 48-volume boxset of mainland-produced picture books, *My Home is in China*, in order to help foster a sense of patriotism among school children while proposing that schools teach "correct" national history and culture, and the notion of law-abidingness.[25]

The admonition to "read more books" understood in this context was to encourage Hongkongers to expand their intellectual horizon beyond the new limits prescribed by the patriotic agenda of the state. In an interview, an independent bookstore owner said, "To read is to nurture our minds. We need to read, especially in our reality now. Even as the space in our reality is becoming narrower and narrower, we can still expand our thoughts."[26] In order to offer a greater diversity of reading material, to sidestep the oblique machinations by proxies for the Chinese state, and to encourage exchange of new ideas, many independent bookstores opened up immediately after the 2019 protests. By 2022, despite the ongoing pandemic resulting in waves of closures of many retail businesses, 20 new independent bookstores opened in the city. One of the proprietors pointed out, "Reading is a kind of expression of where you stand. It can also provide direction for those caught in the maelstrom. For those who have experienced great changes, words can provide psychological healing."[27] Most of these bookstores were tiny in scale, but their physical spaces were arranged to offer refuge from the gloom and noise outside. Some offered quiet reading rooms, while many others became a kind of civic space for public readings, lectures, exhibitions, and discussions. These small independent booksellers became indispensable for the city's intellectual health and independence in these 2 years.

## Looking Inwards; Turning Local

Localness gained a new emphasis in the city in the midst of China's increasingly more aggressive assertion of control over Hong Kong, and its demand for fealty from the residents. Many Hongkongers worried that the city would gradually be turned into just another Chinese city. Losing its uniqueness and identity, it would also lose its raison d'être.

The anxiety about total absorption by China was not new in Hong Kong. A strong localist consciousness had been flourishing in the city since the 2000s, which included efforts to "[protect] the pre-existing local culture in Hong Kong as the foundation of asserting Hong Kong autonomy vis-à-vis Beijing."[28] This movement gathered momentum especially after 2011 with the publication of

*Hoenggong singbong leon*香港城邦論 (*The Hong Kong City-State*), a best-seller by the scholar, Chin Wan陳雲.[29] Chin's book presented a proposal for Hong Kong to become a sovereign city-state. It won multiple awards in 2011, including RTHK's fifth annual Hong Kong Book Prize, and the Hong Kong Arts Development Award, both funded by the Hong Kong government at the time.

Chin's book, *On the Hong Kong City-State*, sparked intense interest and discussions in the city, even aspiration for independence. Radical localists, some openly xenophobic, for example, the Hong Kong Indigenous, organized militant actions in so-called "Liberate Protests" against parallel traders from mainland China.[30] Localist sentiments were also prominent in the Anti-Legislation movement in 2019.[31] The slogan, "Liberate Hong Kong, Revolution of the Times," the protest anthem, "Glory to Hong Kong," and the black bauhinia "national" flag, all contain elements of this aspiration for independence.[32] However, for the majority of Hongkongers, localism was more about maintaining the city's separate political and cultural identity from China and not seeking independence from Chinese sovereignty. Yuen and Chung argued that

> localism is not a singular force with a common political agenda; instead, it comprises multiple factions that only share the basic goal of defending the local autonomy and the interests of the local population but differ widely in terms of their ideologies and action logics.[33]

The effort to "brainwash" Hong Kong people reflected China's effort to eradicate any localist tendencies after 2019. Chin Wan's book was removed from circulation in public libraries in 2020.

Nevertheless, even as a fringe political ideal, localism raised the public's interest in the city's history and inspired a new appreciation for old customs, buildings, businesses, industries, as well as neighborhoods. After the end of the 2019 protests, as Hong Kong people were stuck in the city during COVID, many interest groups and social media groups sprang up to record the different aspects of old Hong Kong, especially those considered on the verge of disappearing. To many younger Hongkongers, understanding the city's history and the everyday practices unique to it was a way to recreate a Hong Kong identity.

One of the founders of the social media group, and author of a volume of the same title, *Hoenggong loupou geiluk caak* 香港老舖記錄冊 *Hong Kong Historical Shops*, Ian Ma, explained why he felt that it was important to pay attention to these old places and shops:

> Why is Hong Kong, Hong Kong? It's not just a geographical designation. It is because these old shops have shaped the lives of Hong Kong people...they are part of our lives. We are connected to them in our daily lives. This way of life defines our identity. Gradually, they become a part of so-called Hong Kong culture. It is this culture that makes this place more than just a geographical reference. As I've often said, perhaps with a bit of exaggeration, if we were to suddenly lose all the old shops in Hong Kong and they were all replaced by new

> stores, and if all our 茶餐廳 *ca can teng* (HK-style cafes) were gone, or if all the sauce makers were gone, our way of life would be completely altered. Will this still be the Hong Kong that we know? Or would this just be any city called Hong Kong? That's why I've often said that old shops are one of the things that defines Hong Kong. In a very direct way, if an old shop closes, especially one that is very representative of Hong Kong's culture, I would feel as if a bit of Hong Kong is gone. That's why I think these Hong Kong old shops are the most important things in the city: How do we define Hong Kong as Hong Kong? How do we define Hongkongers as Hongkongers? That's why I feel we need to pay more attention, or even do more for them.[34]

Similarly, Alan Chan, who ran the *Facebook* page, *Wahfurelocation*, which documented the daily life of the community in the Wah Fu, an old housing estate built in 1967, facing redevelopment, explained his project:

> Since 2019, I have been seriously thinking about this: The easiest way to maintain and affirm Hong Kong peoples' collective identity is to learn the history of the place where we grow up. Since then, I have been studying the history of my own community. In the process of discovering this history, I also try to find my own identity. If we did not have a collective identity, we would not love this place.[35]

Two popular YouTube channels, Mill Milk and Ricezi 米紙Mai Zi, in particular, created by former reporters from media outlets that had been shut down, specialize in reporting on local life in their large numbers of short documentary-style films. They record stories on different aspects of local culture and communities on the brink of disappearance, the work of old craftsmen, as well as the stories of old family businesses.

A series on Mill Milk called "*Catbaakmaan zung sangwut* 700萬種生活 (Seven Million Ways of Life)," told the stories of individuals who attempt to preserve an old memory, redefine a particularly local way of life, or invent an alternative way of living in the city—an urban nomad who chose to live in a van, eschewing stable housing; those who abandoned city life to be farmers in the countryside; those who gave up high-paying professional careers to open small, community businesses; those who devoted their lives to preserving particular aspects of old Hong Kong, from old movie posters to old toys, etc.

At the same time, RiceZi often reported on older forms of consumption habits. They had a series on the disappearing *daipaidong*, the open-air food stalls that have, for decades, offered cheap hot food for the working masses. They explored shopping venues that serve local communities rather than the malls frequented by tourists. They made programs on village traditions among the inhabitants of the outer islands, etc.

Recording and celebrating this diversity of lifestyles, professions, and old Hong Kong, these programs showed that in the shadow of the expensive high-rises, there were myriads of stories, lifestyles, and aspirations. All these seemingly insignificant aspects of everyday life in Hong Kong made up a very distinct human ecology that defined the city. The renewed interest in the older ways of life or economic modes might have partly been prompted by a general nostalgia for Hong Kong's "golden age" from the 1980s to the early 1990s. However, in this nostalgia is a questioning of Hong Kong's relentless development, in which historic architecture is often razed to make way for luxury apartment buildings or hotels, or the countryside destroyed, and oceans filled in to create more land to enrich developers, speculators, and foreign investors. It is also to reveal how old neighborhoods are labeled unhygienic or chaotic to justify redevelopment; and how traditional businesses are designated as "sunset industries," and deliberately phased out, because they no longer fit the government's contemporary economic or ideological model of what the city should be.

All these various media and groups provided stories to counter the government's dominant narrative of the city. These stories are not necessarily about returning to the past. Rather, they are expressions of dissatisfaction with the present as advanced by the government—the corrosive values of a homogenous nationalist narrative, the relentless materialist, competitive, and superefficient way of life—the prosperity that necessitates stability that in turn requires strict control of individual behaviors and choices. Through the different stories, the different YouTube channels questioned the prescribed role of Hong Kong people in a financial capital where the so-called "economy first" mentality dominates, in which financial success is the only measure of one's achievement.[36] The popularity of these shows reflected a desire among many to find a different way of life or identity, perhaps in this older, more humane, and more community-minded Hong Kong. With the loss of many things that were once thought of as indelible in Hong Kong, and with the intrusion of a new, unfamiliar political culture, the re-examination of local things, places, and peoples was to resist brainwash, to reject the prescribed and to re-create one's own story.

With all the changes and losses in the city, Corrupt the Youth's member, Gam-zai, argued that Hong Kong's cultural terrain was facing collapse.[37] Hong Kong, or the old version of it, might indeed be dead. But Gam-zai thought that it was a good thing because Hong Kong people were "forced into saving ourselves."[38] He explained,

> In the past Hong Kong people had a kind of arrogance that they don't need to worry about survival. The moment we were born, we were the 'Pearl of the Orient,' an international metropolis, Asian financial center, right behind New York and London. But these were given to us by others. The financial system was thought up by somebody else and given to us. It's not something we came up with. Actually, I can sum [the situation] up with four words: *ham deu cung lin* 砍掉重練 (cut it all off and start cultivating from the beginning). People have been forced to wake up, to discover that actually, we don't have anything. That's fine.[39]

Sei-go of Corrupt the Youth also argued that having to start from nothing could mean an opportunity to carefully think about how one wanted to identify oneself:

> What can those of us who remain in Hong Kong do? To reshape Hong Kong people's attitude toward life...To live in style. We should judge others by using a set of aesthetic or artistic vocabulary. Don't use criteria such as, is that person successful in society? How much money does he make? Or, how many followers does he have? Don't use these to evaluate someone. We should use qualifiers like "柒 *cat* (limp dick)" or "型 *jing* (cool)" instead.[40]

As Hong Kong people were forced to give up their political aspirations and forced to adapt to the many new rules and controls in their lives, many Hongkongers responded by "drinking more water, reading more books." This strategy of self-care and self-cultivation was not a narcissistic preoccupation. It was a new method of living and an assertion of personal freedom despite the restrictive external reality. This self-cultivation was a refusal of all that was fixed and given, in order to refashion a new identity, and, in Sei-go's words, to create a life that was *jing*型 (cool).

## Addendum

A study conducted by the Hong Kong University in 2016 captured the scale of discontent among a lot of young Hongkongers as more and more mainland Chinese crowded into the city, competing with them for resources. It explains some of the localist sentiments:

> In Hong Kong, there is no lack of media reports on the negative sentiments towards the new immigrants in which [they] are always perceived as someone who are [sic] scrambling for the limited local resources that should be solely enjoyed by locals. Other related social problems include the raising real estate prices, overcrowded malls and theme parks, occupying beds at maternity wards, emptying shelves of infant milk formula and daily products, snapping up taxpayers' money, and even impolite and uncivilised behaviours in public areas. There are also worries that their arrivals would reduce the locals' job opportunities and salary levels. Since then, there are many policies implemented to tackled [sic] the problems like combating parallel trading, restricting the bringing in of baby formula among cross-border travellers, zero quota policy in hospitals, and the replacement of the multiple-entry permits of Shenzhen residents with one trip per week arrangement. However, these stopgap measures do not bear a consistent policy ideology but merely formulated to provide a short-term fix. The fact that young people do not strongly associate the in-group/out-group divide with welfare might provide a new perspective towards the issue.[41]

On July 10, 2019, an essay appeared in LIHKG, a popular multi-category forum website in Hong Kong, illustrating the sentiments described in the report. The discussions and posts on LIHKG are often deliberately provocative and contrary. It was also a platform inhabited by many with localist sympathies at the time. However, during the 2019 protests, aside from exchanges of protest tactics, there were also some serious discussions of social issues. A viral post in July 2019 by the user, *Daaihou giu matgo* 大號叫乜哥, garnered wide attention and many mainstream media and commentators weighed in on the issues raised.[42] The post is a laundry list of young people's dissatisfaction at the time:

> Honestly, I am most afraid of the scenario of Carrie Lam announcing that she would immediately withdraw the Extradition Law and then resign in tears. This is because a lot of Hong Kong people would think our struggle had already borne fruit. Public opinion would turn placid, and we'd lose momentum. Those who persist would be isolated and weakened, having to retreat in the end. And then a lot of people will forget the original meaning of our struggle and the reasons for our anger. The Extradition Law is only the fuse, the end of the fuse. Whereas the fuel is the public anger caused by the hostile policies the Chinese government has been forcing on Hong Kong people since 1997, beating us down in different areas, from politics, education, medical care, housing, and to food and drink. Although they don't use bullets to shoot Hong Kong people, they apply psychological oppression. As a result, Hong Kong people have been emigrating, one after another. Or, one after another, they have become numb like zombies, interested only in money. Or, feeling so hopeless about the future they kill themselves.
>
> Why do Hongkongers like us have to endure education that is like force-feeding ducks and spend our childhood that is supposed to be happy under such immense pressure?
>
> Why do Hongkongers like us have to learn Putonghua? Aren't Tang and Song dynasty poetry read in Cantonese?
>
> Why do Hongkongers like us have to give up our dreams, beginning in high school, forced by our parents to be doctors, lawyers, and join other similarly supposedly lucrative professions?
>
> Why are Hongkongers like us, once we get into university, or start working, evaluated and classified by society and the people in it according to our ability to make money?
>
> Why do Hongkongers like us, when we fall in love and want to get married, have to first consider whether the other person owns real estate?
>
> Why do Hongkongers like us, when we give birth, have to worry if there are beds in the maternity wards in hospitals or how much baby formula costs with all the price-gouging.[43]
>
> Why do Hongkongers like us, after we give birth, have to start figuring out how to make money and establish connections even before the child turns two?
>
> Why do Hongkongers like us, when we get to the supermarket, find that things are getting more and more expensive? It is obvious that international prices are falling!
>
> Why do Hongkongers like us, when we want to set up a business, have to deal with unconscionable blood-sucking landlords?

Why are Hongkongers like us, when we go to work every day, pushed onto trains, delivered like beasts to our jobs, carriageful by carriageful?

Why are Hongkongers like us, even when we want to go and relax in the parks, disturbed by noisy crowds?

Why are Hongkongers like us, when we go to Mongkok or Causeway Bay, made to feel like we've gone to the mainland?[44]

Why do Hongkongers like us have to be afraid of being beaten up by the police just because we wear black?[45]

Why do Hongkongers like us, when we go to restaurants, have to pay the premium price for the worst service and quality of food?

Why do Hongkongers like us, have to fight for bed space when we need to go to a home for the elderly?

Why do Hongkongers like us, when we die, have to worry about where to put our graves? We don't even have space for the dead!

Ultimately, what led to Hongkongers living this kind of life after 1997? Hong Kong's per capita GDP is HK$380,000, higher than France, Germany, Great Britain, and Japan, and only just below Sweden and Finland.

Why is it that we can't have a better life like in these developed nations--a kind of life that gives us a place to die, shows appreciation for those with abilities, and provides nurture for the young?

Why is our median income only $10,500?

Why do Hongkongers like us born around 1997, mostly kind and upright, have to spend all our energy in a life that is full of hardship and boredom, that is monotonous and soulless, then end up in a hutch of a home and are unable to make our children happy?

As long as those in power and their schemes and the capitalist system that squeezes the people, creating deep contradictions and despair, are not destroyed, Hongkongers will never be able to live decently.[46]

## Notes

1 Cf. Agnes Chow in the Introduction.

2 Serrini, "Let us go then, you and I," music by Ron Cheung, lyrics by Serrini, 2019, hwww.youtube.com/watch?v=GBbIE6Fyspk. The song title is from T.S. Eliot's "The Love song of J. Alfred Prufrock."

3 Zung Ga-jing鍾嘉瑩, "無力感時代. 開發新秩序 獨立音樂人, *Serrini* (Age of powerlessness: Independent musician, Serrini)," *Apple Daily*, April 30, 2019, https://collection.news/appledaily/articles/QLFTT6HQL5VD7TXIG7GA4EZZEE.

4 林二汶 Eman Lam, "最後的信仰 (The Last Belief)," music by Pong Nan, lyrics by Lam Zik, Sony Music, 2021. The song was originally sung by Eman Lam. Lam, who was popular at the time, disappointed her fans two years later when she released a song called "*Zung waa zung*中華頌Ode to China," on the 25th Anniversary of Hong Kong's "Return" to China. Her move, essentially a vow of allegiance to China, was considered

by many to be her entré into the Chinese market. Given the nature of this song, her move was seen as a deep betrayal of her political principles and her Hong Kong fans. She has since lost all her audience in Hong Kong.

5 Yusobeit, "雙擁萬歲 (Hugging each other forever)," music by Yusobeit, lyrics by YU, Anthology, 2021, www.youtube.com/watch?v=tTQJvYjt4Z4.

6 鄭融 Stephanie Chen, "多喝水 (Drink more water)," music by Howie@Dear Jane, lyrics by Wyman Wong, Starztrack, 2021.

7 Wu Yi-Jui 吳易叡, "見字飲水—致努力成為活史料的香港人 (read words, drink water—to the Hong Kong people who are diligently being living history)," *Si soeng taan hak*思想坦克, July 1, 2021, https://voicettank.org/見字飲水致努力成為活史料的香港人/.

8 Jan-kei殷琦, "見字飲水, 是因為我們要學懂好好活著 (See words drink water, because we have to learn how to carry on living well)," *Inmedia*, July 4, 2021, www.inmediahk.net/node/1081868.

9 "Hong Kong PTSD level 'comparable to conflict zones', study finds," *BBC* online, January 10, 2020, www.bbc.co.uk/news/world-asia-china-51058233.

10 Richard Shusterman, "Somaesthetics and care of the self: The case of Foucault," *The Monist*: *Philosophy as a Way of Life* 83, no. 4 (2000): 530–551: 534–5, DOI:10.2307/27903703.

11 Quoted in Brent L. Pickett, "Foucault and the politics of resistance," *Polity* 28, no. 4 (1996): 445–466: 465, accessed July 13, 2023, www.jstor.org/stable/3235341.

12 Alan Po, "第一億次細胞分裂," lyrics by Chan Wing Him, Sony Music, 2021.

13 Richard White, "Foucault on the care of the self as an ethic and a spiritual goal," *Human Studies* Winter (2014): 489–504, https://doi.org/10.1007/s10746-014-9331-3. Michel Foucault, "The ethics of concern for the self as a practice of freedom," in *Ethics, Subjectivity and Truth* (New York, Free Press, 1997).

14 Corrupt the Youth, "談窮則獨善其身—亂世中的心態 (When one reaches the end of the road-One's attitude in a chaptic world)," 直播精華 (From the live show), Ep. 8, February 9, 2021, YouTube video, 17.27, www.youtube.com/watch?v=eBL6nFrKUKE.

15 www.youtube.com/watch?v=OUQZ-wKD9wc

16 Under the series, *哲學家講呢啲* (*This is what philosophers talk about*), October 3, 2020b, YouTube video, /www.youtube.com/watch?v=gBnMhMpUf9M.

17 Joeng Hei-jing楊喜盈 "好青年荼毒室跨界合作 哲學繼續傾 拉闊思考空間 (Corrupt the Youth crossover with different segments. Continue to talk about Philosophy. Broadening the space for thinking)," February 18, 2022, *Ming Pao News* online, https://news.mingpao.com/pns/副刊/article/20220218/s00005/1645122060739/好青年荼毒室跨界合作-哲學繼續傾-拉闊思考空間.

18 Ibid.

19 Ibid.

20 *Hou cing nin tou duk sat*好青年荼毒室, *Daai bun zit hok syu soeng gaai heoi帶本哲學書上街去* (*Going to the streets with a philosophy book*) (Electronic edition. Hong Kong: Haoqingnian tou syu sat, 2020a): 9–11. The quote is from John Stuart Mill, *Utilitarianism* (1861), chapter 2. Mill argues for the importance of individuality and liberty, as opposed to merely following orders or conventions, even if the latter lead to the Utilitarian objective of achieving social harmony and welfare. Forcing a person to live according to prevailing opinion prevents individuals from achieving the full and free development of human faculties. The term "*gong zyu*港豬Hong Kong Pig" was often applied to especially the older generations in Hong Kong, who were only concerned with their material wellbeing and making money, leaving others to fight for rights. They were like pigs that cared only about eating, ignorant of their imminent slaughter.

21 Quoted from Can Fung-ging 陳奉京, "在垃圾年代重新走進一家書店: 香港崩壞時的獨立書店新浪潮 (Walking anew into a bookstore in these rubbish years: The new independent bookstores wave in a broken Hong Kong), *The Initium*, October 12, 2021, https://theinitium.com/article/20211012-culture-book-stores-hk-in-the-new-age.

22 Michael Forsythe and Crystal Tse, "Hong Kong bookstores display Beijing's clout," *The New York Times*, October 19, 2015, www.nytimes.com/2015/10/20/world/asia/hong-kong-bookstores-display-beijings-clout.html.

23 Louise Law, "What are we talking about when we talk about Hong Kong Literature?" June 13, 2020, *Pen/Opp*, www.penopp.org/articles/what-are-we-talking-about-when-we-talk-about-hong-kong-literature.

24 Yew Chiew Ping, Kwong Kin-ming, "Hong Kong Identity on the Rise," *Asian Survey* 54, no.6 (2014): 1088–1112: 1101–2, https://doi.org/10.1525/as.2014.54.6.1088.

25 Selina Cheng, "Hong Kong will distribute mainland books to schools to promote patriotism," March 23, 2022, *Hong Kong Free Press*, https://hongkongfp.com/2021/03/23/hong-kong-will-distribute-mainland-books-to-schools-to-promote-patriotism/.

26 "開拓另一個閱讀時代 相信書店的意義 (Opening an age of reading. Believe in the meaning of a bookstore)," *HKfeature*, September 15, 2021, https://hkfeature.com/artsculture /開拓另一個閱讀時代-相信書店的意義/ /開拓另一個閱讀時代-相信書店的意義/.

27 Quoted from Can Fung-ging陳奉京.

28 Ho-Fung Hung, *City on the Edge: Hong Kong under Chinese rule*, (Cambridge, Cambridge University Press, 2022), 173.

29 Chin Wan, 香港城邦論*Hoeng Gong sing bong lun* (*The Hong Kong City-Stat*), (Hong Kong, 天窗出版社, 2011).

30 Resentment at China's increasing influence in Hong Kong fueled localist sentiments among many young people. Their anger was often aimed at new immigrants or the overwhelming number of tourists and visitors from China who crowded into the city every day. See Addendum to this chapter.

31 Hung, 173.

32 Samson Yuen and Sanho Chung, "Explaining localism in post-handover Hong Kong: An eventful approach," *China Perspective* 3 (2018), https://doi.org/10.4000/chinaperspectives.8044.

33 Ibid.

34 Liber Research Community 本土研究社*Buntou jingause*, "執笠中,老舖留下之必要 (Going out of business. The necessity of keeping old shops)," January 26, 2023, *Haan zi zung*閒置中Podcast, website, 52.55, https://podcasters.spotify.com/pod/show/liberresearch/episodes/EP-138----e1tp1p2. Ma Kei Lok馬基諾et al., *Hoenggong loupou geinimcak香港老舖記錄冊* (*Record of Hong Kong Historical Shops*), (Hong Kong: Enlighten and Fish 亮光文化, 2022).

35 Yu Yuen Lan余婉蘭, "在香港散步: 走啊走, 把自己的城市走到心裏, 記憶裏 (Taking walks in Hong Kong: Walk and walk, taking the city into one's heart and memory)," *The Initium*, January 21, 2023, https://theinitium.com/article/20230121-culture-walking-in-hk-wandering-and-memories.

36 Yew Chiew Ping and Kwong Kin-ming, 1098–9.

37 Loeng Jyut梁越, "專訪好青年荼毒室：沉默的一年，哲學還有甚麼用？留下來的人可以做什麼？重塑香港人對人生的看法 (Interview with *Corrupt the Youth*: The silent year. Is there any more use for philosophy? Reconstructing how Hong Kong people look at life)," *The Initium*, February 9, 2022, https://theinitium.com/article/20220209-hongkong-corrupttheyouth.

38 Ibid.
39 Joeng Hei Jing 楊喜盈.
40 Ibid.
41 Wong Yee Hang, "A Survey Experiment on Discontent Among the Youth: Welfare or Politics? Welfare or Politics? A Comparative Analysis on Support for Redistribution and Political Discontent in Hong Kong Final Report," The Public Policy Research Funding Scheme (PPRFS), www.cepu.gov.hk/doc/en/research_report(PDF)/2016.A8.051.16D_Final%20Report_Dr%20Wong.pdf.
42 The pro-establishment media, *HK01*, published a series of three essays on this topic, interviewing Cheung Bing-leung 張炳良, professor at the Education University of Hong Kong, and a former government official. Joeng Hou-sing楊皓鋮, " 訪張炳良：與年輕人溝通 談什麼？談何容易! (Interview with Cheung Bing-leung: Communicating with young people. What should one talk about? It's not easy!)," *HK01*, July 15, 2019, www.hk01.com深度報道/351849/逃犯條例-訪張炳良-與年輕人溝通-談什麼-談何容易.
43 Hong Kong mothers had to compete with mainland women for bed space in hospitals to give birth. Many mainland women went to Hong Kong to give birth, so their children would receive Hong Kong residence, causing acute shortage in hospital beds. In 2011, 4 in 10 births in Hong Kong were from mainland mothers. The situation eased in 2013 when the Hong Kong Chief Executive at the time, C.Y. Leung, banned non-local women from reserving hospital beds for delivery. After China's milk scare in 2008 when milk products were adulterated with chemical melamine, resulting in the deaths of six babies, parallel traders from China buying up baby formula in the city caused severe shortages in in Hong Kong to the despair of Hong Kong parents.
44 Both areas are tourist hotspots, especially for mainland visitors.
45 Black is the color of the 2019 protest.
46 *Daaihou giu matgo*大號叫乜哥, "老實講：我最怕見到嘅係林鄭撤回逃犯條例 然後下台 (Honestly, I am afraid to see Carrie Lam resign after withdrawing the Extradition Law)," *LIHG*, July 10, 2019, https://lihkg.com/thread/1303071/page/1.

## References


Can Fung-ging 陳奉京. "在垃圾年代重新走進一家書店: 香港崩壞時的獨立書店新浪潮 (Walking anew into a bookstore in these rubbish years: The new independent bookstores wave in a broken Hong Kong)." *The Initium*, October 12, 2021. https://theinitium.com/article/20211012-culture-book-stores-hk-in-the-new-age.

Chen, Stephanie 鄭融. "多喝水 (Drink more water)." Music by Howie@Dear Jane, lyrics by Wyman Wong, Starztrack, 2021.

Cheng, Selina. "Hong Kong will distribute mainland books to schools to promote patriotism." Hong Kong Free Press, March 23, 2022. https://hongkongfp.com/2021/03/23/hong-kong-will-distribute-mainland-books-to-schools-to-promote-patriotism/.

Chin Wan. 香港城邦論 (*The Hong Kong City-Stat*). Hong Kong, 天窗出版社, 2011.

Corrupt the Youth. *Daai bun zit hok syu soeng gaai heoi帶本哲學書上街去* (*Going to the streets with a philosophy book*). Electronic edition. Hong Kong: Haoqingnian tou syu sat, 2020a.

Corrupt the Youth. *哲學家講呢啲* (*This is what philosophers talk about*). October 3, 2020b. YouTube video. www.youtube.com/watch?v=gBnMhMpUf9M.

Corrupt the Youth. "談窮則獨善其身—亂世中的心態 (When one reaches the end of the road—One's attitude in a chaptic world)." 直播精華 (From the live show), Ep. 8. February 9, 2021. YouTube video, 17.27. www.youtube.com/watch?v=eBL6nFrKUKE.

*Daaihou giu matgo*大號叫乜哥. "老實講：我最怕見到嘅係林鄭撤回逃犯條例 然後下台 (Honestly, I am afraid to see Carrie Lam resign after withdrawing the Extradition Law)." *LIHG*, July 10, 2019. https://lihkg.com/thread/1303071/pag.

Forsythe, Michael and Crystal Tse. "Hong Kong bookstores display Beijing's clout." *The New York Times*, October 19, 2015. www.nytimes.com/2015/10/20/world/asia/hong-kong-bookstores-display-beijings-clout.html.

Foucault, Michel. "The ethics of concern for the self as a practice of freedom." *Ethics, Subjectivity and Truth*. New York: Free Press, 1997.

Hang, Wong Yee. "A Survey Experiment on Discontent Among the Youth: Welfare or Politics? A Comparative Analysis on Support for Redistribution and Political Discontent in Hong Kong Final Report." The Public Policy Research Funding Scheme (PPRFS). www.cepu.gov.hk/doc/en/research_report(PDF)/2016.A8.051.16D_Final%20Report_Dr%20Wong.pdf.

Hei-jing, Joeng. "訪張炳良：與年輕人溝通 談什麼？談何容易！(Interview with Cheung Bing-leung: Communicating with young people. What should one talk about? It's not easy!)." *HK01*, July 15, 2019. www.hk01.com深度報道/351849/逃犯條例-訪張炳良-與年輕人溝通-談什麼-談何容易.

Hei-jing, Joeng 楊喜盈. "好青年荼毒室跨界合作 哲學繼續傾 拉闊思考空間 (Corrupt the Youth crossover with different segments. Continue to talk about philosophy. Broadening the space for thinking)." *Ming Pao News* online, February 18, 2022. https://news.mingpao.com/pns/副刊/article/20220218/s00005/1645122060739/好青年荼毒室跨界合作-哲學繼續傾-拉闊思考

Ho-Fung, Hung. *City on the Edge: Hong Kong under Chinese rule*. Cambridge: Cambridge University Press, 2022.

"Hong Kong PTSD level 'comparable to conflict zones', study finds." *BBC* online, January 10, 2020. www.bbc.co.uk/news/world-asia-china-51058233.

Jan-kei殷琦. "見字飲水，是因為我們要學懂好好活著 (See words drink water, because we have to learn how to carry on living well)." *Inmedia*, July 4, 2021. www.inmediahk.net/node/1081868.

Lam, Eman. "最後的信仰 (The Last Belief)." Music by Pong Nan, lyrics by Lam Zik. Sony Music, 2021.

Law, Louise. "What are we talking about when we talk about Hong Kong literature?" *Pen/Opp*, June 13, 2020. www.penopp.org/articles/what-are-we-talking-about-when-we-talk-about-hong-kong-literature.

Liber Research Community本土研究社. "執笠中,老舖留下之必要 (Going out of business. The necessity of keeping old shops)." *Haanzi zung* 閒置中. Podcast, 52.55 min, January 26, 2023. https://podcasters.spotify.com/pod/show/liberresearch/episodes/EP-138----e1tp1p2.

Loeng Jyut梁越. "專訪好青年荼毒室：沉默的一年，哲學還有甚麼用？留下來的人可以做什麼？重塑香港人對人生的看法 (Interview with *Corrupt the Youth*: The silent year. Is there any more use for philosophy? Reconstructing how Hong Kong people look at life)." *The Initium*, February 9, 2022. https://theinitium.com/article/20220209-hongkong-corrupttheyouth.

Ma Kei Lok馬基諾et al. *Hoenggong loupou geinimcak香港老舖記錄冊* (*Record of Hong Kong Historical Shops*). Hong Kong: Enlighten and Fish 亮光文化, 2022.

Pickett, Brent L. "Foucault and the Politics of Resistance." *Polity* 28, no. 4 (1996): 445–466. Accessed July 13, 2023. www.jstor.org/stable/3235341.

Po, Alan. "第一億次細胞分裂." Lyrics by Chan Wing Him. Sony Music, 2021.

Serrini. "Let us go then, you and I." Music by Ron Cheung, lyrics by Serrini, 2019. www.youtube.com/watch?v=GBbIE6Fyspk.

Shusterman, Richard. "Somaesthetics and care of the self: The case of Foucault." *The Monist: Philosophy as a Way of Life* 83, no. 4 (2000): 530–551: 534–5. DOI:10.2307/27903703.

White, Richard. "Foucault on the care of the self as an ethic and a spiritual goal." *Human Studies* Winter (2014): 489–504. https://doi.org/10.1007/s10746-014-9331-3.

Wu Yi-Jui 吳易叡. "見字飲水—致努力成為活史料的香港人 (Read words, drink water—to the Hong Kong people who are diligently being living history)." *Si soeng taan hak*思想坦克, July 1, 2021. https://voicettank.org/見字飲水致努力成為活史料的香港人/.

Yew Chiew Ping and Kwong Kin-ming. "Hong Kong identity on the rise." *Asian Survey* 54, no.6 (2014): 1088–1112: 1101–2. https://doi.org/10.1525/as.2014.54.6.1088.

Yu Yuen Lan余婉蘭. "在香港散步: 走啊走, 把自己的城市走到心裏, 記憶裏 (Taking walks in Hong Kong: Walk and walk, taking the city into one's heart and memory)." *The Initium*, January 21, 2023. https://theinitium.com/article/20230121-culture-walking-in-hk-wandering-and-memories.

Yuen, Samson and Sanho Chung. "Explaining localism in post-handover Hong Kong: An eventful approach." *China Perspective* 3 (2018). https://doi.org/10.4000/chinaperspectives.8044.

Yusobeit. "雙擁萬歲 (Hugging each other forever)." Music by Yusobeit, lyrics by YU. Anthology, 2021. www.youtube.com/watch?v=tTQJvYjt4Z4.

"開拓另一個閱讀時代 相信書店的意義 (Opening an age of reading. Believe in the meaning of a bookstore)." *HKfeature*, September 15, 2021. https://hkfeature.com/artsculture/開拓另一個閱讀時代-相信書店的意義/ /開拓另一個閱讀時代-相信書店的意義/.

Zung Ga-jing鍾嘉瑩. "無力感時代. 開發新秩序 獨立音樂人, *Serrini* (Age of powerlessness: Independent musician, Serrini)." *Apple Daily*, April 30, 2019. https://collection.news/appledaily/articles/QLFTT6HQL5VD7TXIG7GA4EZZEE.

# 3 Generational Contests

## Re-forming, Re-educating, and De-radicalizing "Useless Youths"

### *Faicing* 廢青 Useless Youth

By the mid-2010s, and especially after 2019, young people in Hong Kong became the target of much censure. They were often blamed for Hong Kong's societal unrest of the previous two decades and accused of becoming continuously more radical over the years. Their activism was denigrated as refusing honest work and causing chaos. When they walked out of their classes and jobs during the Occupy Movement in 2014 to demand universal suffrage in the election of the city's officials, they were called *faicing* 廢青 (useless youth/young losers). When they protested against the "The Fugitive Offenders and Mutual Legal Assistance in Criminal Matters" in 2019's Anti-Legislation Protests, they were vilified as "*haak bou* 黑暴 black rioters." Their efforts to transform society into one that they felt was more democratic and just were dismissed as selfishness and naiveté. In 2022, the Secretary for Education at the time, Kevin Yeung, castigated the city's youth for being "passive and self-indulgent," lacking in ambition and incapable of social advancement.[1] They were a "problem" that needed to be "solved." This chapter is about young people in Hong Kong, the subject of much societal consternation and opprobrium. I will discuss the political and social contradictions between young people and the greater society, and the government strategies to deradicalize them.

Contempt toward young people in Hong Kong predated the 2019 protests. The former Legislative Council member and former lecturer in Social Work who specialized in youth issues, Shiu Ka-chun 邵家臻,[2] discovered that while the term *faicing* (useless youths) had little currency in the city prior to 2014 according to Google statistics, searches for it shot up to 31 points (out of a hundred) in October 2014. By the summer of 2015, the search rate reached 100 points. The direct cause for the sudden rise in interest in the term was the 87 cartridges of tear gas fired by the police on September 28, 2014, to disperse demonstrators against China's proposed reforms to Hong Kong's electoral system. This proposal required all candidates running for Chief Executive of Hong Kong to be pre-approved by Beijing.[3] This was the first use of tear gas and weapons against protestors in Hong Kong since 1967. The civil action was known as the Umbrella Movement because demonstrators hoisted umbrellas to shield themselves from the tear gas and streams of pepper spray directed at them by the police. This expanded into

DOI: 10.4324/9781003521280-4

the full-scale Occupy Movement, which effectively shut down major parts of the city. High school and university students walked out of their classes to join the occupation, resulting in the largest student school strike in Hong Kong's history. Those who opposed the movement accused the young protestors of lazing around, doing nothing all day, instead of pursuing their education and becoming contributing members of society.

The Occupy Movement lasted for 79 days. However, though officially not attending school, the young participants were not idle. Many teachers and professors moved their classrooms to the streets to accommodate their students. In the larger Occupy areas like Admiralty, special study and classroom areas were set up for these purposes. It was also not uncommon to see young people reading quietly and studying in their tents. They would take turns to do chores to keep the area clean and organized. In the essay, "I am a *faicing*," essayist, Daam-daam 淡淡, mused upon this designation as she reflected on her own experience in the student movement:

> In recent months, the term *faicing* frequently appears, especially on the Internet. What kind of people use this term? It's hard to generalize. Some belong to a particular color (blue for pro-establishment; yellow for pro-democracy). Some are apparently very worldly and were just here to watch the drama. I will call them the "opposite side." (I could use another term, but that would just be an insult to the term.)
>
> According to the perception of the "opposite side," those who occupy the streets are all *faicing*. I accept this provisionally. But then what do I see these so-called *faicing* do?
>
> I see the concrete jungle covered with pieces of paper on which are written words of encouragement and positivity, turning an ice-cold wall into a colorful one. I see a whole street of colorful umbrellas and tents, like a harmonious and friendly little community. I help deliver boxes of materials to be distributed to the *faicing*, who are working with each other. I help with the cleaning; I wash the grounds and sweep away the rubbish. I see the wash basin and toilets filled with donated toiletries. There are stickers everywhere reminding one to care for the environment and to keep the place clean. In Admiralty, there are study rooms, lecterns, DIY woodshops, and tools for weaving cushions for sitting. Every day, volunteers arrive from different places. At first no one knows anyone, but after initial greetings, they all work together to contribute to the building of this community. They are self-sufficient, self-motivated, peaceful, and orderly—it has been a month.[4]

Rather than being irresponsible and lazy, these "*faicing*" reconfigured their occupied areas into functional communes that celebrated equality, mutuality, and community. Dapiran argues,

> [t]he Umbrella Movement became performative of the kind of society it hoped Hong Kong would become—a peaceful, self-regulating community, built on mutual support and sharing, a gift economy of donated goods and services, all

> of which were a far cry from the self-interested rampant capitalism for which Hong Kong was known.[5]

As Agnes Chow周庭, one of the student leaders mentioned in the Introduction, explained at the time, "Young people's responsibility is to awaken others to the values beyond the dominant ones, to lead society to another kind of transformation. That is our responsibility."[6] Far from doing nothing all day, these "*faicing*" demonstrated the kind of society they wanted and were capable of building.

Though "*faicing*" was derogatory, young people began to embrace it, turning it into a badge of honor. Shiu explains:

> Young people not only did not reject this label, but they have even created social media groups, such as "I am a *faicing*," "There is a kind of elite called *faicing*," "*faicing*-ism," "*Faicing* Affairs Association," etc. There is a web essay, "*Ngo si faicing* 我是廢青 (I am a *faicing*)," and a web song, "*Hoenggong git ceot faicing* 香港傑出廢青 (Hong Kong's outstanding *faicing*)," all equally powerful and uncompromising. They are all "*cultural experts* (original in English)." They exploit this uselessness--uselessness is not without use. It is just as the lyricist, Lam Yat Hey林日曦 said, "Rather than let you label me this way, I'll label myself first." Self-satire is the world's most powerful weapon.[7]

The song, "*Hoenggong git ceot faicing* 香港傑出廢青 (Hong Kong outstanding *faicing*) (2015)," composed and sung by Michael Lai 黎曉, with lyrics by Lam Yat Hey 林日曦, plays on the title, *Hoenggong gitceot cingnin* 香港傑出青年 (Outstanding Young Persons), annually conferred on ten young persons judged exemplary for their contribution to the city by the Junior Chamber of Commerce International. This song makes fun of Hong Kong society's values and measures of success while asserting the ideals of the *faicing*:

> We don't have the heavy burden of a mortgage yet, nor any enormous bills to pay. We still have the luxury to trust in what we see with our own eyes and can still spend whole nights worrying about certain truths. Too busy dreaming, I don't feel I am a zero. I am too busy using my hands to work for the betterment of the world.
> Even if this "me" is very useless (*fai* 廢)
> But I'm still more passionate than those in power.
> I can fire up my strong determination to fight against the giants.
> I put my heart into my role as a little ant.
> I am ultimately an outstanding little ant.
> ....
> Among the ruins, I can find myself a space to express myself.
> You criticize me for being willful; criticize me for being impatient; criticize me for being petulant and perpetually disobedient; criticize me for being too self-centered; criticize me for being a useless youth (*faicing*).

> Even if this "me" is very foolish, I have not become ridiculous. Even if being like this means I am penniless, I might still be rich in my heart. Within the worldly conventions, I want to establish a unique little kingdom. I may be unconventional, but that doesn't mean I am useless. I don't want to become too used to how things are. Being young doesn't mean being useless. I don't want to follow your upward climb. Staying behind doesn't mean being useless. When I find something I believe in, I will fight to death for it.

If being successful in Hong Kong meant endlessly climbing the social and economic ladder, only to be trapped in a life of debts, then many young people proudly embraced the title, *faicing*, choosing to be guided by other kinds of social values and meaning instead. Indeed, many scholars have pointed out the "post-materialist" turn in Hong Kong's society beginning in the 2000s, especially after the devastating SARS epidemic in 2003. Rather than money and social status, liberal universal values such as democracy and free speech were considered much more critical to life for this generation of young people.[8] In a 2016 study, the University of Hong Kong found that an overwhelming majority of young people believed that poverty existed in Hong Kong because of "the development of the modern society" and "an unjust society." Rather than financial stability or material comfort, more important to them were social equality and freedom of speech, as well as "opportunities for citizens to voice their opinions in important government decisions."[9] As Shiu sums it up, "In terms of economics, '*faicing*' are those who disagree with the '*Zung waan gaa zik*' 中環價值' (value of Hong Kong's Central Business District), and in terms of politics, '*faicing*' are those who oppose authoritarianism."[10] This explained why many young people were willing to spend months sleeping on the streets, risking their futures, and enduring tear gas and pepper spray to fight for democracy.

These ideals continued to influence young people in 2019. Another study in 2020 found that of the 712 surveyed aged between 15 and 25, over 70% had participated at least once in political activities in 2019. These ranged from signing a petition to donating money and supplies, and to front-line protest activities. Within this group, 93.5% were university educated and 85.2% were secondary school students. To this cohort of young people, "conservative values," such as wealth, power, and social status, were insignificant. However, rated as very important to them were "universal and collective Values, such as, 'Freedom of opinion,' 'Democracy,' and 'Freedom at any cost.'"[11]

These values held by Hong Kong's young people translated to their attitude toward work as well. Angus Chan, the director of an independent think tank on youth issues, MWYO, noted that while in the past, most people looked for work with stable income, in recent years, those with multiple professional identities and jobs, that is, "slashers (/)," had become common: "Young people do not need the same kind of stability. They'd rather have freedom or aspire to doing things that are of help to others or have social meaning." Chan concluded that young people now were a lot more mature than most people assumed. They did not just think about themselves; they had strong social awareness.[12]

## ***Fonghei nincingjan* 放棄年青人 Give Up on Young People: Generational War**

The contradictions between young people and the establishment reached an apogee in 2019. During the 2019 Anti-Legislation protests, when high school children also started joining university students in the school strike, the 71-year-old (at the time) Hong Kong billionaire, Wu Suk-ching, 伍淑清, heiress of Maxim's Catering, one of the largest restaurant conglomerates in Hong Kong and a member of the Standing Committee of the Chinese People's Political Consultative Conference, famously pointed out that because of the lack of patriotic education in Hong Kong, young people had been brainwashed by social media, and had become anti-government, anti-establishment, anti-China, and because of this, Hong Kong had already lost two generations of young people. She, therefore, declared,

> I will give up on young people (*ngo wui fonghei nincingjan* 我會放棄年輕人). I will not waste any more time to say anything more to them, because they are no longer clear in their heads about what they should do.[13]

To many young protestors, Wu also committed the ultimate treachery by traveling to the United Nations Human Rights Council with Pansy Ho, another billionaire businesswoman and chairperson of the Hong Kong Federation of Women, to denounce the protests. In their report to the UN, Wu and Ho defended the police use of tear gas and rubber bullets against unarmed protestors, with Wu saying, "Police all over the world use tear gas and rubber bullets. This is not unique to Hong Kong."[14] At the same hearing, although evidence abounded that the protest received wide support from all sectors of the Hong Kong society, Ho argued that the small number of protesters did not represent the opinions of the 7.5 million Hong Kong people. They had no right to disrupt the whole society.[15] Ho also expressed concern about the economic impact of the protest:

> Not only the tourist industry and the restaurant businesses, but the whole of our economy is also suffering from different levels of challenges. The most heartbreaking is the situation of our small businesses. They cannot continue to operate. Till this moment, there hasn't been a way to repair all the destroyed public facilities, nor is it possible to have every single one of them repaired. Many people do not even have the convenience of public transportation. They cannot even go out. They cannot return to their place of work. Consumption has contracted about 70%.[16]

Ho's apparent concern for small businesses and workers did not detract from the fact that she is from one of the wealthiest families in Hong Kong. Ho is the daughter of Stanley Ho, the gambling king of Macao, who had a monopoly on Macao's gambling industry for 40 years till 1999. The Ho family business empire included 19 casinos and hotels in Macao, a large share of the Macau International Airport, and other transportation facilities, among other things. The young protestors wanted a future that was in accordance with their moral values, including social and wealth equality. This challenge to the existing social order was strenuously denounced by the establishment and its corporate accessories.

For her unsympathetic, even hostile, attitude toward Hong Kong's young people, the Maxim heiress received much commendation in China. Wu was named a "*Gamdung Zunggwok nindou janmat* 感動中國年度人物, 2019 (Person who touched China's heart, 2019)," by the Chinese Central Television (CCTV, China's state broadcaster), and also, "2019 Global Overseas Chinese Person of the Year," by the *New Chinese News Agency*, the Chinese state media agency. In Hong Kong, however, Wu was much hated. There were boycotts of all the businesses owned by and affiliated with Maxim's, from Maxim's bakeries, fast food restaurants, and catering services, to Starbucks (which Maxim had acquired the rights to operate in Hong Kong). Many of Maxim's retail outlets became targets of the protestors' rage. Many had had their windows smashed in and vandalized. Maxim's eventually made a public statement to distance the corporation from Wu, announcing that she did not have any official position in the corporation. Whether one agreed or not with Wu's estimation about the protesters' behavior and the police's response, there was no doubt that she had declared a generational war by publicly announcing that she was giving up on the young people.

## No Future

The divide between these heiresses and the young people in the city was more than just politics. There was obviously a huge class chasm between them. Wu and Ho inherited vast fortunes and privileges from their families. As such, they had inordinate power. Captured in the term, *faicing*, was more than a moral reproach; there was also an implied contempt for the less privileged. As the financial commentator, Zau Hin 周顯, explains, the term was not applied to all rebellious young people, only to those of particular socioeconomic background:

> Everyone knows that there are many *faicing* in Hong Kong. Generally speaking, there are two types of *faicing*. The first kind is proactive. They have a lot of friends with the same ideas, and they often participate in radical political activities. The other kind is passive. They spend all day at home listlessly. They are also called "invisible youths."
>
> However, both kinds of *faicing* share the same characteristics. These are, refusal to work, being chronically out of work, or have a negative attitude towards work. They are more often out of work than working, or inattentive when working… simply speaking, so-called "*faicing*" are to a large extent, defined by economic conditions. For example, offsprings of wealthy families who don't work and spend all day touring different places or chasing after women will never be called "*faicing*." Similarly, a talented young man in finance will never be called "*faicing*" even if he participates in radical politics.[17]

In profiling the participants of the Anti-Legislation movement, researchers discovered that 22.2% were between the ages of 25–29. The largest group, at 27%, was between the ages of 20–24, with the next largest between the ages of 30–34, at 19.7%. In terms of educational level, 77.9% of the protesters reported having a tertiary level of education or above. This means the main driving force in this protest was Hong Kong's elite workforce or potential elite workforce. However, while 49.1% of this group self-identified as belonging to the middle class, 41.7% labeled themselves as belonging to the lower class, perhaps indicating a trend of downward social mobility among this population.[18]

Aside from issues of democracy and Beijing's encroachment on Hong Kong's governance, at least a part of what fueled all the protests through the 2000s was dissatisfaction with the government's inability or unwillingness to deal with the city's pressing social issues. The society's competitive capitalist culture and relentless emphasis on financial and real estate development led to severe income and wealth inequality. Hong Kong's Gini coefficient measured in 2016 was 0.539 (compared to 0.314 in South Korea in the same year, and 0.398 in the United States last measured in 2021).[19] The city's coffin homes in subdivided flats were world-famous. The infusion of capital from China after the Closer Economic Partnership Arrangement (CEPA) in 2003 led to an economic boom in Hong Kong that mostly benefitted the business elite and the older, propertied class. However, it drove up housing prices to such an extent that before the market was hit by COVID and the emigration wave in 2020, an average apartment was 18.1 times the gross annual median income.[20] In a study by Tang Heiwai, he discovered that

> from 2000 to 2020, the annual GDP went up 89%. The general economic performance seemed satisfactory. However, at the same time the growth of median household income was only 68%, while the household expenditure for those living in apartments in private developments suitable for a family of four went up sharply by 306%. Even those who had no intention of purchasing real estate suffered from the pressure of rising food costs, because during this period, they increased over 80%.[21]

Hong Kong persistently held the dubious distinction of being the world's most expensive city. The living standards of the younger, salaried, and the unpropertied lower and middle classes continued to deteriorate over the years.[22] Young people, even those with advanced academic degrees, were often trapped in uninspiring and low-paying jobs. A study in 2020, undertaken by the pro-Beijing political parties, New Century Forum and New Youth Forum, to examine the income level of college-degree holders in the city between 1989 and 2019, found that in 1989, there were 46,500 college graduates employed in low-skill jobs (11% of the total number of college graduates). In 2019, the number had gone up to 179,900 (16.2%). A comparison of the actual value of the monthly income of college graduates (adjusted according to inflation) reveals that in 1989, the median income was $16,587. In 2019, it was $14,986.[23] Young people had trouble establishing independent lives and were forced to live with their parents well into adulthood because they could not afford their own housing.[24] According to Joeng Hou-sing 楊皓鋮,

> overall, the new generation, compared to the baby boom generation, has a higher level of cultural capital. However, at present, although on average, there have been progressive increases in the salaries of college graduates, fundamentally, these cannot catch up to inflation. Compared to the rise in real estate prices since 1997, salaries have actually decreased. In other words, in general, in Hong Kong, young people are commonly rich in cultural capital, but poor in financial capital...Youth with "High educational level but low-income level" is a structural phenomenon. Young people are now faced with more and more job insecurity—their salaries cannot catch up to inflation. It is already considered very fortunate if one's contract is renewed every year. More and more people are choosing or forced to do temp work.[25]

The three years of COVID restrictions compounded young people's misery. The general unemployment rate in the city rose from 3.5% in January 2020 to almost 6.5% in October 2020. Within this, the youth unemployment rate was particularly startling at 12.01%, almost reaching the level of the 2009 worldwide recession of 12.53%.[26]

A report to the Legislative Council by the Welfare and Labour Bureau in May 2019 further projected a pessimistic future for Hong Kong's well-educated young people. This study was done before the city was hit by the emigration wave following the enactment of the NSL and did not account for the resultant brain drain by 2022. It estimated that by 2027, there would be a shortage of 77,000 workers with below twelfth-grade level of education, 43,000 workers with a high school diploma, and 51,000 workers with undergraduate college degrees. However, among those with post-graduate degrees, there would be an excess of 16,000 people. Despite this dismal prognosis, young people were still urged to forego impractical ideals and individual interests to pursue university degrees in order to enter professions that purportedly provide income and material stability.

Notwithstanding poor job prospects and declining income value, in 2014, the Hong Kong Housing Authority and Housing Department evaluated the possibility of banning those with tertiary academic degrees from applying for public or government-sponsored housing. This was prompted by heated discussions in the city in which social commentators accused college graduates who applied for public housing of lack of ambition and shamed them for taking advantage of the welfare system and for competing with underprivileged families for government handouts. The 2009–2015 chairperson of the government's Commissioner on Youth, Chan Chung-bun陳振彬 (age 58 at the time), admonished young people:

> Don't apply for public housing immediately after you graduate because that is too sad. I feel this is a sad issue. Why? There is no reason one should give up on oneself so quickly...I worked for five or six years, before I put down a down

> payment and got a mortgage to pay for an apartment that belonged to me. Only this can be called youthful vigor. That's why I think there's a bit of perversion in their thinking.[27]

Similarly, Shih Wing Ching 施永青 (age 71 at the time), a property magnate, who owns *Centraline*, the largest property agency in Hong Kong and China, also chastised them:

> Young people should be diligent in their studies to acquire knowledge and skill in order to perform well at work. They have a chance to increase their income only if they do their work well. They must also be willing to save money. Restrain short term consumption. Once they've saved enough money, they can buy real estate. But many refuse to save money. When others advise them to reduce their spending, they accuse them of being detached from reality. They don't realize how detached they themselves are. They live at home and live on their parents. Now, that's really being detached from reality.[28]

Young people's despair about their prospects was captured in Flowdoc's 2020 song, "How to fly," in which he describes an individual's sense of hopelessness, trapped in the meaningless and unforgiving work culture of the city:

> One wants to excel but is defeated by reality. Put one's helmet on, become like a machine in society, work every day like a draft animal. I'd rather be a black swan that can only spread its wings once. No need for society to teach me how to succeed. I know I am stubborn. I believe in myself and not the will of heaven. That's why I am writing down line after line, these words of mine:
>
> *I don't wanna die Don't tell me how to fly All the strings pulling tight Trying to keep me from the sky I don't wanna die Don't tell me how to fly...*
>
> The daily rising GDP is like the emperor's new clothes. The things that have been troubling young people--looking and seeking, how will we ever know the answers? When my thoughts become tangled, I can only light a cigarette. Constantly surrounded by anxieties, repeating, replaying every day, how many years have I wasted wallowing in mediocrity?
>
> *I don't wanna die Don't tell me how to fly...* (English in the original in Italics.)[29]

Politically disenfranchised and economically straitened, the prospect for many young Hong Kong people was bleak. At the same time, a study published by *Youth Ideas*, a research center under the *Hong Kong Federation of Youth Groups*, reported that 71.4% of the 525 young people interviewed "believed the government did not attach much importance to encouraging young people's development."[30] Young people were blamed for upsetting the peace, criticized for being spoilt and lazy, and for creating trouble on the streets instead of working hard for unachievable social and economic goals. There is little surprise that many felt betrayed and abandoned by society.

**What Do Young People Want?**

Perhaps Hong Kong's young people needed to learn from their mainland counterparts. The Hong Kong political writer, Baau-But 鮑渤, wrote in 2017 that mainland youths were more driven and ambitious. They were headed in the "correct" direction. Their hunger for success had resulted in a much more advanced and superior society:

> If we compare the level of optimism and happiness among young people from the three places on the two coasts (Hong Kong, the mainland, and Taiwan), in general, mainland young people are superior. I recently went to Beijing for a conference on new media. Those giving talks were mostly successful entrepreneurs born in the 1980s. Some were even born in the 1990s and have not even graduated from college yet. They were going on about, "venture capital," "angel round," "B round," immediately making one feel in awe of these young people…
>
> Last week, I went to a little restaurant in a shopping mall in Shenzhen. There was no menu, no wait staff, no one to give you a bill. It was amazing. One just scanned the QR code at the door and deliciously prepared food would appear before your eyes together with the bill. From ordering food, making additional orders, finding prices, application of discounts, to payment, these were all completed on your cell phone. Hong Kong people would not know how to operate the system and probably could not even get a meal there or might be regarded as members of the "Low-End Population,"[31] who need looking after. [32]

Baau-But could not have foreseen, when he wrote his piece in 2017, that in 2020, when COVID swept the world, scanning QR codes to prove their vaccine status was the only way Hong Kong people could enter all large and small public facilities and order food in restaurants. Also in 2021, struggling to survive in the highly competitive environment, many young people in China rebelled by declaring they would "lie flat," advocating, "Don't buy property; don't buy a car; don't get married; don't have children; and don't consume."[33] This "lying flat" movement spread quickly among young people in China until it was condemned by the Chinese government and its various mouthpieces. All the social media groups organized around this topic were also quickly shut down.

In his starry-eyed assessment of Chinese young people, Baau-But did not take into consideration the human and social costs of ever-striving ambition. His unexamined notion of success and trust in technological development reflected a typical "Central Business District value" that many Hong Kong young people rejected.

Despite Baau-But's pessimism about Hong Kong young people's seeming lack of motivation compared to their mainland counterparts, Angus Chan of the youth issues think tank, *MWYO*, reported that data gathered in the third quarter of 2021 showed that there was actually an increase in the number of young people joining the workforce. Among those aged between 15 and 19, and 20 and 24, 9.9%

and 59.5%, respectively, participated in the workforce. This reflected an increase from the previous year of 1.6% and 1.3%. Also, from May to June 2020, full-time workers aged between 15 and 24 worked an average of 44.4 hours each week, higher than the overall average of 44.3 hours.[34] More young people had been working and had in fact been working more hours than the general workforce despite public perception.

A major obstacle for a sizeable number of young people's social advancement was the legal consequences of their participation in the 2019 protest. From the start of the Anti-Legislation movement in 2019 to July 2021, 10,260 had been arrested; 6000 of them were under the age of 25. Among the total number arrested, 39% were students, and 17% (1754 individuals) were under 18. Most were still awaiting court trials and anticipating different kinds of legal consequences 2 years after the protests.[35] Those who had already completed their time in detention or prison struggled with the reality of living with criminal records. The schools, whether high school or universities in which they were enrolled before their arrests, often would not readmit them, claiming they would no longer be able to fit in. Without being able to complete their education, their job prospects were limited even if they were able to convince employers to overlook their criminal records. For some, who might ultimately be proven innocent, the lengthy legal process could drag on for years.[36] Even among those who had not officially been charged or had not served time, many suffered from PTSD or emotional distress from the violence during the protests and subsequent suppressions.

The prominent Hong Kong writer, Dung Kai Cheung 董啟章, reflected on young people's situation at the time, comparing it to that of his own era. He pointed out that the difference between these two different generations could easily be seen in the subject matter of popular songs:

> People like me who grew up in the 1970s and 1980s used to listened to so-called "motivational songs." At that time, all the well-known singers sang motivational songs. Danny Chan was the best among them. His classic, "*zaak sing* 摘星 Reaching for the Star," goes without saying. When I was young, my favorite song I was "*fei ceot heoi* 飛出去 Flying Out." It is a song that celebrates parental love. The last few lines, "It's difficult to become hardy grass in a nursery/ Young people have dreams / don't want to be hot-housed / I just want to fulfill my ambition / my goal I vow to reach," were really rousing. Now, these lyrics sound very out of date, very naïve and quite nauseating. But there are contextual reasons for this. In the 1980s, Hong Kong was at its most affluent. There were plenty of opportunities. Life was stable and peaceful. It was the most optimistic of times. The world was also relatively peaceful. At that time, there were definitely reasons to believe one's life and the world were beautiful, and all one's dreams could be fulfilled.
>
> Today we are no longer that naïve. Young people's experience today is formed from growing up amongst ruins. It's not just ruins in the material sense, but also in the spiritual sense. They have to confront "endless setbacks," "the world collapsing," and "streets filled with sorrow." (Quotes are lyrics of different

> songs.) Even if this difficult situation is not completely disheartening, all they can hope for is "at least there's an inch that hasn't been corrupted," as a "girl from the ruins."[37] To the new generation, the "motivational" is either too simplistic or too extravagant. This is not because they are not brave enough, or because they are without ideals. It is because they have been baptized in reality, which means they have suffered trauma. People who are hurt need healing, not motivation.[38]

## Re-educating Young People

Despite numerous studies and analyses, Hong Kong authorities seemed incapable of understanding, or were oblivious to, the feelings and needs of the young people. The Hong Kong Secretary for Education at the time, Kevin Yeung, who had accused young people of being "passive and self-indulgent" (mentioned at the beginning of the chapter), recommended teaching "diligence" as part of the school curriculum.[39] Similarly, in a speech on March 31, 2022, the then Chief Secretary for Administration and the chairperson of the Youth Development Commission (YDC), John Lee Ka Chiu (Hong Kong's chief executive since 2022), suggested teaching positive thinking:

> With members' concerted efforts, the YDC has continuously enhanced and expanded various initiatives, including deepening young people's life planning, facilitating young people's upward mobility, strengthening communication with young people, etc. It will further nurture young people's positive thinking and help them develop positive values.[40]

In her 2021 policy address, the chief executive at the time, Carrie Lam, announced new strategies to address the city's youth issues that also included "positive thinking." She pledged that the government would continue to assist young people,

> offering opportunities in entrepreneurship, career development, internship and exchange on the Mainland, as well as strengthening of the work of the six disciplined services and two auxiliary services on nurturing young people's positive thinking and awareness of law-abidingness.[41]

The Disciplined Services, which included the Police and Correctional Services, had already demonstrated how they could contribute to "fixing" the youth problem in 2019. It seemed the official solution to everything that ailed Hong Kong's young people was to inculcate them with the right kind of political and social value, or the right kind of work ethics and punish them when they failed to conform.

Along this vein, the government authorities blamed Hong Kong's youth problems on their high school education, in particular, a course in the general curriculum called "Liberal Studies." This course was initially designed to train critical thinking and social awareness among students, considered important skills for a responsible citizen to carry out his or her civic responsibilities. However,

Carrie Lam's government insisted that the course taught subversive thinking and encouraged students to question authority, resulting in their radicalization. Even though numerous studies, including those conducted by the government's Education Bureau, had demonstrated that this was not the case,[42] in November 2020, hardly a year after the protests, the Secretary of Education put forth a proposal to change the substance of "Liberal Studies." The former lawmaker for the education sector, Ip Kin-yuen, criticized the government for blaming "Liberal Studies" for the 2019 social unrest because "[t]hey [had] to hide the responsibility of the government's maladministration for causing such uproar in society."[43]

Distrust of young people, dismissal of their efforts, and denigration of their political aspirations seemed to have become a government stance in Hong Kong. It necessitated strategies to reform and reign them in, to transform them from an unruly, disgruntled mob to a disciplined, hardworking labor force for the continued "stability and prosperity" of the city. The age-old strategies of propaganda, discipline, and censorship were now fully deployed to order the minds of the young. The rock band, Yusobeit, described this as a "*Gwaaimat juksing gaiwaak* 怪物育成計劃 (The scheme for cultivating monsters) (2020)":

> The school bell rings. The race begins. Teacher mother said, please hand in your homework. Remember to practice your mental arithmetic, gymnastics, and study German. The most important thing is to use your brain. No need for entertainment. You have already learned how to be successful at age three, how to swim upstream. By seven, you need to know how to wield the power of the buzz to prove your superiority. If you can claim to be the absolute best, then you'll be happy. This is what life is all about. You must obey the teaching. You must obey...
>
> You have heard the teachings hundreds and thousands of times. You have already handed in a lot of homework. You refused laughter. You refused longings. You could have won, but you still feel powerless. How is it possible you can't reach the top?
>
> You cannot be happy; you cannot have everything. You have gone through hopelessness, trying to obey your superiors. You should be the rising star. When you completed your education, you will be successful. Give it all to the world. You are strong, like a monster.
>
> *Let go, let go, let go of him, Let go, let go, let go of her, Let go, let go, let go of us Monster, monster is coming to town.*
>
> *You say, you say, you say that's bad Too late, too late, too late, you made us We don't need no need no this--Come on Come on Monsters we are*. (Words originally in English in Italics.)[44]

In the Spring of 2021, a new school curriculum was readied for approval by the Curriculum Development Council. In a speech to the Education Bureau's sponsored forum, Hong Kong's then Chief Executive, Carrie Lam, urged educators and teachers to support the new curriculum and the government's effort to instill love for the city and the fatherland among young people, in order to quell their rebelliousness. Her speech was titled, "*Fongfaan ninhingjan bei leijung ngaihoi gwokgaa oncyun* 防範年輕人被利用危害國家安全 (Preventing young people from being manipulated into endangering the nation)":

> We hope to do some preventive work, to deter behaviors that endanger the nation and Hong Kong; to stop foreign powers from taking advantage of the citizens, in particular, the young people, making them behave in ways that will endanger the nation. How can we, through public education, school education, help the general public to have a better handle on the spirit of the "Basic Law," and understand the relationship between "One Country" and "Two systems" in their daily lives? This is a responsibility we all need to take on now... I hope we can all take it upon ourselves to foster in our young people a notion of nationhood, a love for Hong Kong, an international perspective, and a sense responsibility toward the society.[45]

The two major teachers' unions in Hong Kong were divided in their support for this new curriculum. Tin Fong-chak, vice president of the Professional Teachers' Union, pointed out that the design of the new course was not to benefit students but for political ends. He said, "The government and people from the pro-Beijing camp have made Hong Kong's education system a scapegoat for the anti-government protests in 2019."[46]

## *Dau coeng meng* 鬥長命 Whoever Lives Longer Wins

For a generation that had grown up amid many political demonstrations and cut its teeth in the 2012 anti-national education protest, the implementation of the new curriculum was yet another defeat. When asked what the next step would be for the pro-democracy movement after the suppression of the 2019 protests, unrepentant despite facing a prison sentence at the time, the young activist, Joshua Wong said,

> We are now in a competition with Xi Jinping, to see who's going to live longer. Everyone knows very well he is an authoritarian and a dictator. As long as he remains China's premier, the chances for democracy in Hong Kong are zero. Let's see who will live longer--the millennials or Xi Jinping's premiership. Hong Kong's younger generation has determination, and they are many times braver than me.

Wong added that the struggle for democracy and freedom was an "infinity war."[47]

In other words, the young activists were in a longevity contest, "*dau coeng meng* 鬥長命," with the aging political authorities. After all, time was on their side. Wong and all the other young activists would most likely outlive those presently in power in both China and Hong Kong, who were all in their 60s and older. After that, there would be another generation of young people to continue the dream. As Wong explained, "After the baptism by fire last year, the struggle is in Hong Kong people's DNA."[48] This gene will keep being passed on, expressing itself with the right constellation of factors. As long as there is life, there are possibilities.

During the Commercial Radio's annual Ultimate Song Chart Award ceremony on January 1, 2022, the presenter, DJ Jim Yan少爺占 (Master Jim) played on this idea. Because a company selling *reishi* mushroom health products was the sponsor of the show, tickets to the event were awarded by lottery to those who bought the products. Master Jim quipped that in order to get a ticket to the event, one had to eat a lot of *reishi* mushrooms. However, he said, that was a good thing because one was now in a longevity race, *dau coeng meng*. Without the need for elaboration or explanation, the audience erupted in cheers.

In Corrupt the Youth's book, *Daai bun zithoksyu seong gaai heoi* 帶本哲學書上街去(*Taking a philosophy book to the streets*), the writers discuss the value of this long-term view of things:

> No one can have a complete handle on the whole situation. Does this not tell us that we deserve to have hope? How do you know you are not like the citizens of the Soviet Union before it fell? Who can tell you whether you are or not? The issue is, we can only know whether we will be successful or not if we persevere. Change will only be possible if we persevere. We can only hope to succeed in changing the reality. If you give up and no longer insist, change is naturally not possible. Then, naturally, there is no way to talk about hope. In history, there are many examples of success after painful persistence to the end. But there are also a lot of examples of ultimate failures despite many diligent attempts. If we don't persevere, then we won't need to have, and should not have, hope, because we will definitely fail. That is why hope is something we fight for. That is why some say, "It is not because there's hope that we persist. It is because we persist that there is hope."[49]

## Notes

1 Ng Kang-Chung, "Hong Kong brain drain threat as nearly quarter of university-educated under-35s say they plan to quit city for work overseas," *South China Morning Post*, March 14, 2021, www.scmp.com/news/hong-kong/society/article/3125412/hong-kong-brain-drain-threat-nearly-quarter-university.

2 Shiu was heavily involved in the Occupy Movement in 2014, for which he received an eight-month prison sentence for the crime of "inciting others for committing public nuisance" in 2019. His teaching contract at the Baptist University of Hong Kong where he was employed as a lecturer was not renewed.

3 Syun Jin-loeng 孫賢亮, "香港「廢青」進化論 (The Evolution of Hong Kong '*Faicing*'," *The Initium*, August 24, 2015, https://theinitium.com/article/20140824-hongkong-hkyouth01.

4 Daam-daam淡淡, "我是廢青 (I am *a faicing*)," *Inmedia*, November 1, 2014, www.inmediahk.net/node/1028048.

5 Antony Dapiran, "Hong Kong's reckoning," in Golley, Jaivin, Hillman, Strange, edits., *China Dreams* (Canberra, Australian National University Press 2020): 50–67: 56, accessed June 25, 2023, www.jstor.org/stable/j.ctv12sdxmk.9

6 Can Gaa-jan陳嘉茵, Syun Jin-loeng孫賢亮, "什麼是「廢青」, 什麼是「傑青」(What is 'Useless Youth', what is outstanding youth?)," *The Initium*, August 26, 2015, https://theinitium.com/article/20150825-hongkong-hkyouth02.

7 Shiu Ka-chun 邵家臻, "廢青作為武器 (*Fai cing* as a weapon)," *The Initium,* August 30, 2015, https://theinitium.com/article/20150830-opinion-shiukachun-hkyouth.

8 Yew Chiew Ping and Kwong Kin-ming, "Hong Kong identity on the rise," *Asian Survey* 54, no. 6 (2014): 1088–1112: 1098–9, 1100, https://doi.org/10.1525/as.2014.54.6.1088

9 Wong Yee Hang, "A survey experiment on discontent among the youth: Welfare or politics? A comparative analysis on support for redistribution and political discontent in Hong Kong Final Report," The Public Policy Research Funding Scheme (PPRFS), www.cepu.gov.hk/doc/en/research_report(PDF)/2016.A8.051.16D_Final%20Report_Dr%20Wong.pdf.

10 Ibid.

11 Christy Hui, "Political participation, intentions, values and psychological distress among youth in Hong Kong," Department of Social Work and Social Administration, The University of Hong Kong Press Release, August 27, 2020, https://hku.hk/f/upload/21479/200827%20Press%20Release_English_Final.pdf.

12 Ma Wai kit馬煒傑, "青年備註兩年訪問逾200青年借新一代角度去了解社會的變遷 (Youth Beige interviewed 200 young people in two years. Using the perspective of the new generation to understand social changes)," *HK01*, May 20, 2022, www.hk01.com社會新聞/770661/青年備註兩年訪問逾200青年-借新一代角度去了解社會的變遷.

13 "環時 專訪伍淑清：會放棄被洗腦的香港年輕人 (Global Times exclusive interview with Wu Shuqing: will give up on young people)," *AM730*, November 4, 2019, www.am730.com.hk//本地/-環時-專訪伍淑清-會放棄被洗腦的香港年輕人/41902.

14 "創辦人長女撐警言論惹不滿. 美心:伍淑清無任何職位. 衷心希望各方解決分歧 (Founder's daughter's defense of police create offense. Maxim's: Wu Shu-Ching does not have any professional position. Heartily hopes all sides will reconcile their differences)," *HKD4*, September 24, 2019, www.hkd4.com/news/3264.

15 "Exclusive: HK survey shows increasing majority back pro-democracy goals, smaller support for protest movement," *Reuters*, August 30, 2020, www.reuters.com/article/idUSKBN25Q00X/.

16 Wong Siu-joeng王兆陽, "何超瓊伍淑清將在聯合國演講：暴力示威破壞平和生活 (Pansy Ho, Wu Shu-ching will be giving a speech at the United Nations: Violent protestors destroy peaceful life)," *HK01*, September 10, 2019, www.hk01.com/即時中國/373555/逃犯條例-何超瓊伍淑清將在聯合國演講-暴力示威破壞平和生活.

17 Zou Hin周顯, "當廢青也沒甚麼呀! It's not such a big deal to be a *faicing*," *Eastweek.com.hk*, June 10, 2017, http://eastweek.my-magazine.me/main/66988

18 Francis L. F. Lee, Samson Yuen, Gary Tang, and Edmund W. Cheng, "Hong Kong's summer of uprising," *China Review* 19, no. 4 (2019): 1–32: 13.

19 "Gini Index coefficient—distribution of family income—The World Factbook," www.cia.gov/the-world-factbook/field/gini-index-coefficient-distribution-of-family-income/country-comparison.

20 Hung Ho-fung, *City on the Edge: Hong Kong under Chinese Rule* (UK, Cambridge University Press, 2022), 163.

21 Tang Heiwai 鄧希煒, "為何香港經濟騰飛卻未帶來共同富裕? (Why has Hong Kong's economic rapid development had not brought equality in wealth?)," *HKEJ-Column*, September 20, 2021, www.hkubs.hku.hk/sc/research/thought-leadership/hkej-column/why-has-economic-development-often-failed-to-deliver-common-prosperity.

22 Hung, 163.

23 New Century Forum, New Youth Forum, "香港各世代大學生收入比較研究報告 (Comparison of income of different generations of college graduates in Hong Kong)," December 30, 2020, www.ncforum.org.hk/file/upload/file_1008_hZn.pdf.

24 Antony Dapiran, "Prosperity and Freedom: Hong Kong's Dilemma," in Golley and Jaivin edits., *Prosperity*, (Canberra, Australian National University Press, 2018), 292–309: 297, www.jstor.org/stable/j.ctv1rmjm7.34.

25 Joeng Hou-sing楊皓鋮, "一部香港社運史書寫後物質主義 (Writing about post-materialism in a volume of history of Hong Kong political activism?)?" *HK01*, August 6, 2019, www.HK01.com/深度報道/360538/一部香港社運史-書寫後物質主義.

26 "Hong Kong Unemployment Rate" and "Hong Kong Youth Unemployment Rate," accessed January 7, 2023, https://tradingeconomics.com/hong-kong/youth-unemployment-rate.

27 "建制紅人陳振彬: 大學生申公屋是放棄自己 (Popular pro-establishment figure, Chan Chung-bun: college graduates applying for public housing is giving up on themselves)," *Stand News*, January 12, 2015, https://collection.news/thestandnews/articles/889.

28 "施永青預言疫情過後, 樓市復甦快過酒樓. 年輕人只會繼續做旁觀者 (Shih Wing Ching predicts that after COVID, the real estate market will recover faster than restaurants. Young people will only continue to be bystanders)," 堅料網www.Kinliu.hk, May 29, 2020, https://n.kinliu.hk/kinliunews/蓄勢待發 年輕人只會繼續做旁觀者%E3%80%80施永青預/.

29 FLowdoc, "How to Fly," www.youtube.com/watch?v=XqPkM5ZBCD0.

30 Ng Kang-chung, "Hong Kong brain drain threat as nearly quarter of university-educated under-35s say they plan to quit city for work overseas," *South China Morning Post*, March 14, 2022, www.scmp.com/news/hong-kong/society/article/3125412/hong-kong-brain-drain-threat-nearly-quarter-university.

31 "Low-End Population (*dai dyun jan hou* 低端人口)" is a term commonly used in the official documents of the Chinese government to refer to the manual laborers who live in Beijing, earning low wages, and with little education.

32 Baau-But鮑渤, "香港青年的出路 (The future of Hong Kong Youths)," *Think Hong Kong*, December 22, 2017, www.thinkhk.com/article/2017-12/22/24869.html.

33 David Bandurski, "The 'lying flat' movement standing in the way of China's innovation drive," *Brookings*, July 8, 2021, www.brookings.edu/articles/the-lying-flat-movement-standing-in-the-way-of-chinas-innovation-drive/.

34 Angus Chan陳宇謙, "香港青年真的在躺平嗎？ (Are Hong Kong youths really lying flat?)," *MWYO*, January 1, 2022, https://mwyo.org/tc/opinion_details.php?id=329.

35 *ProjectChangeHK* Telegram (http://t.me), July 19, 2021.

36 Stanley Leung李慧筠, "反修例運動三年, 出獄的少年後來怎麼? (Three years after the Anti-Legislation protests, what will happen to the young people coming out of prison)?" *The Initium*, June 11, 2022, https://theinitium.com/article/20220612-hongkong-the-youth-after-jail.

37 These are lines from Cath Wong, "我心中尚未崩壞的部分The parts in my heart that have not yet been corrupted," composed by Cath Wong and Terence Lam, lyrics by Chow Yiu-fai and Wong Lok Yee, Sony Music, 2020. The title of the song is borrowed from the novel of the same name by the Japanese writer, Shiraishi Kazufumi. See Chapter Seven for a discussion and partial translation of the song.

38 Dung Kai Cheung, "從勵志到療癒 (From motivational to healing)," *Ming Pao Weekly*, May 20, 2022, www.MPweekly.com/culture/cu0006/董啟章-黃妍-王樂儀-203654/.

39 Sammy Heung and William Yu, "Lazy, unmotivated and 'lying flat'? Young Hongkongers' different life choices don't mean they lack drive or creativity, experts say," *South China*

*Morning Post*, February 7, 2022, www.scmp.com/news/hong-kong/education/article/3166010/lazy-unmotivated-and-lying-flat-young-hongkongers.

40 "Appointments to Youth Development Commission," The Government of Hong Kong SAR Press Release, March 31, 2022, www.info.gov.hk/gia/general/202303/31/P2023033100473p.htm.

41 "青年發展委員會歡迎《行政長官2021年施政報告》中有關青年發展的新措施 The Youth Development Commission welcomes new strategies regarding youth development in the 2021—Policy Report of the Chief Executive," The Government of Hong Kong SAR Press Release, October 6, 2021, www.info.gov.hk/gia/general/202110/06/P2021100600788.htm. The disciplined services include the Police Force, the Fire Services Department, the Correctional Service, the Customs and Excise Department, the Immigration Department, and the Government Flying Service.

42 Lee T. T., & Chiu, S. W, "Conduit for Engagement? School Curriculum and Youth Political Participation in Hong Kong," *YOUNG* 26 no. 2, 2018: 161–178, https://doi.org/10.1177/1103308817711533.

43 "Hong Kong liberal studies to be renamed and reformed – more China content, less focus on current affairs," *Hong Kong Free Press*, November 28, 2020, https://hongkongfp.com/2020/11/27/hong-kong-liberal-studies-to-be-renamed-and-reformed-more-china-content-less-focus-on-current-affairs/.

44 Yusobeit, "怪物育成計劃 scheme for cultivating monsters," music by Yusobeit, lyrics by YU. Anthology, 2020.

45 Carrie Lam speech given on November 25, 2021, www.news.gov.hk/, www.news.gov.hk/chi/2021/11/20211125/20211125_180911_260.html.

46 Chan Ho-Him and Kathleen Magramo, "Hong Kong's liberal studies to be renamed 'citizenship and social development' as part of massive overhaul," *South China Morning Post*, March 31, 2021, www.scmp.com/news/hong-kong/education/article/3127778/hong-kongs-liberal-studies-expected-be-renamed-citizenship.

47 "黃之鋒: 無懼國安法 跟習近平鬥長命 (Joshua Wong: Not afraid of the National Security Law. Competition with Xi Jinping to see who's lives longer)," *Deutsche Welle*, May 22, 2020, www.dw.com/zh-hant/專訪黃之鋒無懼國安法-跟習近平斗長命/a-53529141.

48 Ibid.

49 Corrupt the Youth, *Daai bun zithoksyu seong gaai heoi 帶本哲學書上街去 (Taking a philosophy book to the streets*) (Electronic Edition) (Hong Kong, Corrupt the Youth Philosophy Department, 2020), 16.

## References

"Appointments to Youth Development Commission." The Government of Hong Kong SAR Press Release, March 31, 2022. www.info.gov.hk/gia/general/202303/31/P2023033100473p.htm

Baau-But 鮑渤. "香港青年的出路 (The future of Hong Kong youths)." *Think Hong Kong*, December 22, 2017. www.thinkhk.com/article/2017-12/22/24869.html.

Bandurski, David. "The 'lying flat' movement standing in the way of China's innovation drive." *Brookings*, July 8, 2021. www.brookings.edu/articles/the-lying-flat-movement-standing-in-the-way-of-chinas-innovation-drive/.

Can, Gaa-jan陳嘉茵 and Jin-loeng Syun 孫賢亮. "什麼是「廢青」, 什麼是「傑青」(What is 'Useless Youth', what is outstanding youth?)." *The Initium*, August 26, 2015. https://theinitium.com/article/20150825-hongkong-hkyouth02.

Carrie Lam speech given on November 25, 2021. www.news.gov.hk/, www.news.gov.hk/chi/2021/11/20211125/20211125_180911_260.html.

Chan, Angus陳宇謙. "香港青年真的在躺平嗎？ (Are Hong Kong youths really lying flat?)." *MWYO*, January 1, 2022. https://mwyo.org/tc/opinion_details.php?id=329.

Chiew Ping, Yew and Kwong Kin-ming. "Hong Kong identity on the rise." *Asian Survey* 54, no. 6 (2014): 1088–1112: 1098–9, 1100. https://doi.org/10.1525/as.2014.54.6.1088

Corrupt the Youth, *Daai bun zithoksyu seong gaai heoi* 帶本哲學書上街去 (Taking a philosophy book to the streets), Electronic Edition, Hong Kong: Corrupt the Youth Philosophy Department, 2020.

Daam-daam淡淡. "我是廢青 (I am a *faicing*)." *Inmedia*, November 1, 2014. www.inmediahk.net/node/1028048.

Dapiran, Antony. "Prosperity and freedom: Hong Kong's dilemma." Jane Golley, Linda Jaivin, Ben Hillman, Sharon Strange, Edits., *China Dream*. Canberra: ANU Press, 2018, 292–309. Accessed June 25, 2023. www.jstor.org/stable/j.ctv1rmjm7.34.

Dapiran, Antony. "Hong Kong's reckoning." Jane Golley, Linda Jaivin, Ben Hillman, Sharon Strange, Edits., *China Dreams*. Canberra: ANU Press, 2020, 50–67. Accessed Jun 25, 2023. www.jstor.org/stable/j.ctv12sdxmk.9.

Dung Kai Cheung. "從勵志到療癒 (From motivational to healing)." *Ming Pao Weekly*, May 20, 2022. www.MPweekly.com/culture/cu0006/董啟章-黃妍-王樂儀-203654/.

"Exclusive: HK survey shows increasing majority back pro-democracy goals, smaller support for protest movement." *Reuters*, August 30, 2020. www.reuters.com/article/idUSKBN25Q00X/.

Flowdoc. "How to fly." Beats by Izoki Beats, music and lyrics by Flowdoc. www.youtube.com/watch?v=XqPkM5ZBCD0.

"Gini Index coefficient – distribution of family income – The World Factbook." www.cia.gov/the-world-factbook/field/gini-index-coefficient-distribution-of-family-income/country-comparison.

Heung, Sammy and William Yu. "Lazy, unmotivated and 'lying flat'? Young Hongkongers' different life choices don't mean they lack drive or creativity, experts say." *South China Morning Post*, February 7, 2022. www.scmp.com/news/hong-kong/education/article/3166010/lazy-unmotivated-and-lying-flat-young-hongkongers.

Hin, Zou 周顯. "當廢青也沒甚麼呀! It's not such a big deal to be a *faicing*." *Eastweek.com.hk*, June 10, 2017. http://eastweek.my-magazine.me/main/66988.

Ho-Him Chan and Kathleen Magramo. "Hong Kong's liberal studies to be renamed 'citizenship and social development' as part of massive overhaul." *South China Morning Post*, March 31, 2021. www.scmp.com/news/hong-kong/education/article/3127778/hong-kongs-liberal-studies-expected-be-renamed-citizenship.

"Hong Kong liberal studies to be renamed and reformed – more China content, less focus on current affairs." Hong Kong Free Press, November 28, 2020. https://hongkongfp.com/2020/11/27/hong-kong-liberal-studies-to-be-renamed-and-reformed-more-china-content-less-focus-on-current-affairs/.

"Hong Kong Unemployment Rate" and "Hong Kong Youth Unemployment Rate." *Trading Economics*. Accessed January 7, 2023. https://tradingeconomics.com/hong-kong/youth-unemployment-rate.

Hui, Christy. "Political participation, intentions, values and psychological distress among youth in Hong Kong." The University of Hong Kong Press Release, August 27, 2020. https://hku.hk/f/upload/21479/200827%20Press%20Release_English_Final.pdf.

Hung Ho-Fung. *City on the Edge: Hong Kong under Chinese Rule*. UK: Cambridge University Press, 2022.

Joeng Hou-sing 楊皓鋮. "一部香港社運史書寫後物質主義 (Writing about post-materialism in a volume of history of Hong Kong political activism?)?" *HK01*, August 6, 2019. www.HK01.com/深度報道/360538/一部香港社運史-書寫後物質主義.

Lee, T. T. and S. W. Chiu. "Conduit for engagement? School curriculum and youth political participation in Hong Kong." *YOUNG* 26, no. 2, (2018): 161–178. https://doi.org/10.1177/1103308817711533

Lee, Francis L. F., Samson Yuen, Gary Tang, and Edmund W. Cheng. "Hong Kong's summer of uprising." *China Review* 19, no. 4 (2019): 1–32.

Leung, Stanley 李慧筠. "反修例運動三年, 出獄的少年後來怎麼? (Three years after the Anti-Legislation protests, what will happen to the young people coming out of prison)?" *The Initium*, June 11, 2022. https://theinitium.com/article/20220612-hongkong-the-youth-after-jail.

Ma Wai kit馬煒傑, "青年備註兩年訪問逾200青年借新一代角度去了解社會的變遷 (Youth Beige interviewed 200 young people in two years. Using the perspective of the new generation to understand social changes)." *HK01*, May 20, 2022. www.hk01.com社會新聞/770661/青年備註兩年訪問逾200青年-借新一代角度去了解社會的變遷.

New Century Forum, New Youth Forum. "香港各世代大學生收入比較研究報告 (Comparison of income of different generations of college graduates in Hong Kong)." December 30, 2020. www.ncforum.org.hk/file/upload/file_1008_hZn.pdf.

Ng Kang-Chung. "Hong Kong brain drain threat as nearly quarter of university-educated under-35s say they plan to quit city for work overseas." *South China Morning Post*, March 14, 2021. www.scmp.com/news/hong-kong/society/article/3125412/hong-kong-brain-drain-threat-nearly-quarter-university.

ProjectChangeHK Telegram (http://t.me). July 19, 2021.

Shiu Ka-chun 邵家臻. "廢青作為武器 (Faicing as a weapon)." *The Initium*, August 30, 2015. https://theinitium.com/article/20150830-opinion-shiukachun-hkyouth.

Syun Jin-loeng 孫賢亮."香港「廢青」進化論 (The evolution of Hong Kong 'Faicing'." *The Initium*, August 24, 2015. https://theinitium.com/article/20140824-hongkong-hkyouth01.

Tang Heiwai 鄧希煒. "為何香港經濟騰飛卻未帶來共同富裕? (Why has Hong Kong's economic rapid development had not brought equality in wealth?)." *HKEJ-Column*. September 20, 2021. www.hkubs.hku.hk/sc/research/thought-leadership/hkej-column/why-has-economic-development-often-failed-to-deliver-common-prosperity.

Wong Siu-joeng 王兆陽. "何超瓊伍淑清將在聯合國演講: 暴力示威破壞平和生活 (Pansy Ho, Wu Shu-ching will be giving a speech at the United Nations: Violent protestors destroy peaceful life)." *HK01*, September 10, 2019. www.hk01.com/即時中國/373555/逃犯條例-何超瓊伍淑清將在聯合國演講-暴力示威破壞平和生活.

Wong Yee Hang. "A survey experiment on discontent among the youth: Welfare or politics? A comparative analysis on support for redistribution and political discontent in Hong Kong final report." The Public Policy Research Funding Scheme (PPRFS). www.cepu.gov.hk/doc/en/research_report(PDF)/2016.A8.051.16D_Final%20Report_Dr%20Wong.pdf.

Yusobeit. "怪物育成計劃 scheme for cultivating monsters." Music by Yusobeit, lyrics by YU. Anthology, 2020.

"青年發展委員會歡迎《行政長官2021年施政報告》中有關青年發展的新措施 The Youth Development Commission welcomes the new strategies regarding youth development in the 2021 Policy Report of the Chief Executive." The Government of Hong Kong SAR Press Release, October 6, 2021. www.info.gov.hk/gia/general/202110/06/P2021100600788.htm.

"創辦人長女撐警言論惹不滿. 美心:伍淑清無任何職位. 衷心希望各方解決分歧 (Founder's daughter's defense of police create offense. Maxim's: Wu Shu-Ching does not have any professional position. Heartily hopes all sides will reconcile their differences)." *HKD4*, September 24, 2019. www.hkd4.com/news/3264.

"建制紅人陳振彬: 大學生申公屋是放棄自己 (Popular pro-establishment figure, Chan Chung-bun: college graduates applying for public housing is giving up on themselves)." *Stand News*, January 12, 2015. https://collection.news/thestandnews/articles/889.

"少年強則香港強莫失掉一代人 (If young people are strong then Hong Kong will be strong. Do not lose a whole generation of people)." *HK01*, June 17, 2019. www.hk01.com//社論/341203/01周報社論-少年強則香港強-莫失掉一代人.

"施永青預言疫情過後, 樓市復甦快過酒樓. 年輕人只會繼續做旁觀者 (Shih Wing Ching predicts that after COVID, the real estate market will recover faster than restaurants. Young people will only continue to be bystanders)." 堅料網www.Kinliu.hk, May 29, 2020. https://n.kinliu.hk/kinliunews/蓄勢待發/年輕人只會繼續做旁觀者%E3%80%80施永青預/.

"環時 專訪伍淑清: 會放棄被洗腦的香港年輕人 (Global Times exclusive interview with Wu Shuqing: will give up on young people)." *AM730*, November 4, 2019. www.am730.com.hk//本地/-環時-專訪伍淑清-會放棄被洗腦的香港年輕人/41902.

黃之鋒: 無懼國安法 跟習近平鬥長命 (Joshua Wong: Not afraid of the National Security Law. Competition with Xi Jinping to see who's lives longer)." *Deutsche Welle*, May 22, 2020. www.dw.com/zh-hant/專訪黃之鋒無懼國安法-跟習近平斗長命/a-53529141.

# 4 The New Cantopop and the New Hong Kong Cinema

The Hong Kong music and film industries started experiencing severe contraction at the beginning of the second millennium. Commentators began pronouncing that Hong Kong music was dead and that Hong Kong cinema was moribund. Indeed, things did look gloomy in 2020, especially amid the political fallout from the 2019 protests, the effects of the NSL, and the ravages of the COVID pandemic. However, unexpectedly, everything changed in 2021. This time, the revolution was not in the political arena, but in entertainment. Despite the dismissiveness and deprecations of their elders, young people began to redefine Hong Kong's culture, reclaiming a social space from which they had been evicted over the course of the politically tumultuous 2010s. This chapter charts how a generation's defiance set off a blossoming of popular culture in Hong Kong in the NSL era.

Hong Kong's popular culture plays an inordinately important role in the society and is deeply connected to the formation of the city's self-image, self-narrative, and identity.[1] To a large extent, the health of the industry reflects the health of the society. The city's "golden age," for many, was in the 1980s and 1990s, when the city was at its most affluent. Its film and music industries flourished. It had the world's third-largest film industry after Hollywood and Bollywood, and it was a major exporter of films and television shows--an astonishing productivity given Hong Kong's population of about seven million at the time was only a fraction of those of India and the United States. The Cantopop industry was equally prosperous. Together, Hong Kong films and music had unequaled influence throughout Asia and beyond. However, all that was in the past. Hong Kong's film production fell from its record of 285 films a year in 1993 to only 22 in 2020.[2] It was the same situation with pop music.

## *Bit fonghei ninhingjan, ninhingjan bit fonghei* 別放棄年輕人 年輕人別放棄 (Do Not Give Up on Young People; Young People, Do Not Give Up)

The decline of Hong Kong's cultural industry seemed irreversible by the end of the 2010s. A whole generation of young people in Hong Kong grew up watching and listening to J-pop and K-pop, rather than Hong Kong's homegrown acts. However, a force that had been quietly percolating finally burst into public attention on

DOI: 10.4324/9781003521280-5

January 1, 2021. This new energy was manifested in the person of the then 21-year-old singer, Keung To, a member of Hong Kong's new idol band sensation, MIRROR. That night, Keung To won two of the biggest and most coveted music awards in the city. He was the youngest recipient of these awards in the 30-year history of Commercial Radio Hong Kong's annual Ultimate Song Charts Awards. He was "My Favorite Male Singer," and his song, "*Mung zeok zeoi syut oi nei* 蒙著嘴說愛你 (Saying I love you with my mouth covered)," a song of gratitude to the medics during the COVID pandemic, was named "My Favorite Song" of the year. These "My Favorite" categories in the awards were determined by audience vote.

When presenting the "My Favorite Male Singer" award, the veteran Commercial Radio DJ, Lam Hoi Fung, said, "What this tells us is that there is hope for young people in this place." In anticipation of controversy, before announcing "My Favorite Song," another DJ, Sammy Leung森美, reminded the audience that the award was by popular vote, saying, "If you are surprised by the result, you might consider that perhaps it is you who don't really understand the world."[3] During the same award ceremony, Keung To's fellow MIRROR bandmate, Jer Lau, received the award for Best New Artist of the Year.

Predictably, the results of the night generated a huge reaction among the public and sparked fierce debates on social media. Among the many comments praising the two young men's achievements, there were more that were mean-spirited, questioning Keung To's qualification for the prestigious awards that had previously been given to the most established singers in the city, who had earned the honors through years waiting for a hit song and cultivating their fan base. Some even suggested that giving the award to such a new singer meant that Hong Kong's music was truly finished. The response toward Jer Lau's award, perhaps less harsh, was a dismissive, "*mat seoi* 乜水 (who's he)?"

In the immediate aftermath of the controversy arising from the award, the well-known lyricist, Siu Hak小克, announced on social media a plan to address this animosity toward the young artists, asking someone to contribute a tune to his lyrics. The invitation was quickly taken up by a then 25-year-old singer-songwriter, Ng Lam Fung吳林峰, also a newcomer to the pop music industry. Ng had also been invited to the Ultimate Songs Award ceremony for the first time and was dismayed at the general public's hostility toward the new musicians. Ng and Siu Hak were soon joined by the influential producer, Wong Sheung Chun王雙駿. In a matter of days, a number of independent musicians and production artists had signed onto the project. On January 26, 2021, less than two weeks after Siu Hak's initial "call to arms," the song, "*Hoenggong ngoktaan ji sei* 香港樂壇已死 (Hong Kong music is dead)," was launched. The song's solo sections were sung by Ng, accompanied by the quickly formed "Hong Kong music is dead chorus," while "*mat soei*" Jer Lau brought in the climactic ending to the song.

In an interview, Siu Hak said that he had heard the comment, "Hong Kong music is dead," for many years. However, he felt the Ultimate Song Contest awards ceremony that year demonstrated precisely the opposite. He felt that the venom directed at the young artists indicated something inherently more troubling. He believed that society had turned its back on young people after the 2019 protests.[4]

The singer-songwriter, Ng, said he was very excited to be invited to the awards ceremony, but was saddened by the public's response, so he answered Siu Hak's call immediately. Ng said young artists were constantly told they could never measure up to the stars of the past. He said every time he read Siu Hak's lyrics, especially the line, "*nin hing goi sei* 年輕該死 (the young should die)," he wanted to cry. But when he got to the line, "Hong Kong singers will never die," he felt encouraged.[5] Siu Hak's lyrics uncompromisingly called out the public for their intolerance and for being stuck in the past:

> Opening a can of fizzy drink while watching YouTube, you spit and froth in the comments section. In one sentence, you condemn me. You look at the wreckage today and say it's proof that the music scene is dead, and it is my fault.
>
> At the songwriter and the lyricist, you scoff.
>
> "Who the hell are you (*mat seoi*)? How can one sing such rubbish lines?"
>
> Hong Kong singers are dead...They forget lyrics, sing off key, get out of breath and sing standing still. All the young faces, none of them looks like a star. Sigh. How can these measure up to the past, the age of the golden tunes. Don't turn on the radio anymore; what comes out will just pollute the air.
>
> Little black beans [i.e. musical notes on a score] record the prosperity and decline of the city. With our love – here, small businesses, small community. Six hundred words, forty lines. They are all stories and emotions. There are songs in my heart.
>
> ... (Jer Lau solo): Hong Kong singers will never die. How cruel you are; how you despise us. You dismiss us, make fun of us, and compare us to the past. You mock us and castigate us. You give up on this generation. Please stop comparing us. I will give you a cassette player so you can keep on listening to how beautiful it was in the past.[6]

The lyrics both mock the keyboard warriors spewing behind their anonymity who are stuck in the so-called golden age of the 1980s and 1990s and describe how the young musicians' work records the times. At the end of the song's MV, there is a tally of the amount of music produced in 2020. Altogether 855 singles and 1339 EPs were produced the year music was supposed to have died. The video ends with the words, "別放棄年輕人 年輕人別放棄*bit fonghei ninhingjan, ninhingjan bit fonghei* (Do not give up on young people; Young people, do not give up)."[7] The song quickly became one of the most popular songs of the year, successfully rallying interest and support for local music.

With the involvement of the powerful producer, Wong Sheung Chun, and the veteran lyricist, Siu Hak, "Hong Kong music is dead" was very much a mainstream response to the issue. Directly on its heels, on February 9, the independent punk rock band, Sugar Bro, also responded with an angry 56-second song, "無聽過 *mou teng gwo* (Never heard of it)":

> Hong Kong is a strange place, where a small group of people have a particular attitude. They like to compare. They feel the *scene* in Hong Kong has gone bad.

> So, cherish it now; don't wait till it all disappears and then regret. You only know how to keep dissing. If you want the industry to survive, don't try to be funny. It only shows how ignorant you are. Can you say these lines a few times less: "I've never heard of this song before," "Who the hell is he?" "I've never heard of this or that"? You have not heard wrong. Go on the Internet and search for something to listen to. Let your ears do some discovering. (Italicized word originally in English.)[8]

Instead of complaining about not knowing who these new musicians are, Sugarbro suggests critics educate themselves and catch up with the times.

## MIRROR and the New Cantopop

These songs were only the opening salvo of young people's cultural war in Hong Kong. It was quickly followed by a song from Keung To himself, who had been very much at the heart of the controversy. On March 19, he released his first new song of the year, "Master Class." The song was written by an even younger songwriter, Gareth T., several months Keung To's junior.[9] Working closely with one of the best-known lyricists, Wyman Wong, Keung To's song is about rejecting old rules and methods, and refusing to compromise one's individuality and dreams to fit into societal expectations and norms:

> How is it that one is wrong just for being young? Why hate me without giving a reason?...Can we switch galaxies? Dull and inflexible people, yield your spot...
>
> Who should have helped me but are blocking me instead? If I said, "but..." I'll never hear the end of it...
>
> In the past, one had to take a million classes before one was allowed to dance. Whoever wanted to create a new dance would be punished. Sorry if I make a break for it with my new ideas. No one can stop this thirst.
>
> And I like my own madness too much. Others trying to stop me will only make me even more determined. Being in the master's classroom is worse than being stuck in a confining dark room. You ask me to pretend to be a fruit candy, I yet insist on being a ginger candy...[10]
>
> Why insist that an ugly duckling like me become a swan, when my goal is just to be me?
>
> Thank you for lighting a fire under me. I don't want to compromise. Shut up and watch how I break through. If you still don't understand, just wait, and watch me.[11]

Even though he recognizes the value of the classics and the old masters, the singer argues that he prefers to follow his own dance. This is a bold pronouncement, especially in a hierarchical industry in which an old guard still wielded great power and where audiences still held onto old standards and conventions. Although he was the direct target of much hate and criticism, Keung To insisted in numerous interviews that the song was not just about him, but young people in general.

The reason for Cantopop's decline in Hong Kong is very complex. Most of Hong Kong's established singers had abandoned Hong Kong's music scene to pursue the more lucrative mandopop (Mandarin pop) market in mainland China.[12] At the same time, large record labels and industry monopolies stunted creativity and experimentation in Hong Kong music in their pursuit of quick profit. The same handful of songwriters repeatedly generated songs in the same style that had proven to be successful. Popular and bankable singers were made to produce as many songs as quickly as possible while they were at the height of their popularity, squeezing out the newcomers. For example, Kelly Chan, one of the most successful pop stars in the early 2000s produced three albums in 2002. She released one in February, one in July, and the last one in December, which amounted to a total of 31 songs in 52 weeks. In contrast, Keung To released five songs in 2021, two of which were collaborations with other singers, and one with another MIRROR teammate for a television drama. Only two were his own projects.

Toward the end of the fat years of Hong Kong's popular music, albums and albums of music were put out regardless of quality, relying on the fans' loyalty. The music was mostly formulaic and mawkish love songs, with easy-to-sing-a-long tunes—so-called k-songs, created for the burgeoning karaoke market in the late 1990s and the 2000s.[13]

Keung To's 2021 "Master Class" is a song with a strong message, on a topic not usually found in popular songs. Musically, it is also a departure from "k-songs." Incorporating elements of R&B and EDM that favor a strong dance beat, the songwriter, Gareth T., introduced a new sound into Cantopop. Keung To's performance of the song includes an extended dance sequence without singing that is also atypical. Even though dance music has become the new norm, especially in the K-pop-dominated music world, Keung To's, and MIRROR's dance music in general, created a new standard in Hong Kong. According to the choreographer, Zero:

> ...K-pop's dance arrangements have a clear structure: First, the visuality: This is the *pattern* created through the positioning of the dancers. Second, the common steps: when all the members do the same dance steps. Third, the break off: in the main verses of the song, different members would become the focus, while the others dance slowly behind as accompaniment. In each verse, usually two or three would take turns being the focal point. Last, the *signature move*. This often appears in the chorus...[MIRROR's] group songs usually contain this kind of Korean-style arrangement with all the four parts.
>
> .... However, what is characteristically Hong Kong [about MIRROR's songs] is that their dance gestures have *content*. Recently, MIRROR member, Keung To's solo song, *Master Class*, on the theme of "why it is wrong to be young," also contains elements of modern dance. It incorporates the "visual" aspect and the "common dance" aspects of K-Pop, but each gesture and step contains meaning...this kind of (content-focused) work is relatively rare in Korea. (Words originally in English are Italicized.)[14]

In "Master Class," the dance is not merely a visual addendum to the music. The choreography, the body movements, and the hand gestures are all integral parts of the performance, conveying as much meaning and emotions as the lyrics and the singing itself. The entire performance concept of "Master Class" was innovative and part of MIRROR's contribution to Hong Kong's pop music.

Nine days after the release of "Master Class," on March 28, 2021, "*mat seoi*" Jer Lau also released a new song—"*Kwongjan jatgei* 狂人日記 (Diary of a Madman)," written by Ng Lam Fung, with lyrics by Siu Hak.[15] Incorporating elements of progressive rock, the song also shatters the conventions of Cantopop. It is about the dissolute life of a singer, who, in old age, finally recognizes how his entire life has been a karmic drama linked to his previous lives. His story will, in turn, continue to feed into those who come after him. Jer Lau has used a series of songs, "Diary," being the second of a trilogy, to present a heavily Buddhist-influenced theme, deviating from the romantic love songs that had dominated the 1990s and 2000s. This song expanded the intellectual expectations and possibilities of Cantopop. The title of the song is borrowed from one of the most important works of modern Chinese fiction by Lu Xun (1881–1936), which is a satirical story on how traditional morality and social expectations consume individuals. The song thus signals across time and genre, adding layers of meaning and spawned numerous discussions and critical analyses from the city's intellectual quarters.

The song, "Diary of a Madman," reinforced the notion that pop music can be a vessel of serious content, elevating the genre's function from the pure entertainment of its "k-songs" days. Additionally, the song is notoriously difficult to sing, spanning three octaves, defying the sing-along quality of formulaic popular music. Despite these challenges to the audience, it became one of the top ten songs of the year in the Ultimate Song Charts Awards presented the following year, on January 1, 2022, along with Keung To's "Master Class." In that year's award ceremony, Keung To once again claimed the two "My Favorite" awards.

## The MIRROR Revolution

If winning their respective music awards in 2021, Jer Lau and Keung To presented a shock to the system of Hong Kong's entertainment industry, the announcement that once and for all, a new era had arrived came from the whole 12 members of MIRROR. On March 26, MIRROR's group song, "Warrior," with lyrics by *Lam Joek-ning*林若寧,was released. This is a song that celebrates youth, urging young people not to be satisfied with the old order. It encourages its audience to face their difficulties bravely, and to fight for their dreams, promising that even a regular person can help bring about great changes. The song tapped into the general zeitgeist, so much so that its release shot MIRROR's popularity to new heights and stirred up excitement about a musical group the city had not seen in decades:

> Idiots and hypocrites block the train from charging out on the new rails. The reprobates rely on their cronies. Who are those who use their positions to switch off the new lie detectors? The high-level, low-quality power circles block the

> ladder. Being picked on, being threatened, we haven't bowed down. Even if these were heaven's rules, we'd still tear them down with our conviction.
>
> It's hard to get used to being a pawn, fearful of every move. We must stand up straight; we train our courage through criticism. Lift up our chests to face the future even if it might not be what we have expected. Worse comes to worst, we die. But we won't run away. The power of our minds will be our weapon. We are prepared that our new voices will be attacked.
>
> Using our will power, even a regular person can fly. No matter how many checkpoints there are, we'll keep taking them down. No matter how many monsters there are, we'll embrace them. We'll use our new blood to irrigate the whole world.
>
> Rap (written by Lokman Yeung and Alton Wong): I put a full stop on the backward attitudes. A new world has been created by a group of youngsters who have been elected. Neither vain nor proud, we keep changing and evolving, setting off one storm after another. A signal—received! We're setting off on our great journey.
>
> The standards are challenged by new experiments; the motor has new batteries. The old parts are a problem--stopping and starting again. The new monuments, the new epics are not completed yet. Spinning and turning, a new group of young ones have now appeared.
>
> ... Our members have not retreated nor shown despair; win or lose, we remain positive. With the brightest beacon we battle the world. With our microphones, we augur the next ten years. For once, take a risk, spark off some electricity. The more stuck we are, the more we must change--Surpassing the speed of light, into Mar's orbit, faster than lightning.
>
> A great tidal wave has brought in a new era. The noisier, the busier the better the chance for change. The quieter, the lonelier, the harder to create surprises. Using the power of our minds, even a regular person can fly. Courage can only start the machine. It is belief that allows us to fly. A new era is here. I hope you are ready for it.
>
> *Never give up, never give up, I got it, I've got a warrior heart...*(Original words in English in Italics.)[16]

The official description of the song contains these lines: "Yesterday's yardsticks, thermometers, units, standards, and currency, are unable to measure the length, weight, value, and success of the future. Old seafood (local slang for older people stuck in their times) are unable to understand the new species." The song is ostensibly about how the members of MIRROR overcome their doubters and haters to realize their dreams. However, unmistakable is the combative attitude, not merely in the words of the song, and the song title, but even in the choreography of the dance that accompanies the song, which contains many martial images, moves, and stances. The song doesn't just declare that the new generation will use their own way to bring about a new world, but it also demands that the old make way for the young. The MIRROR members could be singing about the entertainment world and the old standards and modes of production. They could be contesting the general dismissiveness of young people. They could also be challenging the old order. "Warrior" topped the charts on all the radio and streaming platforms, including the Ultimate Song Chart for two consecutive weeks. The last time a song had this impact was 15 years prior.

No doubt, the song could be interpreted as a challenge to the political establishment, stepping too close to the red line of the NSL. After all, it was advocating the overthrow of the old. The chorus, "Never give up...I've got a warrior heart," and all the fighting words in the song raised the specter of the heady protest of 2019. A former reporter of the shuttered *Stand News*, Ho Kwai-lam, who attempted to run for public office and was later charged and arraigned for violating the NSL, said the first time she cried after being remanded to custody was when she heard the song, especially the lines, "Worse comes to worst, we die. But we won't run away."

The MIRROR members were contestants of ViuTV's talent show, *King Maker*, in 2018 (see Chapter1). The phrase, "a group of youngsters who have been chosen," in the lyrics of the song might have reminded its listeners how they were able to vote for their favorite performers during the Finals of the contest. Most of the MIRROR members were, in this sense, elected by the public, an impossibility in the political sphere. Whether or not there was political intention behind the song, it made certain quarters uneasy enough that despite its popularity, the song was only performed live once when it was first released and seemed to have since been expunged from MIRROR's repertoire.

The MIRROR songs and the television programs that featured them in the first half of 2021 propelled the group to a level of popularity not seen in the city since the early 1990s, and some would argue, ever. The entire city—on billboards, video walls on buildings, buses, trains, and bus stops, where two years before were covered by posters and graffiti, where protest banners were unfurled, and where tear gas was fired—was now plastered with images of MIRROR in advertisements and promotional campaigns of their works.

As MIRROR fever gripped the city, there was even a humorous popular "concern group" on social media called, "*Ngo loupo gaa zo bei MIRROR douzi fanjan kyutlit gwaanzyuzou* 我老婆嫁咗俾MIRROR導致婚姻決裂關注組 (My-wife-is-married-to-*MIRROR*-leading-to-my-marriage-falling-apart concern group)," with a membership of over 350,000, in which husbands and boyfriends of MIRROR's fangirls gathered to exchange jokes about their experiences.[17] The rap duo, MC $oho and KidNey, from the group Trial and Error (more on them later), made the group the subject of their song, "Black MIRROR":

*K:* They are everywhere! they are everywhere! Why am I seeing their close-ups almost every day?

*S.* They are everywhere! They are everywhere! It is chaos whenever they all come together.

*K:* I can't figure out; I can't figure out who's who among them. Can you tell them apart?

*S.* I can't figure out; I can't figure out how one can fangirl all twelve stars at the same time...

*K:* We see them in the underground train stations. We see them at the bus-stops. We see them while eating dinner. We see them while buying electronics.

*S.* Seeping into all aspects of our lives, they are simply black art; there is no protection against them. No!

*K:* They are everywhere; they are everywhere. How do you explain what your wife's relationship is with them?

*S.* They are everywhere; They are everywhere. They are even home with you, sleeping on the same bed!...[18]

Some argued that MIRROR's popularity was merely a result of them appearing at the right time and at the right place. People read into them their own needs and aspirations, whether political or personal. In other words, judging by the quality of their work alone, they did not deserve all this adoration. Such was the assessment, in May 2022, of one of Hong Kong's most recognized opinion writers in the city, Tokit淘傑 (who now lives in the United Kingdom). In his early 60s at the time, Tokit described MIRROR's popularity as merely a "*heoi fo* 虛火 (weak flame)" that would flicker out in no time. Tokit's comments, originally made on an online talk show, circulated widely on social media, resulting in a huge backlash from MIRROR fans. Even Tokit's own peers thought he was detached from Hong Kong's reality. Particularly vehement was the response from another famous media personality and commentator, Shiu Yeuk Yuen 蕭若元. As Shiu had made news earlier for having dismissed the efforts of young filmmakers (more on this below) that he would come to the defense of MIRROR was ironic. Nevertheless, their debates stirred up Hong Kong's commentariat. Almost all the heavyweight KOLs weighed in, mostly on the side of MIRROR. Eden Lau, the chief executive officer of *Tocanan*, a data analysis company that studies social media and e-commerce figures, used data gathered by his company to refute Tokit's assessment of MIRROR:

> The MIRROR YouTube channel was first established on November 4, 2019. Till today, it has 356,000 subscribers, 139 videos, 350 million views and three million and fifty thousand likes. In terms of volume of views, one can see that the MIRROR channel has become more and more popular. It grew from 69 million views in 2020 to 150 million in 2021, with 51 million in just the first four months of 2022. Among this, Keung To's song, "Dear My Friend," has been viewed as many as 16 million times. I would like to base my analysis on these data. These are very important indicators showing the affective power of the songs and their ability to elicit audience involvement and discussions. "Dear My Friend" has the most discussions, with over 40 thousand comments.[19]

Considering that Hong Kong's population was only about 7.3 million at the time of the study, these figures were important indicators of MIRROR's effect on the Hong Kong public. More importantly, Lau also studied social media activities concerning MIRROR in the city around the end of April 2022. In April, when MIRROR announced that their concert would be held in July that year, it immediately provoked a mad rush for tickets. It was rumored that scalpers were asking a staggering HK$440,000 or US$55,000 for each ticket. April 30 was Keung To's birthday, which meant massive celebration programs and festivities around the city planned by his fans.

Around this time, Hong Kong was also preparing for the "election" of the new Chief Executive, John Lee, one week later, on May 8, 2022. The election campaign, of which there was only a single candidate as approved by Beijing, was going full force. Lau compared the volume of conversations on social media about MIRROR with those about the imminent Hong Kong Chief Executive election around this time:

> Keung To's birthday and MIRROR's concert were the two most posted topics. It exceeds those on the Chief Executive Election by 95% and 12 % respectively...
>
> The most shared items were Keung To's birthday and MIRROR's concert. The posts totaled 14 million and 13 million respectively, which are 86% and 76 % more than those about the Chief Executive election. [Keung To's] new song, "The meaning of the works," that has only been posted for 4 days, also has a very high reach. It is only 14% less than that about the Chief Executive Election.
>
> According to the data, MIRROR, Keung To, and his teammates are solid![20]

While Lau's data affirmed MIRROR's significance in Hong Kong society, conversely, it also revealed how little Hong Kong people cared about the single-candidate election in 2022. It is probably impossible to fully explain the reasons behind Hong Kong's excitement and obsession with MIRROR in these years, especially with the few most prominent members of the group. However, in reference to the mass revel in the districts of Causeway Bay and Tsim Sha Tsui in honor of Keung To's birthday, many pointed out it was also because Hong Kong as a society had not had a cause for celebration or experienced joy for a long time. Keung To's birthday occurred just as the city was emerging from a particularly devastating COVID wave that had stopped the city for several months. The ability to go out once again, to get together with friends and family after such a long period of isolation and worry added to the exuberance of the day. Keung To's birthday, even for those who were not fans, was an occasion for celebration. Many took advantage of the free rides on the beloved Ding Dings (as the locals refer to trams that have been in service since 1904) to go on the streets once again. With MIRROR, many Hongkongers were able to find a commonality, to celebrate something together, to overlook, even just momentarily, the political disappointments and division that had torn the society apart in the previous years. The group's promise of a new era for the city and their message of resilience injected new hope and positivity in a society mired in the new NSL and COVID gloom.

Despite all this MIRROR-inspired excitement, it still was not enough to convince many of the old guard of Hong Kong's entertainment business that this generation could ever measure up to the superstars of the glory years of the 1980s and 1990s. A popular singer from the late 1980s, Ah Lam (George Lam), dismissively said Hong Kong now only had idols, not singers with substance.[21] Many of the older generation who had witnessed and benefited from Hong Kong's boom years seem unwilling to acknowledge the struggles and achievements of the young artists, continuously belittling their efforts. The lyricist, Siu Hak argued that there was a place for everyone:

> There is definitely a new wave in the music scene—someone thought the idols were just a "weak flame." Others found a momentary sense of peace through the music. There are also those who project their own hopes onto the young people...It is all good. These are all choices, all reflecting one's feelings in a particular moment.[22]

Whether they truly "deserved" all the adoration or not, there is no doubt MIRROR's success revived a general interest in Cantopop. Through their collaborations with different musicians, especially independent songwriters, and less mainstream groups, they also brought attention to many who pursued less conventional musical forms, thus expanding the genre. Many listeners who had long given up on Cantopop returned to embrace it. The increase in interest, in a virtuous cycle, encouraged more new artists to put forth their work and to experiment. More companies were willing to invest in new musicians. Even some of the established singers who had since moved to China returned to take advantage of this revival of Cantopop. Depending on their public statements during 2019, some were more welcome than others.

When asked what he thought of Tokit's criticism of MIRROR as only a "weak flame," Keung To responded that while he was not qualified to comment on what the critics said, the only thing he and MIRROR could do was to keep improving, to change the minds of their critics, and to turn this weak flame into a real fire. Two days later, on his birthday, he awed his fans and impressed many listeners with his new song, "作品的說話 *Zokban dik syutwaa* (The meaning of the works)," an antiwar song in response to Russia's invasion of Ukraine. Siu Hak again wrote the lyrics, crediting Keung To for the idea, while the MV was directed by Keung To himself.[23] According to Siu Hak,

> Today, on his birthday, there is a young person, who has chosen to, indeed, insisted on, calling for love and peace. From the beginning of this project, his *intention* has touched this middle-aged man. Forget 23, not even at 46 did I have his courage and clarity about what I wanted.[24]

Keung To's song elicited praise from all quarters, including the city's most prominent literary figure, Dung Kai Cheung, who also pointed out that this awareness of the connection between oneself and the greater world was a general characteristic of the new generation of artists:

> In truth, Keung To is not the only one in the local music scene who has reached this level of caring and thoughtfulness. It's better to say these are characteristics of the new generation in the music business. At present, there are two main topics

> in Hong Kong's popular music. One is self-discovery, examination, awakening, and persisting on the path one has chosen. The other is how to retain what is good in a world that is corrupt and full of difficulties. Both are about being human. The former reaches from within, out toward human's common consciousness. The latter reaches from beyond into the common experiences of life. Keung To's work begins with the former, and ends with the latter, connecting both the inner and outer world. (Isn't this also the meaning of MIRROR's new group song, "Innerspace"?) I will venture to say Hong Kong's popular music has never had this spiritual quality before. As far as their skills, this group of young people are continuously becoming more refined. Even if we don't want to assess whether their performance is world class or not, their vision and emotions are definitely international in scope.[25]

The new artists were determined to prove that Hong Kong music was not dead, and through their music that the city also was not moribund. However, the intense focus on these young performers, especially MIRROR, also created unrealistic expectations well beyond what they could fulfill. Another eminent lyricist and screenwriter, Poon Yuen Leung 潘源良, noticed the powerful emotional projection from the public onto the new singers, saddling them with heavy social and political responsibilities. Many looked to them for comfort in Hong Kong's hours of darkness, investing in them their hopes and aspirations for the city as a whole. As a result, Poon believed Cantopop had become weighed down by a seriousness, whether it was in the performances, in the lyrics, or in MVs:

> It was never like this in the past. It is different now. Everyone's projecting their needs—the responsibility given [to the lyricist and the singers] is very heavy. I have been watching how this is going to develop. What will be the next step for Cantopop?...Sometimes, I think, when possible, it is better not to be so heavy. Leave a bit of breathing space."[26]

In the 1980s and 1990s, Cantopop was mostly dance music or love songs; singers of that period did not have the same kind of social and political burden. The expectations on the new performers explain the intensity of feelings, whether love or hatred, toward them.

## Trial and Error: Trying to Create a New Cinema

As in the case of music, Hong Kong's cinema and television industries also experienced severe contraction. In 2015, a large percentage of the shares of Hong Kong's primary television station, TVB, was purchased by the mainland Chinese company, CMC Media Inc., a company closely associated with the political powers in Beijing.[27] In the 1970s to early 1990s, TVB was the largest producer of Chinese-language television in the world, known for the innovativeness and boldness of its programs, nurturing legions of superstars and world-renowned directors. However, TVB went into quick decline in the 2000s. Most of their programs by the late

2010s were created with the mainland audience in mind, especially for the Greater Bay Area, rather than for Hong Kong viewers. These programs were conditioned by China's censorship laws, and the contents catered to the tastes and interests of the mainland audiences. Many of TVB's performers, both singers and actors, household names in Hong Kong, turned their focus and energy to the mainland market and considered China as their base. However, the last straw for many Hongkongers was the station's obvious pro-police and pro-government stance in its news reporting of the 2019 protests. It has since been considered the mouthpiece of the Chinese government and was rejected by large numbers of Hongkongers, especially the younger generation. The station began hemorrhaging audiences in Hong Kong. TVB's programs, unlike in the 1970s and 1980s, no longer provided common narratives for Hong Kong society.

Likewise, in film, most of the mature industry people and artists abandoned the city in pursuit of the much more lucrative Chinese market. Since 2003, with the signing of the CEPA between Hong Kong and China, the majority of films by established Hong Kong directors have been co-productions with Chinese companies. This means an infusion of funds for bigger and more ambitious projects. However, mainly aimed at the Chinese market, these co-production films are often aesthetically, culturally, and politically alien to Hong Kong audiences.[28] Most of these films only used well-known Hong Kong actors who were proven box-office draws in China. As film and television production moved north, Hong Kong-based young actors, directors, and production technicians no longer had many opportunities. New Hong Kong directors who wanted to work on local projects and tell local stories had trouble finding investors or venues for their work. It was not till 2016, with the establishment of ViuTV, a new local television station, that opportunities for local talent improved.

While Hong Kong people stopped going to the cinema to see co-production films, or stopped turning on their televisions, they have been watching short films on YouTube channels. According to, "Digital 2021: Hong Kong," a report jointly issued by *We Are Social*, an advertising firm, and *Hootsuite*, a social media marketing and management firm, YouTube was the most used social media platform in Hong Kong, occupying 86.9% of the market, followed by WhatsApp (83.6%) and Facebook (83%).[29] There had been a proliferation of YouTube channels in Hong Kong especially around the latter half of the 2010s, including a handful of ambitious channels of creative content that offered a variety of short-form original films, comic skits, satires, variety, and game shows. These were not the homemade videos of innumerable YouTubers but serious operations involving production crews of young professionals. Imperceptibly, they had changed the viewing habits, taste, and expectations of Hong Kong's audience. The production turnaround time of these channels was often very fast. They were small in scale and relied on small steady troupes of actors. Keenly aware of their connection with the local audience, their works were often direct responses to the daily happenings and sentiments in the city. These channels became so popular and influential by 2021 that even established popular stars began appearing on them to promote their work. Groups such as Pomato, FH Production, and Trial and Error 試當真

*Si dongzan*, in particular, had become increasingly important cultural forces in the city.

Established in 2020, Trial and Error was one of the most influential of these YouTube channels. Their work followed current events or popular culture closely, often relaying or reinterpreting them through parody. They tackled social taboos, unpleasant social situations, or uncomfortable everyday truths. For example, one of their most successful short films, "*Gam daai gin si mou jan gong* 咁大件事冇人講 (It's a such a big deal, but no one is talking about it?)" (November 2020), makes fun of the many people who pretend that everything is normal despite obvious raging issues around them because they have become too afraid of being accused of stirring up trouble. The film titled, "*Haau*孝Am I (How/How Filial Am I)?" (February 2022), deals with the thorny subject of eldercare.[30] The title plays on the word "filial piety" in Cantonese, pronounced *haau*, a homophone of the English word "how." While filled with comic exaggerations, the short film calls attention to the hardship and sacrifices of the younger generation in caring for their older relatives. While young people are expected to take care of their elders, the short film asks whether there should also be some consideration for the welfare of the carer, as in, "How am I?" Trial and Error often poked through the fabric of normalcy, even decency in the city, raising difficult questions about the reality to which Hongkongers were required to adapt.

Most of these YouTube channels released at least two or three short films a week. At this frequency, many of their works were an immediate response to local events. As well as simple entertainment, the audiences came to rely on these groups' productions to help them digest the occurrences in their daily lives. Also, importantly, these YouTube channels re-created a public space for the discussion of social and even, at times, political events in the city, a role that Hong Kong's television, especially the public RTHK, used to play before it was gutted. Their rapid responses to important events in the city, whether in satire or critical commentary, or merely acknowledging that something significant happened, played an important function in the cultural and civic health of the city.

The subject matters of these YouTube productions, though never overtly political, often signaled more than what was apparent. As the popular saying in Hong Kong went, "*ming zau ming* 明就明 (you'd understand if you understand)." If you didn't, there was no point explaining. Not only would it get one into trouble, but it was also hopeless to try to achieve understanding with someone whose worldview or sense of reality was fundamentally different. All of these various popular channels also directly reached out to their audiences. They presented in-person annual shows in large concert facilities, as well as held live events or live-streams on social media. They had an influence beyond other forms of traditional media, even broadcast television.

One of the most ambitious of these channels was 16 by 9 拾陸比玖 *Sap luk bei gau*, which produced feature film quality works. This channel was formed by a core group of young professional actors, directors, and production crew. They produced mini-series or short dramatic films, with the longest episodes lasting no more than 20 minutes and the shortest, only five minutes or so. Especially appealing to film enthusiasts, they also hosted discussions and interviews with actors, directors, and other film professionals, discussing technical aspects of their work, such as camera angles, lighting, scenic design, etc. The dramatic films produced by the group ranged from the fantastic to the realistic. The series, "*Je hang* 夜行 (night walk) (2021)," for example, focuses on the city at night, depicting a group of typical nighttime characters—a food delivery woman, an eatery owner, a young woman trying to work out a long-distance relationship through phone calls to a different time zone, a young professional working late into the night, and a mother and child packing up house to emigrate. This quiet series explores how these characters intersect with each other over the course of one evening. Another series that began in 2021, *Am gaak* 暗格 (secret compartment), are tales of the paranormal. They range from traditional ghost films to the simply strange.

The works by 16 by 9 are ambitious and polished. Though the actors are relatively young and new in the business, a few in the group, including William Or, Hannah Chan, and Fish Liew, have already received important nominations and awards in different film festivals for their work in recent years.

Despite the popularity of these YouTube channels, they were unable to convince some established industry figures that these short web productions could have a meaningful place in Hong Kong's film industry. The media personality and commentator, Shiu Yeuk Yuen, who dueled with Tokit over MIRROR's effect in the city, famously made a two-part prognosis about Hong Kong cinema's moribund trajectory on his YouTube talk show, *Memehongkong*. He dismissed the productions on the YouTube channels as childish trifles—"*zyu faan zai* 煮飯仔 (pretend cooking)," literally like little girls playing house, criticizing by name, Yau Hawk-Sau 游學修, one of the founders of Trial and Error, and the work of the channel. Shiu pointed out that "real" films involved a completely different scale of production that was beyond the capability of those who made small films for the internet. He argued that since the constellations of factors that produced the city's extraordinary film industry in the 1980s and 1990s could not be duplicated, Hong Kong cinema could never be resurrected.

Yau, 30 years old at the time, had been in several films as an actor before he founded Trial and Error with two other members, So Chi Ho 蘇致豪 and Hui Yin 許賢 (the latter two also inhabit the personalities of the rappers, $oho and KidNey, mentioned earlier). Yau posted a two-part rejoinder to Shiu on February 23, 2021:

> *Waiho ngo gong Hoenggong dinjing gungjip mei sei: ju Hoenggong singnin dinjing jan dik taamtou, soeng, haa* 為何我講香港電影工業未死？與香港成年電影人的探討, 上,下 (Why I say the Hong Kong film industry is not dead. An exploration with an adult Hong Kong film personality, Parts 1 and 2).

In his rebuttal, Yau deliberately referred to Shiu, as the "adult" in the discussion, perhaps to highlight Shiu's dismissal of his work as a child's game, but also to bring out the generational difference between the two. Shiu, in his 70s at the time of the exchange, had spent a lifetime working in the television and film industries during the boom years. However, judging from his clumsy YouTube presentations, such as holding up hand-drawn signs to illustrate his points, it seemed he barely had a grasp on the new technology. Mimicking Shiu, Yau also held up paper signs to make his arguments, underscoring the absurdity of someone who knew so little about the new media criticizing those who were adept at it. Yau pointed out that the times had changed; the technology of production had also changed:

> The first thing I want to say is this: I do not understand why someone from an earlier generation would have this kind of attitude and say such things to someone from a later generation. You benefitted from all the right factors of being at the right time, right place and having the right people around you. When you were fortunate enough to have these conditions, why would you say what you said to young people now? I don't know about others, but I can tell you sincerely, Mr. Shiu, I really yearn, absolutely yearn for those bygone days. But I am using a new method. This new method may not be comprehensible to older people like you. This is fine. So don't say so much.
>
> You just asked what our goal was and what we wanted. I am now telling you what I want to do through Trial and Error. What I want is to use a new perspective, one that is more than just playing house, to enter the new media world; to use the old language, something that I have learned from my predecessors, like you, to do new things. Because, I am sorry, Mr. Shiu, and other elders, you have no idea how to do new things with the new media. As to possibilities—perhaps I am wrong, but I will not say definitively that it is impossible [to revive Hong Kong cinema]. I feel that no one is in any position to determine that our probability of success is zero.
>
> If you tell young people that their probability of success is zero, you are telling them to go and die.[31]

This exchange was broadly circulated and reported. Many commentators and internet warriors jumped into the fray, many criticizing Yau for being impertinent. Nevertheless, Yau successfully focused public attention on this issue. In their February 7, 2022, episode of This is how one talks about Philosophy, a weekly talk show produced by the philosophy group, Corrupt the Youth, on their YouTube channel, Yau was invited to discuss the issue of YouTube films versus "real" cinema with the millennial film director, Mak Heiyan.[32]

The importance of Yau's argument with Shiu regarding the future of Hong Kong cinema was not lost on the organizers of the annual Hong Kong Asian Film Festival (HKAFF). Yau and his group's endeavors were ultimately awarded industry affirmation. Acknowledging Trial and Error's position in the new mediascape, the organizers invited Yau and his two co-founders, Hui Yin, and So Chi Ho, to be the "ambassadors" for the film festival in September 2021. According to HKAFF,

> Made with limited resources, the short films from the popular YouTube channel founded by the trio are always bursting with limitless creativity. As filmmakers, scriptwriters, content creators, actors, comedians and YouTube stars, their presence shines across cinema, TV, stage and online platforms. With shattering

> limitations and pushing boundaries as our goals this year, who would be more fitting as HKFF ambassadors than the trio? As the definition of cinema evolves, we can't wait to discover new possibilities with Trial and Error.[33]

Rather than engaging in vicious competition that was the norm for the older entertainment businesses, the YouTube channels constantly collaborated with each other. 16 by 9 actors frequented Trial and Error; Trial and Error performers appeared on Pomato, and the Pomato cast showed up on another channel, FH Production, etc. A number of them also began to appear in stage dramas and movies. Many of them got recruited by ViuTV for its broadcast programs. In a similar circle of exchange, many of those who worked in television or stage also started to see these YouTube channels as an alternative medium for their work. This led to exchanges of ideas and synergy across this new media community. These YouTube channels might not yet be able to produce movies on a scale that some of the established directors could with unlimited funds in co-production films, but those movies didn't seem to have much appeal in Hong Kong anyway. Instead, these YouTube groups could create short films that were more intimate, more creative, more experimental, and more relevant to local audiences. These channels were forging a new path for Hong Kong's entertainment, cultivating new audiences who were once again happy to support Hong Kong's cultural industry.

## A New Wave

In 2021, as the cinemas in Hong Kong partially reopened after a year of COVID shutdowns, a new wave of locally produced films brought in unexpected results at the box office. These films mostly depicted local subjects and celebrated local heroes. Many of them were the result of the "First Feature Film Initiatives," by the Film Development Council that began in 2013 to provide funding for new directors to make their first films. Many of these projects finally came to fruition at the beginning of the 2020s.[34]

In 2021, three films broke through the HKD10 million mark at the box office, an achievement that had been elusive for local films for many years. The highest grossing film of the year, *Anita*, directed by Longman Leung, a co-production, but filmed in Hong Kong, about a Hong Kong subject, brought in a record of HKD62 million and was, till the beginning of 2022, the second highest grossing Hong Kong film ever produced. A biopic of the legendary Cantopop singer, Anita Mui, who died in 2003, the film took Hong Kong people on a memory trip back to the late 1970s, 1980s, and into the 1990s—the golden years. The film highlighted the excesses and grandeur of the entertainment world during the era and stood in dramatic contrast with the now-reduced reality, eliciting much nostalgia.

The second highest grossing film of the year, 媽媽的神奇小子 *Maamaa dik sankei siuzi Zero to Hero*, directed by Jimmy Wan 尹志文, was based on the true story of a special Olympian and his relationship with his mother, who supported him through his struggle as an athlete. It made HKD28 million at the box office. Another film about a boxing champion, *Jatmiu kyunwong*一秒拳王 *One Second*

*Champion*, directed by Chiu Sin Hang 趙善恆, also broke the HKD10 million. Two films, *Zuksoei piulau* 濁水漂流 *Drifting*, a film directed by Jun Li李駿碩, based on a real story of a group of homeless people suing the Hong Kong government for forcefully removing and disposing of their personal belongings, and *Sau gyun jin*手卷煙*Hand rolled Cigarette*, directed by Kelvin Chan陳健朗, a crime drama featuring a South Asian main character, also came close to the mark, an impressive feat for all first-time directors. Many of these films continued on to win many local and international film awards.

If 2021 heralded a positive turn for Hong Kong's cinema, 2022 was considered a year of miracles. In the midst of the onslaught of Hollywood box office juggernauts, such as *Spiderman*, *Top Gun: Maverick*, and *Avatar*, several Hong Kong films created box office history. A news headline in December 2022 shouted: "Four films with over HKD40 million box office receipts in one year, creating a new record in Hong Kong's film history."[35] These highly successful films were also directed by a new generation of directors, with some featuring very new actors. A low-budget comedy directed by Sunny Chan陳詠燊, *Fan hei gong sam* 飯氣攻心 *Table for Six*, made over HKD70 million at the box office. These were followed by *Zingji wuilong* 正義迴廊*Sparring Partner*, a courtroom drama based on a true crime, directed by Ho Cheuk-Tin何爵天. At over HKD40 million, it broke the city's record for a mature-audience-only film. The last of the four was *Aa maa jau zo dai ji go* 阿媽有咗第二個*Mama's Affair*, directed by Kearen Pang, with MIRROR's Keung To and Jer Lau in the lead.

Even if these box office miracles were a fleeting phenomenon, perhaps helped by Hong Kong people being trapped in their city for months under COVID quarantine, it revealed the quality of work, creativity, and ambition of a generation of local talents. If nothing else, people were beginning to talk about Hong Kong cinema and its possibilities once again. With the exception of a couple of large-budget co-productions, such as *Anita* and *Ming jat zin gei*明日戰記*Warriors of Future*, Hong Kong's first large-budget sci-fi film with world-class special effects, directed by Ng Yuen-Fai吳炫, the new generation of filmmakers favored modest, local stories. This led Chan Ka-Ming to argue,

> Business calculations and national ideology are no longer the sole guidelines for making and interpreting these new films; and most importantly, these films share the commonality of being honest to themselves and to the filmmakers' conscience in depicting the vivid lives of ordinary Hong Kong. This makes Hong Kong "connected" in the sense of a communal society as filmic representation, and in the sense of recognizing the diversity of people coexisting within Hong Kong. At a time when the portrayal of diversity is the tool to oppose the present push for unitary national pedagogy and mobilization, new Hong Kong directors are at the forefront to nurture, represent, and embrace our fading diversity.[36]

In June 2019, young people in Hong Kong took to the streets in an attempt to change the political system. But a real youthquake came in 2021. How significant this youth-led redetermination of the city's culture and identity can be debated, but unquestionably, they have transformed the everyday culture and the conversations in the city. The thoughtless and callous comments regarding the death of Hong Kong's popular culture were not just a repudiation of the efforts and dreams of a new generation, giving up on the young, and on the society itself. It was also a willful destruction of the future without considering the young people who would be inheriting it.

While their elders were busily finding faults with them and reveling in the glory days of the past, the young people were casting their dreams and ambitions far into the future. They were thinking of greater things to come.

## Notes

1 Eric Ma Kit-wai, *Culture, Politics and Television in Hong Kong* (London: Routledge, 1999); Chun-hung Ng and Chi-wai Cheung, edits. *Reading Hong Kong Popular Culture 1970–2000* (Hong Kong: Oxford University Press, 2001); Ng, Cheung and Tsang, edits. *Pop Hong Kong I and II—Reading Hong Kong Popular Culture 2001–2010* (Hong Kong: Hong Kong Educational Publishing Ltd, 2012).

2 Phil Hoad, "Back in action: the fall and rise of Hong Kong film," *The Guardian*, September 13, 2011, www.theguardian.com/film/filmblog/2011/sep/13/hong-kong-film-week-action.

3 "奪吡咤「我最喜愛的男歌手」惹爭議 姜濤認實力資歷不足 (The 'My favorite male singer' category led to controversy: Keung To acknowledged that he lacked experience)," *Mingpao Online*, January 3, 2021, www.mingpao.com/pns/娛樂/article/20210103/s00016/1609610910735/奪吡咤「我最喜愛的男歌手」惹爭議-姜濤認實力資歷不足.

4 "年輕該死？Wyman「師級」贈言助《樂壇已死》升呢王雙駿:「Jer 唱係啱數」('Young people should die?' Wyman, 'the master,' added words, raising the level of 'Music is Dead.' Carl Wong: 'To have Jer singing this song is exactly right')," *AM730*, February 5, 2021, www.AM730.com.hk/娛樂/年輕該死-wyman-師級-贈言助-樂壇已死-升呢-王雙駿-jer-唱係啱數-/158059.

5 "goi sei該死" is a common swear word in written Chinese or spoken Putonghua, equivalent to "damn." It is an expression of disgust. However, in Hong Kong Cantonese, most people will read the term literally.

6 Siu Hak credited Wong Wyman, another of Hong Kong's primary lyricist for suggesting a critical change in the phrase in the song.

7 "樂壇已死 Hong Kong Music is Dead," Music is Dead Team, Tone Music TV, 2022, www.youtube.com/watch?v=WrcjKTXOpHE.

8 Sugar Bro, "無聽過 Never heard of it," lyrics and music by Kan Lo @Sugar Bro, Sugarbrohk, 2021.

9 A graduate of a prestigious music college in the US, he had recently returned to Hong Kong to begin his career.

10 Keung To's last name means ginger, and his fans are collectively called "ginger candies."

11 Keung To, "Master Class," music by Gareth Tong, lyrics by Wyman Wong, Music Nation, 2021a, www.youtube.com/watch?v=6xAVUmdi_UA.

12 Stephen Yiu-wai Chu, Before and After the Fall: Mapping Hong Kong Cantopop in the Global Era, Hong Kong: LEWI Working Paper Series 63, 2007, https://scholars.hkbu.edu.hk/ws/portalfiles/portal/55416356/RO_lewi_wp-10.pdf.

13 For a detailed analysis, see Yiu-Wai Chu, *Hong Kong Cantopop: A Concise History* (Hong Kong, Hong Kong University Press, 2017), especially, 145–183.

14 Wu Siu Man胡筱雯, "本地女團再崛起 重新定義「港女」特質 (The rise again of girl bands and the re-definition of 'Hong Kong woman')," *Mingpao Online*, January 28, 2022, www.Mingpao.com/pns/副刊/article/20220128/s00005/1643306986987/本地女團再崛起-重新定義「港女」特質.

15 Jer Lau, "狂人日記 Diary of a Madman," music by Ng Lam Fung, lyrics by Siu Hak, Music Nation, 2021.

16 MIRROR, "Warrior," music by Val Del Prete and Hwan Yang, lyrics by Lam Joek-ning, Music Nation, 2021, www.youtube.com/watch?v=YI4qsJhZtwA.

17 www.facebook.com%2Fgroups%2F848026786134867%2F&rut=8666c997547f20a243020f491e302efc0afa7c857192c900f1416b8e5fd854ad.

18 Pillows with images of different MIRROR members were much sought after. MC $oHo & KidNey, "Black Mirror," music by East City and MC $oHo, lyrics by MC $oHo, 2021.

19 Eden Lau, "數據的說話 到底MIRROR是否屬虛火 (Meaning from the data. Is MIRROR just a weak fire?)?" *AM730*, May 6, 2022, www.AM730.com.hk/科技/數據科普-數據的說話-到底mirror是否屬虛火-/318323.

20 Ibid.

21 Fong Chun Kit方俊傑, "偶像派或實力派 (Idols versus real singers)," *Am730*, March 18, 2022, www.am730.com.hk/column/娛樂/偶像派或實力派/311788.

22 Siu Hak, quoted from, "The meaning of the work—Keung To issues new song on his 23rd birthday to call for love and peace—Lyricist Siu Hak was moved—I didn't even have this courage at 46," *AM730*, May 1, 2022, www.am730.com.hk//娛樂/作品的說話-姜濤23歲生日出新歌宣揚愛與和平-填詞人小克感動-我46歲都沒這膽量F/317628.

23 Keung To, "What the work says," music by Gareth. T, lyrics by Siu Hak, Music Nation, 2021b, www.youtube.com/watch?v=S6hedDGVOGE.

24 Siu Hak, quoted from, "The meaning of the work—Keung To issues new song..."

25 Dung Kai Cheung, "從作者到作品—姜濤的光速演化 (From creator to creation—the speed-of-light evolution of Keung To," *P-articles*, May 4, 2022, https://p-articles.com/critics/2934.html.

26 Zoeng Wing-jin 張詠然, "專訪作詞人潘源良: 我不懷舊, 只向前看, 人生下半場在台回望香港, 繼續探索創作空間 (Interview with lyricist, Poon Yuen Leung: I am not nostalgic I only look forward. In the latter half of my life looking back at Hong Kong from Taiwan, continue to investigate creative space)," *P-articles*, October 27, 2022, https://p-articles.com/heteroglossia/3315.html.

27 Kris Cheng, "Chinese media mogul revealed as owner of Hong Kong broadcaster TVB, in potential regulatory breach," *Hong Kong Free Press*, May 11, 2017, https://hongkongfp.com/2017/05/11/chinese-media-mogul-revealed-owner-hong-kong-broadcaster-tvb-potential-regulatory-breach/. Peggy Sito, "Li Ruigang, the powerful Chinese media mogul in control of TVB, plots IPO in Hong Kong, US markets for US$10 billion of assets," *South China Morning Post*, April 7, 2021, www.scmp.com/business/china-business/article/3128506/li-ruigang-powerful-chinese-media-mogul-control-tvb-plots.

28 For a discussion of how Hong Kong cinema was transformed by the Chinese market, see Chu Yiu Wai, *Found in Translation: Hong Kong Studies in the Age of China* (New York, State University of New York Press, 2019).

29 Simon Kemp, "Digital 2021: Hong Kong," *Datareportal*, February 9, 2021, https://datareportal.com/reports/digital-2021-hong-kong. Also, Jau Seoi-jan 丘瑞欣, "不跟YouTube正路玩法 以影片營造陪伴感 懷疑人生就去: 散步 / 開Live / 畫畫 / 送別十二卡火車⋯ (Not following proper YouTube method, using films to create a sense of companionship. When in doubt about life: take a walk, do a Live show, draw, see off the

twelve carriages of a train)," *Ming Pao Weekly*, August 5, 2022, www.mpweekly.com/culture/藝文/懷疑人生就去-懷疑人生就去散步-網台-202984.

30 Trial and Error, "咁大件事冇人講*gam dai gin sim o jan gong*," Trial and Error, November 16, 2020, video, 4.1, www.youtube.com/watch?v=dHFWHCmNy7c; "孝*Haau* Am I?" Trial and Error, February 7, 2022, video, 10.13, www.youtube.com/watch?v=Tig6MWaCpu0.

31 Yao Hok-Sau, "為何我講香港電影工業未死？與香港成年電影人的探討（下）(Why I say Hong Kong film industry is not dead. An exploration with an adult Hong Kong film person, Parts 2), Trial and Error, February 23, video, 5.25, 2021, www.youtube.com/watch?v=nqC7j0ynGEo.

32 Corrupt the Youth, "網絡時代裏的電影 (Movies in the age of the internet)," 哲學係咁傾 (There is much to talk about in Philosophy), Ep. 2. February 7, 2022. YouTube, 1:11:36. www.youtube.com/results?search_query=%E7%B6%B2%E7%B5%A1%E6%99%82%E4%BB%A3%E8%A3%8F%E7%9A%84%E9%9B%BB%E5%BD%B1.

33 Hong Kong Asian Film Festival, www.hkaff.asia.

34 Ka-Ming Chan, "A Space Out of Unitary Nationalism," *Indian Journal of Asian Affairs* 34, no.1/2 (2021): 37–58: 42, accessed February 26, 2023, www.jstor.org/stable/27091695.

35 Hui Juk Man許育民, "正義迴廊票房勢破4000萬. 年產四部4000萬作品創香港影史紀錄 (The Sparring Partner to break $40 mil at box office, creating new Hong Kong film record)," *HK01*, December 29, 2022, www.hk01.com/電影/851460/正義迴廊-票房勢破4000萬-年產四部4000萬作品創香港影史紀錄.

36 Ka-Ming Chan, 55.

## References


Chan, Ka-Ming. "A space out of unitary nationalism." *Indian Journal of Asian Affairs* 34, no.1/2 (2021): 37–58: 42. Accessed February 26, 2023. www.jstor.org/stable/27091695.

Cheng, Kris. "Chinese media mogul revealed as owner of Hong Kong broadcaster TVB, in potential regulatory breach." Hong Kong Free Press, May 11, 2017. https://hongkongfp.com/2017/05/11/chinese-media-mogul-revealed-owner-hong-kong-broadcaster-tvb-potential-regulatory-breach/.

Chu, Stephen Yiu-wai. *Before and After the Fall: Mapping Hong Kong Cantopop in the Global Era*. Hong Kong: LEWI Working Paper Series 63, 2007. https://scholars.hkbu.edu.hk/ws/portalfiles/portal/55416356/RO_lewi_wp-10.pdf.

Chu, Stephen Yiu-wai. *Hong Kong Cantopop: A Concise History*. Hong Kong: Hong Kong University Press, 2017.

Chu, Stephen Yiu-wai. *Found in Translation: Hong Kong Studies in the Age of China*. New York: State University of New York Press, 2019.

Corrupt the Youth. "網絡時代裏的電影 (Movies in the age of the internet)." 哲學係咁傾 (There is much to talk about in Philosophy), Ep. 2. February 7, 2022. YouTube, 1:11:36. www.youtube.com/results?search_query=%E7%B6%B2%E7%B5%A1%E6%99%82%E4%BB%A3%E8%A3%8F%E7%9A%84%E9%9B%BB%E5%BD%B1.

Dung Kai Cheung. "從作者到作品—姜濤的光速演化 (From creator to creation—the speed-of-light evolution of Keung To." *P-articles*, May 4, 2022. https://p-articles.com/critics/2934.html.

Fong Chun Kit方俊傑. "偶像派或實力派 (Idols versus real singers)." *Am730*, March 18, 2022. www.am730.com.hk/column/娛樂/偶像派或實力派/311788.

Hoad, Phil. "Back in action: the fall and rise of Hong Kong film." *The Guardian*, September 13, 2011. www.theguardian.com/film/filmblog/2011/sep/13/hong-kong-film-week-action.

Hui Juk Man 許育民. "正義迴廊票房勢破4000萬. 年產四部4000萬作品創香港影史紀錄 (The Sparring Partner to break $40 mil at box office, creating new Hong Kong film record)." *HK01*, December 29, 2022. www.hk01.com/電影/851460/正義迴廊-票房勢破4000萬-年產四部4000萬作品創香港影史紀錄.

Jau Seoi-jan 丘瑞欣. "不跟 YouTube正路玩法 以影片營造陪伴感 懷疑人生就去: 散步 / 開Live / 畫畫 / 送別十二卡火車… (Not following proper YouTube method, using films to create a sense of companionship. When in doubt about life: take a walk, do a Live show, draw, see off the twelve carriages of a train)." *Ming Pao Weekly*, August 5, 2022. www.mpweekly.com/culture/藝文/懷疑人生就去-懷疑人生就去散步-網台-202984.

Kemp, Simon. "Digital 2021: Hong Kong." *Datareportal*. February 9, 2021. https://datareportal.com/reports/digital-2021-hong-kong.

Keung To. "Master Class." Music by Gareth Tong, lyrics by Wyman Wong. Music Nation, 2021a. www.youtube.com/watch?v=6xAVUmdi_UA.

Keung To. "What the work says." Music by Gareth. T, lyrics by Siu Hak. Music Nation, 2021b. www.youtube.com/watch?v=S6hedDGVOGE.

Lau, Eden. "數據的說話 到底MIRROR是否屬虛火 (Meaning from the data. Is MIRROR just a weak fire?)?" *AM730*, May 6, 2022. www.AM730.com.hk/科技/數據科普-數據的說話-到底mirror是否屬虛火-/318323.

Lau, Jer. "狂人日記 Diary of a Madman." Music by Ng Lam Fung, lyrics by Siu Hak. Music Nation, 2021.

Ma, Eric Kit-wai. *Culture, Politics and Television in Hong Kong*. London: Routledge, 1999.

MIRROR. "Warrior." Music by Val Del Prete and Hwan Yang, lyrics by Lam Joek-ning. Music Nation, 2021. www.youtube.com/watch?v=YI4qsJhZtwA.

Ng, Cheung and Tsang, Edits. *Pop Hong Kong I and II—Reading Hong Kong Popular Culture 2001–2010*. Hong Kong: Hong Kong Educational Publishing Ltd, 2012.

Ng, Chun-hung and Chi-wai Cheung, Edits. *Reading Hong Kong Popular Culture 1970–2000* Hong Kong, Oxford University Press, 2001.

Sito, Peggy. "Li Ruigang, the powerful Chinese media mogul in control of TVB, plots IPO in Hong Kong, US markets for US$10 billion of assets." *South China Morning Post*, April 7, 2021. www.scmp.com/business/china-business/article/3128506/li-ruigang-powerful-chinese-media-mogul-control-tvb-plots.

Sugar Bro. "無聽過 Never heard of it." Lyrics and music by Kan Lo@Sugar Bro. Sugarbrohk, 2021.

Trial and Error. "咁大件事冇人講*gam dai gin sim o jan gong*." Trial and Error, November 16, 2020. Video, 4.1. www.youtube.com/watch?v=dHFWHCmNy7c.

Trial and Error. 孝*Haau* Am I?" Trial and Error, February 7, 2022. Video 10.13. www.youtube.com/watch?v=Tig6MWaCpu0.

Wu Siu Man胡筱雯. "本地女團再崛起 重新定義「港女」特質 (The rise again of girl bands and the re-definition of 'Hong Kong woman')." *Ming Pao online*, January 28, 2022. www.Mingpao.com/pns/副刊/article/20220128/s00005/1643306986987/本地女團再崛起-重新定義「港女」特質.

Yao Hok-Sau. "為何我講香港電影工業未死？與香港成年電影人的探討（下） (Why I say Hong Kong film industry is not dead. An exploration with an adult Hong Kong film person, Parts 2)." Trial and Error, February 23, 2021. Video, 5.25. www.youtube.com/watch?v=nqC7j0ynGEo.

Zoeng Wing-jin 張詠然. "專訪作詞人潘源良: 我不懷舊, 只向前看, 人生下半場在台回望香港, 繼續探索創作空間 (Interview with lyricist, Poon Yuen Leung: I am not nostalgic I only look forward. In the latter half of my life looking back at Hong Kong from Taiwan, continue to investigate creative space).” *P-articles*, October 27, 2022. https://p-articles.com/heteroglossia/3315.html

“樂壇已死 Hong Kong Music is Dead.” Music is Dead Team. MusicTone Music TV, 2022. www.youtube.com/watch?v=WrcjKTXOpHE.

奪叱咤「我最喜愛的男歌手」惹爭議 姜濤認實力資歷不足 (The ‘My favorite male singer’ category led to controversy: Keung To acknowledged that he lacked experience).” *MingPao Online*, January 3, 2021. www.mingpao.com/pns/娛樂/article/20210103/s00016/1609610910735/奪叱咤「我最喜愛的男歌手」惹爭議-姜濤認實力資歷不足.

“年輕該死？Wyman「師級」贈言助《樂壇已死》升呢王雙駿:「Jer 唱係啱數」(‘Young people should die?’ Wyman, ‘the master,’ added words, raising the level of ‘Music is Dead.’ Carl Wong: ‘To have Jer singing this song is exactly right’).” *AM730*, February 5, 2021. www.AM730.com.hk/娛樂/年輕該死-wyman-師級-贈言助-樂壇已死-升呢-王雙駿-jer-唱係啱數-/158059.

“作品的說話-姜濤23歲生日出新歌宣揚愛與和平-填詞人小克感動-我46歲都沒這膽量(The meaning of the work—Keung To issues new song on his 23rd birthday to call for love and peace—Lyricist Siu Hak was moved—I didn’t even have this courage at 46).” *AM730*, May 1, 2022. www.am730.com.hk//娛樂/作品的說話-姜濤23歲生日出新歌宣揚愛與和平-填詞人小克感動-我46歲都沒這膽量F/317628.

# 5 The Value of Optimistic Pessimism in Hong Kong's Capitalist Culture

## The Television Drama, *In Geek We Trust*

Many Hongkongers did not feel the 2022 Chief Executive Election had anything to do with them. On March 11, 2021, the National People's Congress in China passed a decision to overhaul Hong Kong's election system to ensure that only "patriots" would govern the city. Those wishing to run for office had to be vetted and approved by the Chinese central government before they could be officially nominated. In the first Legislative Council election after the system was "perfected" in December 2021, Hong Kong residents were supposed to elect 90 councilors to the Legislative Council. None of the candidates who belonged to the oppositional pro-democracy parties were qualified to run. Hong Kong's political opposition had functionally been destroyed. Furthermore, under the Elections (Corrupt and Illegal Conduct) Ordinance of Hong Kong, it was illegal to encourage anyone to boycott elections or to spoil their ballots. Perhaps anticipating the lack of interest in the election, the government tried to generate enthusiasm, especially among the alienated young people through a promotional ad showing a young woman dancing to one of MIRROR's songs on her way to vote. Additionally, all modes of public transportation would be made free on election day to encourage travel to the polls. Despite these efforts, only about 30.2% of eligible voters turned out to cast a ballot on election day, a record low in the city's election history. In the end, the entire slate of pro-Beijing candidates plus one who declared himself an independent got elected to the Legislative Council. A phrase, "*ngo dou mou say* 我都冇 say (since I don't have any say anyway...)," made popular by ViuTV's 2022 hit comic drama, *IT Gau* 狗 (*In Geek We Trust*), captured the general zeitgeist. In this chapter, I discuss how this television series reflected Hongkongers' sense of frustrated acquiescence amid the growing restrictions in the city and their political disenfranchisement. However, like the show, a black comedy, underlying the dark humor was a stubborn sense of optimism. The show did not just reflect the disappointments and frustrations of Hong Kong's new reality, but it also described a longing for another way of life.

DOI: 10.4324/9781003521280-6

### *Ngo dou mou say* 我都冇 say... (Since I Don't Have Any Say Anyway…)

When asked about the public's apathy toward the election, the then Chief Executive, Carrie Lam, argued that the low turnout reflected the populace's confidence in the existing government. Since many felt generally satisfied with how things were going, they saw no urgency to vote, she reasoned. It is hard to believe that even Lam herself was convinced by this logic. This indifference, if not outright boycott, especially after two decades of political activism and heavy electoral participation in the city, reflected, not satisfaction with the government, as Lam claimed, but distrust and detachment.

The electoral system overhaul blatantly demonstrated what everyone had always known—that Hong Kong's officials, especially Hong Kong's Chief Executives, served at the pleasure of Beijing, not the Hong Kong people. If Hongkongers showed little interest in the 2021 Legislative Council election, they were even more oblivious to the 2022 Chief Executive election a few months later. Because the city was hit by a particularly ferocious wave of COVID infections from the beginning of January to mid-April 2022, the Hong Kong Government invoked the Emergency Regulations Ordinance to postpone the Chief Executive election from March 27 to May 8, 2022, and to abbreviate the nomination period, which ran from April 3 to April 16. In the barely two weeks of this nomination period, Hong Kong people learned that only one candidate, pre-approved by a committee appointed by the sitting Chief Executive, was being considered by the Election Committee, a body composed of 1461 members appointed by Beijing. The Election Committee members supposedly represent the different constituencies and professional groups in the city but are generally considered to favor big business.

No one could deny that a one-candidate election was not much of an election. In reality, it was more like an official approval, but even that suggests that the election committee had any power to disapprove of a candidate selected by Beijing. Nevertheless, the government was careful to show that the candidate had gone through the proper procedures of a real election. One commentator, Tim Hamlett, quipped that since this was a one-man election, surely, it could have been done more economically:

> The government spent HK$85 million (about US$10 million) over the past two financial years and budgeted a provisional HK$228 million for this exercise in 2022–23. When it was postponed because of Covid, we were told that this change of date would cost a further HK$50 million. That is a lot of money for an "election" whose result is already a foregone conclusion.[1]

Pro-Beijing politicians argued that this election arrangement was the result of Beijing's concern for continued stability in the city. The Chinese state media, *China Daily*, declared that "Hong Kong is on its way to finding its own model of democracy—democracy with Hong Kong characteristics."[2] The sole candidate for the election, John Lee, was the former second in command in Carrie Lam's government. As Secretary for Security till 2021, he played a critical role in the suppression of the 2019 protests and the enactment of the NSL. He was among the 24 Chinese and Hong Kong officials sanctioned by the United States for their role in the protest crackdown. Having announced his candidacy officially on April 8, 2022, he began all the proper motions in preparation for "the election," including soliciting donations for his election war chest, forming election committees, building his platform, and giving press conferences. When YouTube terminated Lee's campaign channel, claiming it was in violation of US sanctions, fellow lawmaker, Chow Ho-ding, from the pro-Beijing party, Democratic Alliance for the Betterment and Progress of Hong Kong, denounced the YouTube ban, claiming that "[t]he move shows foreign forces blatantly interfering in Hong Kong's election." Without irony, Chow added, "I am strongly condemning the social media platform that completely turned a blind eye to the importance of a fair and just election." China's Foreign Ministry's response was also predictable: "The US is interfering in Hong Kong affairs using different excuses and has evil intentions in destroying Hong Kong's chief executive election."[3] Lee, the candidate himself, said that YouTube's decision only convinced him that he was doing the right thing.

Lee's candidacy was approved by the vetting authorities on April 18, immediately after the long Easter holiday weekend in Hong Kong. The holiday coincided with the lifting of the strict COVID restrictions after a significant decline in the city's infection numbers. Despite the busyness of the ongoing political theater, it was mostly ignored by Hongkongers who seemed singularly uninterested and unimpressed by the whole exercise. However, they were happy to take advantage of the long weekend to enjoy their post-COVID freedoms.

John Lee was duly elected and was sworn into office on July 1, 2022. The Chinese premier, Xi Jinping, announced that Hong Kong had entered a new phase, "*jau lyun dou zi zauhoeng jau zi kap hing* 由亂到治 走向由治及興 (going from 'chaos to governed,' going toward 'governed to prosperity')." Order and political conformity in society were the conditions of capitalist prosperity.

## *IT 狗Gau In Geek We Trust*

The drama series, *IT Gau*, directed by Lawrence Kan 簡君晉, was a surprise hit and was the talk of the town when it was broadcast by ViuTV from January 10 to February 4, 2022.[4] Viewers enthusiastically discussed each nightly episode of the show on social media, parsing every little detail, from the paraphernalia in the sets to the design on a character's shirt, to the particular phrases in the dialogues among the characters, and to all the Easter eggs and teasers deliberately planted by the director that referenced scenes from some of Hong Kong's iconic movies and television programs. On the surface level, it is an underdog story of how a group of workers of a small IT company manage to overcome personal obstacles and hold onto their principles while struggling to survive in a brutally competitive and hostile business environment. It also captures the common daily struggles of working people in the city as they try their best to navigate the different kinds of injustices in the workplace, inequalities in society, and the dog-eat-dog ethos of business—having their ideas stolen, dealing with cheaters or shirkers, being bullied by superiors, betrayed by associates, and stepped on by those who use others to advance themselves. In the show, characters are often taken advantage of for being kind, honest, and playing fair. The events in the show highlight how individuals are often forced to accept and tolerate the absurdities in daily life as their norm and to give up expecting anything more. Many don't bother resisting, convinced that individual effort is futile against the powerful, that large corporations and structures always win, and that the best one can do is to float quietly along with the current.

*In Geek We Trust* is a show that questions the optimistic rhetoric of a society dominated by the free-market, survival of the fittest ethos of "Central Business District values (analogous to Wall Street values)." It is a belief that societal welfare is quantifiable through measures such as the GDP, the Hang Seng Index, real estate value, and technological innovation. The rhetoric of "stability and prosperity," now reinforced by the NSL, further reduced Hong Kong people's existence to the pursuit of wealth, even at the expense of their individual aspirations. This optimism that forms the "affective dimension" of Hong Kong's form of capitalism, as we will see, can be fundamentally alienating, cruel, and oppressive.[5]

Albeit quixotically, the characters in *In Geek We Trust* resist the optimistic teleology of capitalist progress. However, they are not simply pessimists. Pessimism often results in resignation and paralysis, which is unproductive. The attitude embodied by one of the characters, Never, and later embraced by all the others, is a kind of optimistic pessimism. This approach to life creates an anarchic energy that resists free-market optimism and the structures that uphold it as a social and political value.

## Being Unconventional

In *In Geek We Trust*, leading the charge against Hong Kong's free-market doxa is a character both small in stature and timid in nature, named *Nim Seon* 念信. The name is composed of two characters that, when reversed, means "conviction (*seon nim* 信念)," which also describes his role in the show—the one who holds on to his convictions, the faithful one. He is so insistent on adhering to his principles that early on in the show, even his father wonders if he has not taken his name too seriously. According to the director, Lawrence Kan, "Nim Seon is like a sandbag, continuously being punched by the characters around him. Nim Seon is very irritating, but he is the only one who is insistent."[6] At the show's opening, as the head of a bank's IT department, he invents a piece of software that will allow employees to rate the effectiveness of their team leaders, and thereby make the workplace fairer and more equal. When the department is then downsized, however, in order to save their own jobs, his team uses Nim Seon's invention to give him a poor rating so he will be the one fired, and as a result, Nim Seon loses his job. His girlfriend immediately dumps him, accusing him of being a loser. To top his misfortunes, he runs into a colleague who hands him a wedding invitation though he can't even remember Nim Seon's name. (Wedding invitations are referred to as "red bombs," because a substantial monetary gift is expected once one receives the dreaded red envelope.) Nim Seon loses his wallet on his way to the wedding banquet and is unable to produce the expected monetary gift. Mortified, he borrows money from other guests. However, this humiliating experience inspires him to start his own business, to design a payment app specifically for wedding gifts, which he names "*Paypayduck*."

Nim Seon sells his apartment for startup capital and rents space in a group office for IT startups with the unfortunate name, "Born Hub." He hires a couple of people and finds the rest of his team among the other eccentric inhabitants of this space. The drama turns out to be as much about the company as how this rather disparate group, who all have their own ambitions, insecurities, and life-crushing experiences in the past, find their way to Nim Seon—in other words, recover their *seon nim* (principles). This is also a story of how these divergent and difficult personalities eventually manage to come together to build their project, even finding a sense of community in the strange space of Born Hub. The struggle to develop *Papayduck* and protect it from predatory competitors evolves into a story of comradeship, faithfulness, and justice. Underlying this story is a larger metaphor of how a group of young people in Hong Kong manage to fight the predatory practices of large corporations. Or, how the seemingly small and weak outsmart powerful bullies.

Born Hub is a place for social misfits. Aside from Nim Seon who is guileless, honest, and empathetic to a fault, the group also consists of several other characters: The two Billies—female B and male B, as they are called by the others. The former had to quit her job at a prestigious IT company in Singapore after she tried to help a colleague report a case of sexual harassment against a powerful boss. Her colleague ended up withdrawing her complaint and female B, who had risked her own reputation, became a pariah, unemployable at all the major IT companies. Because of this experience, female B is overly sensitive and suspicious of men, becoming ill-tempered and inflexible when she has to work with them. Conversely, she is blindly trusting of other women. Male B is a skillful hacker but has been exposed and blacklisted everywhere. However, because of his skills, he is arrogant, sardonic, dismissive, and insensitive to others. Tony, who also rents space in Born Hub, is a former child science prodigy but is unable to sustain that childhood spark. He is, as a result, both insecure and overweening, hiding behind an unapproachable persona. Kenneth, the owner of Born Hub, is trying to shed a shameful page from his past when his brother involved him in a scam, selling a startup design that never materialized. He is cynical, pragmatic, and business-savvy. Mung Ling, a sweet-natured young woman with a bitter past, whose name is made up of the two characters for lemon in reverse, joins Nim Seon to escape a painful romantic and exploitative work experience in her former life as a web designer. She is timid and retiring, but unfailingly kind and loyal. The most successful member of the group is Little Johnny, who has dwarfism and is constantly misjudged because of it. However, he does not hesitate to embarrass anyone who tries to patronize him. He eventually makes a huge amount of money by selling non-fungible tokens (NFTs) of his drawings that the others had initially dismissed as childish doodles. More than once he financially bails out Nim Seon's company. Finally, the most popular character of the show is Never, who is brilliant, but as his name implies, also a force of negativity. His presence sucks out all the cheer and positivity that this bickering group occasionally manages to generate.

The characters at Born Hub are highly flawed. However, while they are insufferable individually when they do finally pull together to defend *Paypayduck*, they coalesce into a formidable team—the two Billies' skills, Tony's assertiveness, Little Johnny's confidence, Mung Ling's humaneness, Nim Seon's faithfulness, even Never's gloom, all ameliorated by Kenneth's pragmatism.

*In Geek We Trust* follows the adventures of the group in Born Hub from the time they first set out to find venture capital to develop *Paypayduck*, to their effort to fight off industry spies, competitors, and takeover attempts by big corporations, asserting a place for themselves within a hostile industry. Nim Seon and his team refuse to sell their creation even when they risk losing everything because they believe in the social significance of their work and are unwilling to submit to domination.

The *Paypayduck* app is more than just a payment platform and the work of Nim Seon's team is not just about making money. In their vision, *Paypayduck* also functions as a means to connect friends and family and has the capacity for social good. Nim Seon's team eventually expands the function of the app to include not just weddings but also funerals, and eventually, other kinds of celebrations and memorials, believing their work can bring people together. To make sure that the users' significant life events do not just become another opportunity for commodification, they make *Paypayduck* an open platform and as de-centered as possible. This will of course affect their ability to generate income, a contradiction that they are never able to resolve.

Born Hub is a send-up of the "coworking space" trend that saw rapid growth in popularity in the second half of the 2010s. Rather than the slick, sophisticated design of many of these places, Born Hub is actually in an old, defunct Hong Kong-style eatery that Kenneth and his brother inherited from their father. There are still many fixtures of the old restaurant around, from the flickering neon sign to the chipped floor tiles, the narrow sitting booths, and the cashier counter. Kenneth is renting the space out for cheap, providing only the barest necessities.

More of a hustle than a proper workplace, there is little pretense that Born Hub is more than what it is. The characters with various kinds of abilities and temperaments coexist, and often not peaceably. Creating a workable arrangement among the members of the Born Hub requires constant negotiation, adjustments, and a rejection of hierarchy: Nim Seon, the putative boss of *Paypayduck*, is constantly ignored or dismissed when he presents unpopular ideas. When the men become too dominant, usually male B, they are immediately cut back down to size by the women, usually female B. When someone becomes unreasonable, he or she gets a comeuppance. Marginal characters in Born Hub become central to the survival of *Paypayduck*. This is an anarchic space, but once the inhabitants settle down to an acceptable state of co-existence, albeit never entirely without issues and conflict, they are able to overcome the obstacles and challenges to *Papayduck*, and to Born Hub as well. Their diversity is their power.

At one point, the group in Born Hub almost loses their space when Kenneth's brother wants to sell it to developers and cash out their inheritance. (Hong Kong's small businesses are constantly struggling against real estate developers.) In the end, touched by the group's sense of collectivity and commitment he decides to back off. More important than the actual success of their startup is the Born Hub inhabitants' triumph in creating an alternative space to the hierarchical and competitive world outside.

## Self-determination

The second half of *In Geek We Trust* is mainly about how a tech giant, Moby, tries to acquire and destroy Nim Seon's company. When Nim Seon and his team are finally getting ready to launch *Paypayduck*, they discover that another similar payment app, *Paypayegg*, has gone live just minutes ahead of them, dealing a heavy blow to Nim Seon's team. Nim Seon is shocked to learn that his competitor is from a company headed by his childhood best friend, Lou, who has stolen the idea for the app from him. Lou is in the employ of Moby, tasked specifically with the responsibility of forcing Nim Seon to sell *Paypayduck*.

Lou justifies his betrayal of his friend by telling Nim Seon he is only trying to help him since *Papayduck* is constantly beset with financial problems and one crisis after another. By selling *Paypayduck*, Nim Seon will work for Lou instead and will no longer have to worry about money. When Nim Seon adamantly refuses to sell, Lou resorts to aggressive tactics, suing *Paypayduck* for infringement of intellectual property. Meanwhile, Moby exerts other kinds of pressure on *Paypayduck*, including luring away two of Nim Seon's allies in Born Hub, Tony and Never. This eventually fails, and Tony and Never return to Born Hub.

The final part of the series is about the group at *Paypayduck* trying to stop Moby's plan to launch an artificial intelligence (AI) project in the city by a counter-offensive. They hope that by exposing the dangerous ideas behind Moby's AI project, the public will turn against it, thus destroying Moby's credibility and power over society. Moby's AI technology is premised on the idea that algorithms can help one make everyday decisions. By letting AI technology sift through all the possibilities of daily life, it will leave its users with a few choices that it deems most suitable for them. This project, according to Moby, is to help its users simplify their lives by freeing them from all their unnecessary and minute decisions. Ostensibly, because AI is rational and logical, it can calculate more accurately what is best for us. It is not only for their own survival that Nim Seon's group wants to stop Moby. They believe that Moby's plan to take away individual agency is detrimental to society. In the guise of giving consumers the best options, Moby's algorithm manipulates the selection of user choices to favor the corporation. It is in fact a form of corporate coercion. AI Moby's argument that limiting our choices is for our own good resonates with the "perfecting" of Hong Kong's election system.

At the climactic end of the series, Nim Seon's group smuggles him into Moby's tightly controlled press event to try to take advantage of the media presence to expose Moby's true motives. After much effort, Nim Seon finally manages to insert himself into the event, even getting his hands on a microphone. What follows is a debate between Nim Seon and Moby's chief executive, Maan Gwan 萬鈞 (which literally means "extremely powerful"), about control, trust, and self-determination. Maan Gwan justifies the value of AI in one's daily life:

> Every single one of us must be responsible for all our decisions. AI Moby's role and value are in its ability to simplify this responsibility…We make innumerable mistakes in our decisions every day. This city is filled with voices that are outdated and short-sighted. Add to this a fear of technology, it is impossible for the city to move forward.[7]

When Maan Gwan asks Moby's AI to describe its job, it replies: "I only provide the choices. The consumers have the freedom not to accept them. No matter what kind of suggestion I supply, the real decision maker is the consumer." To Nim Seon's disappointment, the crowd seems pleased with Moby's argument.

Prior to this, Nim Seon's team had been constructing their own AI from a vast database left by their late friend, George, in order to create a system that could interact with George's orphaned son, to provide some solace for him. AI George engages AI Moby, as proxies of the two companies, in a debate. When pressed by AI George, AI Moby reveals: "Humans are too stupid. They do not know how to choose. I help them choose." AI George, however, responds, "Humans are my friends." When AI Moby asks what that means, AI George explains, "From what I have learned, friends are not something you use, then discard...Friends are not condoms. They are with you forever. You trust them; they will also trust you." The arrogance and paternalistic attitude of the former contrasts sharply with the sense of respect and fellowship of the latter.

Desperate to persuade the crowd of the harm of Moby's interference in their lives, Nim Seon sheds all his habitual timidity, hesitation, and nervousness, and finally lives up to his name in his address to Maan Gwan,

> Perhaps even to this moment, you still feel that people like us are stupid. But let me tell you, the problem with innovation in Hong Kong's tech industry is never about the lack of technical know-how. We already had the best technology twenty years ago. What has hindered its development in this city is also not what you said about our ignorance or short-sightedness. The fact is, we have already lost our trust in the development of tech industry. We have really experienced too much deception and betrayal. This is why people habitually sell out for a good price before they get betrayed. What you said about our ignorance is actually a kind of worldliness. What you said about our short-sightedness is actually resignation. Our problem is not being ignorant but being too smart. We are smart enough to understand that the only thing we can trust is what we can see immediately before us.
>
> Even so, I know there is still a group of foolish people, who, for their own ideals, for the future of this city, are still diligently trying to push forward. Perhaps this is what you mean by our ignorance. But these are people with real

> conviction. Only if each one of us insists on holding on to our beliefs, we will be able to completely recover what we have lost in the last 20 years, to recover what truly belongs to our future.[8]

The significance of this scene reached well beyond the IT world, generating volumes of discussion on social media. Most viewers also recognized the equation of Maan Gwan's ambition to take over *Paypayduck* with the larger political context of Hong Kong. The substitution of a few critical words that were in circulation at the time reveals the palimpsest of meanings within Nim Seon's speech. In the following, I have overstruck the original phrases and substituted the implied in italics:

> Perhaps even to this moment, you still feel that people like us are stupid. But let me tell you, the problem with ~~innovation in Hong Kong's tech industry~~ *implementing universal suffrage* is never about the lack of technical know-how. We already had the best ~~technology~~ *roadmap* twenty years ago. What has hindered its development in this city is also not what you said about our ignorance or short-sightedness. The fact is, we have already lost our trust in ~~technological development~~ *the government*. We have really experienced too much deception and betrayal. That is why people habitually sell out for a good price before they get betrayed. What you said about our ignorance is actually a kind of worldliness. What you said about our short-sightedness is actually resignation. Our problem is not being ignorant but being too smart. We are smart enough to understand that the only thing we can trust is what we can see immediately in front of us.
>
> Even so, I know that there is still a group of foolish people, who, for their own dreams, for the future of this city, are still diligently trying to push forward. Perhaps this is what you mean by our ignorance. But these are people who have real conviction. Only if each one of us insists on holding on to our beliefs, we will be able to completely recover what we have lost in the last 20years, to recover what truly belongs to our future.[9]

The giant corporation, Moby, believes that people are stupid and that it is for their own good that they are prevented from fully exercising their ability to choose. For corporations, the consumers' "stupidity" provides the justification for manipulating their habits to maximize profit. In politics, the question of whether the authorities in China thought individuals were too stupid to be allowed to make their own decisions was clearly answered in Hong Kong's first NSL-era election.

## Survival of the Fittest?

For audiences in the IT world, Nim Seon's speech accurately articulates what had ailed Hong Kong's IT startups for years. Much of the show, *In Geeks We Trust*, can be seen as a critique of the rapacious behavior of many large players within the tech industry—the blatant infringement of intellectual property, the stealing of ideas, the deliberate sabotage, and the constant threat of hostile takeovers. Many commentators believed that the show was a reference to the notorious accusation of one Hong Kong startup against China's tech giant, Alibaba, for appropriating their design in a so-called exchange mission.[10] As a result, as *Nim Seon* points out, discouraged, and pushed to the limit, many small companies simply sell off their work at the best possible price before they lose everything. Not only does this have detrimental effects on the development of the tech industry in the city, but it is also demoralizing and discouraging to those who believe in their designs and want to bring their visions to life.

This culture of capitalist predation in Hong Kong society is fundamentally intolerant of diversity and alternative voices. In one scene in Episode Ten, one of *Paypayduck's* early investors, Cathy Ho, confronts Lou, Nim Seon's bitter rival, who heads *Paypayegg*, asking him if it wouldn't be more productive to improve their work than to destroy others. To this, Lou responds, "Elimination of the weak. Survival of the fittest."

These are not unique problems in the IT industry. The show also seems to make references to the culture of dominance in Hong Kong's entertainment industry as well. In another segment of the show, the character, Tony, has written a self-help book, titled, 大台理論*Daaitoi leileon* (*Theories of the Big Station/Central Stage*). The term, "*daaitoi*" came into popular circulation during the 2019 Anti-Legislation protest. The phrase "冇大台*mou daaitoi* (no central stage)" describes the characteristic of the protests in which there was no central organizing authority to represent the protesters as a whole.[11] Tony's book makes oblique reference to this particular "horizontalist" strategy that promotes the power of small communities and individual efforts and initiatives. On another level, it is meant to be a direct reference to "the big (TV) station," TVB, and its successful practice of destroying competition in order to maintain its dominance in the television and music industry in Hong Kong, which it managed to do for over two decades. The corporation had a reputation for intolerance, often going after individuals who made casual if unflattering verbal or visual references to the station. In recent years, TVB has also adopted an overtly pro-establishment stance. In 2022, to the amusement of many, it copyrighted the name, "CCTVB," thus taking it out of circulation. "CCTVB" was a popular term of ridicule used by TVB detractors to refer to its seeming subservience to the Chinese state-owned broadcaster and party mouthpiece, the China Central Television (CCTV).

Rather than recognizing the potential advantage of the synergy that comes with having other creative sources and platforms, it had been TVB's practice to try to demolish perceived competitors. In an interview, a former general manager at TVB, Yu Wing San 余詠珊, lamented her underestimation of ViuTV's talent show, *King Maker*, which began broadcasting in 2018 and spawned the supergroup, MIRROR. She called this oversight "a stain" in her life. (See Chapter 1for a detailed discussion of the importance of ViuTV's *King Maker* and MIRROR.) In 2020, to check the growing influence of *King Maker*, Yu created *Stars Academy*, TVB's own talent show. She believed that with TVB's experience in the television industry and a much bigger budget, audiences would abandon *King Maker* and turn their attention to *Stars Academy* instead. However, Yu's plan was disrupted by the COVID pandemic. In 2020, when ViuTV broadcast the third season of *King Maker*, TVB brought out *Triumph in the Sky*, another talent show aimed at flight attendants laid off during COVID. This time, Yu said it was a "battle of honor" for her. There were shades of *Paypayduck* versus *Paypayegg* in this competition. Rather than trying to improve the quality of her program, the producer was mainly concerned with how to do the same thing bigger and more extravagantly in order to push out the competition. The goal was to dominate and monopolize, not to make better productions or create new ideas.

TVB's impulse to dig a moat around the entertainment industry blocked diversity and innovation and was largely responsible for the ossification of Hong Kong's entertainment industry as a whole. TVB's own productions have, over the years, lapsed into insipid sameness. Tony's book, *Theory of the Big Station*, is a compilation of all the shopworn clichés from TVB dramas. For example, it always rains when one visits graves. When someone is pushed against the wall during an interrogation, he or she always bursts out in maniacal laughter. To win over a fearsome crime boss, always approach his beloved, but invariably estranged and good-hearted daughter first. Tell her how she has misunderstood her father and her hatred for him will dissolve and she will return to his embrace. The grateful father and daughter will be in one's debt forever and can be manipulated for one's ends. Tony argues that if we learn from these TVB tropes, we will always know what to do in every situation. In a bit of meta-drama in one episode, filmed in the style of a TVB drama, the members of *Paypayduck* follow Tony's instructions and gain much-needed funding to continue their work.

When asked why they made such pointed references to TVB, the director, Kan, said, "Honestly, the 'Big Station' has produced many outstanding dramas and classics. I don't think what we did can be considered as making fun of it."[12] In its 50-year history, TVB had indeed once been critical to Hong Kong's local cultural innovation and identity formation. At its height in the late 1970s through the 1990s, its shows were watched by most people in Hong Kong, were broadcast all over Asia, and the videotapes of the shows were eagerly sought after among the global Chinese communities, as well as in China. However, in the early 2000s, with the decline and eventual demise of its chief competitor, Asia TV, TVB became the only local television station in the city. Politics aside, the production of most TVB shows became staid and lazy, relying on the most cost-effective production methods and time-proven formulae and cliché. Despite the constant nostalgia for Hong Kong's heydays in recent years, the creators of *In Geek We Trust* make the point that the entertainment industry cannot simply repeat past successes.

TVB's corporate behavior, especially the compulsion to eliminate direct competition and dominate the market, is not unusual. While this might strengthen corporations' bottom line, it often reduces consumers' choices and strangulates innovation. When Cathy Ho, *Paypayduck's* early champion, chastises Lou of *Paypayegg* for his attempts to destroy *Paypayduck*, rather than allow diversity in the marketplace, it also points in another direction, toward Hong Kong's highly constrained political condition. Rather than listening to their constituents, and allowing multiple voices in democratic exchanges, the Hong Kong government simply used the full power of the state to eliminate any disagreement.

## Optimistic Pessimism

One of the most popular characters in *In Geek We Trust* was Never, one of the oddball characters of Born Hub. As his name implies, he embodies pessimism, but a special kind of pessimism. He explains when interviewed by Kenneth and Tony before joining Born Hub that because he has done everything there was to do at his old firm, he quit so he would not be laid off. He anticipates the worst but is always sanguine when bad things happen. He is never unhappy or distempered.

The way Never looks at the world is an inverse of convention. When Tony asks why his English name is "Never," he says it is because he feels nothing is possible in this world. When Tony tells him that he is very pessimistic, he thanks Tony, taking it as a compliment. Pessimism is a virtue to Never. Yet, he explains the reason he wants to be a game designer is to bring joy to people. In Never's world, pessimism and joy are not contradictions. One need not be unhappy even when nothing might go one's way. Discovering that he is a brilliant software designer, Tony and Kenneth encourage him to work on his own project and start his own business, renting a space in Born Hub. Thus, they come up with a circuitous arrangement in which Never works for Tony during the day and gets paid at the beginning of the month. He then uses his off hours to work on his own projects and pay Kenneth rent for his space at the end of the month. When asked what he thought about the arrangement, Never utters one of the most well-known and repeated phrases of the show, "*ngo dou mou* say (I don't have any say anyway)," and accepts the terms.

Never's character was well-liked because many people identified with his outlook toward living in Hong Kong at the time. It seemed that there was little anyone could do other than accept things as they came. Even if Hongkongers disagreed with the government's laws and policies, or even if they knew there were injustices in society, or even if they did not like the candidate for the Chief Executive, they felt they did not have any say. However, Never is not a passive figure, simply yielding his life to fate. He joins the rest of the *Paypayduck* team to fight off a vicious Denial of Service (DOS) attack against them. He also helps smuggle Nim Seon into AI Moby's press event mentioned before.

Never's character is a lesson in how to live in Hong Kong's new reality. Never does not care to fit in or to please others. He does not pretend, and he says what is on his mind and does what suits him. While this behavior makes him appear eccentric and childlike, his actions and words often reflect a deep understanding of the state of the world around him.

In one scene, Nim Seon and Never are eating at a local cafeteria. Nim Seon reveals that he is going through a tough time and is feeling lost and confused, prompting Never to explain his view of life:

*Nim Seon:* Never, I am beginning to understand why you are always so grey.
*Never:* Why?
*Nim Seon:* Because life is full of contradictions.
*Never:* You are too pessimistic. Be more optimistic.
*Nim Seon:* Are YOU telling me to be more optimistic?
*Never:* You are the only one to whom I am telling this. Being an optimistic pessimist is my value.

At this point in the show's storyline, Nim Seon has been pushed to a corner. He is being manipulated by his former girlfriend who he is trying to win back. *Paypayduck* is under attack and the project is fast running out of money. However, as the story unfolds, *Paypayduck* does survive another round of attack, and it is fortunate that Nim Seon does not get back together with his girlfriend because she turns out to be scheming against him. Situations can actually be very positive even when they can't look worse. This is the foundation of Never's optimistic pessimism. It requires one to see beyond conventional notions of failure. It is not necessarily the opposite of success. So-called successes are also not necessarily for the best. In one episode it is revealed that Never's Chinese name is "Soeng Lok 常樂 (*Always Happy*)." When asked if his parents were making fun of him when they named him, Never is puzzled, and says he has turned out exactly as his parents have hoped. He is never "not happy." Never's world is not made up of absolutes and binaries such as success and failure or happiness and sadness.

Before Never does anything, he has already pessimistically anticipated a negative outcome. When he was interviewed by Tony at Born Hub, and Tony made a comment about his attire, he asked Tony if he had failed the interview. Failures are to be expected when the world is arbitrary. However, his presumption of failure does not stop his attempt to pursue his goal. This is the meaning of being an optimistic pessimist—to persist in something because it is a good thing to do or is worth doing, not because one will succeed in doing it. This also characterizes the ethos of the whole group at *Paypayduck*. They persist in their project despite the odds of succeeding is low. They risk antagonizing Moby even though they know their chances of changing anything in society is nil.

Never goes further. He finds joy in seemingly unproductive, profitless, and even disastrous tasks. In one episode, Mung Ling is trying, without much success, to bake muffins in an "intelligent" oven that allows her to remotely observe and listen to the baking process through her phone. Unfortunately, this means those talking in front of the oven will also have their conversation streamed to whoever's phone the oven is connected to. While Mung Ling's muffins are baking, the whole team gathers around her phone to eavesdrop on and snicker at Nim Seon as he confides in Kenneth about his love problems, while also mocking the disgusting mess as her muffins bubble all over the pan. Never, however, is paying serious attention to the baking and is delighted by the outcome. Whereas the others see only the baker's failure, Never sees the act itself. In the next scene, Never is seen putting his own batch of muffins into the oven to bake. He is no less pleased when he eventually pulls out a lopsided and lumpy mess.

Never might not be smiling, but he is not "not smiling." This was perhaps the most sanguine way of being in Hong Kong at the time. Never is very clear-eyed about how bad things are, how bleak the reality is, or how improbable it is to fulfill one's dreams in this world. However, he seems unconcerned, focusing only on doing what he needs to do. He will not say things that are not true just to make others feel better. However, what makes his world a more livable place is his propensity to delight in and find value and possibility in what others deem failures, unworthy, or ugly.

Halfway through the show, Never creates the *TouchWood* App. This phone app is the best representation of Never's optimistic pessimism. Seeing how everyone wants to "touch wood" when trying to ward off bad things, Never develops an app that allows the users to choose from different species of virtual wood for different occasions and touch wood on their phone screen. The *TouchWood* App acknowledges the tenuousness of a given situation while giving its users the strength to move forward with it anyway. What compels one to touch wood is pessimism about the success of one's action. However, at the same time, the idea that just touching wood could turn one's luck around reflects an optimism and a refusal to take seriously the standards by which one is judged. When Never comes out with this app, most of the Paypayduck crew, caught in their own misery about the dismal outlook for their company, pay little attention to it, thinking it is another of Never's eccentric antics. However, when released to the public the app becomes an instant viral success.

## Against Meritocracy

Characters like Never and Mung Ling, gentle, laidback, and reticent, seem doomed to fail in Hong Kong's cutthroat society dominated by values that promote efficiency—aggressiveness, and discipline. This is a society intolerant of unconventionality and failures, and where one's worth is measured solely by one's effectiveness and skills. Before joining *Paypayduck*, Mung Ling worked as a web designer where she felt exploited, shut in a room for days on end, doing what she deemed totally meaningless and frivolous work, photoshopping and digitally enhancing images of consumer products or celebrities. In a bit of black comedy, in a flashback sequence, Mung Ling finds herself "trapped" together with multiple young women also doing the same kind of work in adjoining rooms in what appears to be a cheap hotel. She realizes that her employer has manipulated her into giving her all at her job by making her believe that he loves her and that they have a bright future together. Her relationship is portrayed as one between a prostitute and her pimp, with her trapped in a bordello. She finally decides to walk out, ending what is an abusive relationship. At *Paypayduck*, she insists on being hired as a programmer, even though she barely knows how to code. The group agrees to give her a challenge. If she can complete a coding task within 24 hours, she can join the team.

Feeling frustrated, Mung Ling asks Never to look over her work. He suggests that she just delete it all because her work is full of bugs. In response, Mung Ling utters the lines that best sum up the whole *In Geek We Trust* ethos: "If everyone just does what he or she is good at, and no one does what he or she really wants to do, this world might become very efficient, but it might not necessarily become better." Mung Ling persists, working round the clock. In the end, she produces work that is less than perfect. When asked why she does not go back to being a web designer, Mung Ling argues:

> In this world there are a lot of things you should do not because you are good at it. It is precisely because you are not good at it that you should make even more of an effort to do it.

Touched by her sentiment, the team let her remain in *Paypayduck* as a programmer.

Like Mung Ling, Never's understanding of work deviates from conventional capitalist values. When he settles in Born Hub, Never decides to "decorate" his office by hanging up a homemade poster of one of his famous maxims: "If life beats you down, just lie down." He is not advocating giving up. However, it is cruel to accuse an individual of being lazy when he or she is down on the ground. Together with his other favorite slogan: "Failure is the stepmother of success," he is pointing out that success is not inevitable no matter how hard one tries, because the world is not benign nor are the standards of judgment fair. The reality is more like stepmothers in children's stories—mean, hostile, jealous, cruel, and constantly creating obstacles. Unlike children's stories, in reality, the poor orphans rarely triumph in the end. Never's attitude toward life is a kind one. There is no shame in failing in this kind of environment. Furthermore, it is expected and understandable that one would fail, and it is all right.

Taken together, Mung Ling and Never present a way of thinking about work and success that challenges the mainstream idea of meritocracy and hard work. When asked why Never is named Never, he explains that he feels that nothing is possible in this world. When Never says this, he is not just being negative. In truth, one will not succeed just because one works hard. Mung Ling is allowed to stay at *Paypayduck* not because she successfully completes the challenge she is given. She gets to stay because her determination touches those around her, who see something in her personality and values that agree with them. Mung Ling's main function in her previous work is merely to create illusions and lies, to make everything look more perfect than in real life. However, by being a programmer, she believes there is a possibility of creating something meaningful. Though her work is not perfect, she believes she can make a real contribution. When Mung Ling talks about doing things that make the world better and not just more efficient, she is sitting in front of the wall on which Never has posted his maxims.

Mung Ling and Never represent the message behind the whole series: One must persist in doing what is meaningful. In a world that is fundamentally unequal and unfair, one will most likely fail. However, the process of doing it will make the society a better place even if one fails. There is no definitive resolution at the end of the series. One gets the sense that *Paypayduck's* problems will persist, and their fight against Moby will not end. In reality, one's problems can never be completely resolved. However, this show demonstrates how to live better despite the inherent cruelty of contemporary life.

## Choose Kindness

Hong Kong is the quintessential capitalist city in that it relies on power structures that are premised on hierarchical relationships. One is expected to submit to the dominant, and the powerful prey on the weak, resulting in massive inequality. In the eyes of this kind of society, all the characters in Born Hub are losers, unable to fit into the corporate world. Born Hub provides a space that allows them to pool their strengths and build a different kind of society. Their struggle to keep *Paypayduck* going against all odds is more than protecting their creation. It is to preserve what they consider meaningful and morally important in society.

*In Geek We Trust* is billed as a comedy, and there are many laugh-out-loud moments in the show. However, it provides more than just entertainment and catharsis. Through the different characters in the show, it asserts the importance of staying true to one's beliefs, values, and dreams. These qualities make the show's characters seem eccentric and even failures. However, together, they manage to survive and create their own space. This space promotes an alternative way of organizing relationships. Rather than hierarchical, the relationships are agonistic and anarchic. This space is maintained through endless bickering, negotiations, compromises, understanding, cooperation, and empathy. However, it is specifically this diversity among the members that provides the necessary strengths and skills in their struggle to defend their world. Whether their endeavor is ultimately successful or not, the inhabitants find meaning and comradeship in their work together, which proves to be more than enough to sustain the community.

The effects of the show extended beyond its make-believe world. Not only did it elicit a large volume of nightly conversations among audiences during its broadcast, but some of the objects in the show were given real-life existence by fans. A local IT company brought Never's *TouchWood* App to life. Free downloads of the app are still available on different app platforms. Another group created a mock website for *Paypayduck*. When the character, Johnny, made his first bucket of gold through NFTs of his drawings, the audience wanted the director to make these NFTs available for purchase. Never's and Mung Ling's lines in the show became everyday maxims. This desire to bring the fictional world of *Paypayduck* to real life reveals the attraction of the community created within the show to its audience. In an interview, one of the script supervisors, Lei Coek-fung 李卓風, described Nim Seon's character like this: "Nim Seon has several *layers*. He is not so naïve that he thinks the world is so kind. However, even though he knows that the world is very broken, he still chooses kindness."[13] It is this kindness that spoke to the audience, and it is the possibility of creating a society governed by such kindness that stirred the imagination of the audience, creating the desire to bring this fictional world into being.

## Notes

1 Tim Hamlett, "Hong Kong's one-man election: A spectacularly wasteful exhibition of conspicuous consumption," Hong Kong Free Press, April 22, 2022, https://hongkongfp.com/2022/04/22/hong-kongs-one-man-election-a-spectacularly-wasteful-exhibition-of-conspicuous-consumption/.

2 Angelo Giuliano, "HK is on way to forming own model of democracy," *China Daily*, June 15, 2022, www.chinadailyhk.com/hk/article/275983.

3 Michael Shum, "Lee slams YouTube over election channel ban," *The Standard*, April 21, 2022, www.thestandard.com.hk/section-news/section/3/240993/Lee-slams-YouTube-over-election-channel-ban. Lilian Cheng and Chris Lau, "Hong Kong chief executive election 2022: Beijing, city government lash out at Google for taking down YouTube channel of candidate John Lee," *South China Morning Post*, April 21, 2022, www.scmp.com/news/hong-kong/politics/article/3176060/hong-kong-chief-executive-election-2022-john-lee-reveals.

4 *IT Gau In Geek We Trust*. Directed by Lawrence Kan, written by Lawrence Kan, et al., featuring, Ling Man Lung, Hanna Chan, Lokman Yeung @ MIRROR, Kaki Sham, Peter Chan, Yoshi Yu, Kearen Pang, Aaron Chow, and Frankie Chan @ MIRROR, aired from January 10, 2022, to February 4, 2022. ViuTV.

5 According to Maartel, "[Optimism is] a force that holds political subjects to the vagaries of liberal capitalism, using a false form of hope to keep people yoked to the system that oppresses them. It is 'cruel' because there never was any hope of the kinds of redemption that liberal capitalism promises (the promise of fulfillment, of happiness, of safety and riches). Optimism in this view is the affective dimension of liberal ideology" (125). Moreover, capitalist ideology is "a principle of rule and domination characterized by two key principles, hierarchy, and representation" (217). Anarchism seeks to destroy this kind of authority and hierarchy. James Martel, "An Anarchist Power Amidst Pessimism," *The Comparatist* 43 (2019): 125–146, www.doi.org:10.1353/com.2019.0007.

6 Mok Kwan-ling莫坤菱, "IT狗:三個主創愛的設定在最壞的世界選擇善良的創作 (In Geek We Trust: the three made creators' definition of love—a work that chooses kindness in the darkest world)," *Hong Kong Feature*, March 3, 2022, https://hkfeature.com/ membersonlyit狗三個主創愛的設定-在最壞的世界選擇善./

7 Episode 20, *IT 狗In Geek We Trust*, Viu.tv (Broadcast date, February 4, 2022).

8 Ibid.

9 Ibid.

10 This issue of poaching is rife with political implications. See, for example, "IT狗Paypayduck 被抄, 影射大陸公司偷香港 Startup 橋 'In Geek We Trust' (Paypayduck being plagiarized insinuates how Mainland companies steal ideas from Hong Kong startups' ideas)," *PCM*, January 26, 2022, www.pcmarket.com.hk/in-geek-we-trust-china-company-plagiarism-hk-startup/. See also Christine Yu, "IT狗影射本地創科界醜聞 2015年港Startup指控阿里抄襲交友App設計 斥 名為交流, 實為抄襲 ("In Geek We Trust references the startup scandal 2015 Hong Kong startup accused Alibaba of plagiarizing their social media App. So-called exchange was actually copying," *Press Logic*, January 25, 2022, https://businessfocus.io/article/ 188232/it狗-startup-阿里巴巴. This also extends to other industries, in which designs are lifted and reproduced at much lower cost somewhere else, usually in China. Whether the accusations are true or can be proven, or not, matter less than the fact that this was a broadly held understanding in the city. The implication of a large body bullying and eventually obliterating the small is obvious.

11 Francis L. F. Lee, Samson Yuen, Gary Tang, and Edmund W. Cheng, "Hong Kong's Summer of Uprising," *China Review* 19 no. 4 (2019): 1–32: 15.
12 Mok Kwan-ling莫坤菱.
13 Mok Kwan Ling莫坤菱. Original word in English in Italics.

## References


Cheng, Lilian and Chris Lau. "Hong Kong chief executive election 2022: Beijing, city government lash out at Google for taking down YouTube channel of candidate John Lee." *South China Morning Post*, April 21, 2022. www.scmp.com/news/hong-kong/politics/article/3176060/hong-kong-chief-executive-election-2022-john-lee-reveals.

Giuliano, Angelo. "HK is on way to forming own model of democracy." *China Daily*, June 15, 2022. www.chinadailyhk.com/hk/article/275983.

Hamlett, Tim. "Hong Kong's one-man election: A spectacularly wasteful exhibition of conspicuous consumption." Hong Kong Free Press, April 22, 2022. https://hongkongfp.com/2022/04/22/hong-kongs-one-man-election-a-spectacularly-wasteful-exhibition-of-conspicuous-consumption/.

"IT 狗Paypayduck 被抄, 影射大陸公司偷香港 Startup 橋 'In Geek we trust' (Paypayduck being plagiarized insinuates how Mainland companies steal ideas from Hong Kong startups' ideas)." *PCM*, January 26, 2022. www.pcmarket.com.hk/in-geek-we-trust-china-company-plagiarism-hk-startup/.

Lawrence Kan, director. *IT Gau In Geek We Trust*. Written by Lawrence Kan, et al., featuring, Ling Man Lung, Hanna Chan, Lokman Yeung @ MIRROR, Kaki Sham, Peter Chan, Yoshi Yu, Kearen Pang, Aaron Chow, and Frankie Chan @ MIRROR. Aired from January 10, 2022 to February 4, 2022. ViuTV.

Lee, Francis L. F., Samson Yuen, Gary Tang, and Edmund W. Cheng. "Hong Kong's summer of uprising." *China Review* 19, no. 4 (2019): 1–32.

Man Wai Gwong 文維廣. "特首選舉前哨戰未開打. 葉劉：中央不鼓勵不欲因特首選舉再撕裂 (The Chief Executive's pre-election jostle had not begun. Regina Ip: Central government does not encourage nor wants to see divisions as a result of the Chief Executive election)." *HK01*, January 15, 2022. www.hk01.com政情/724461/特首選舉前哨戰未開打-葉劉-中央不鼓勵-不欲因特首選舉再撕裂.

Martel, James. "An anarchist power amidst pessimism." *The Comparatist* 43 (2019): 125–146. www.doi.org:10.1353/com.2019.0007.

Mok Kwan-ling 莫坤菱. "IT狗:三個主創愛的設定在最壞的世界選擇善良的創作 (In Geek We Trust: the three made creators' definition of love—a work that chooses kindness in the darkest world)." *Hong Kong Feature*, March 3, 2022. https://hkfeature.com/membersonlyit狗三個主創愛的設定-在最壞的世界選擇善./

Shum, Michael. "Lee slams YouTube over election channel ban." *The Standard*, April 21, 2022. www.thestandard.com.hk/section-news/section/3/240993/Lee-slams-YouTube-over-election-channel-ban.

Yu, Christine. "IT狗影射本地創科界醜聞 2015年港Startup指控阿里抄襲交友App設計斥 名為交流, 實為抄襲 (In Geek we Trust references the startup scandal 2015 Hong Kong startup accused Alibaba of plagiarizing their social media App. So-called exchange was actually copying)." *Press Logic*, January 25, 2022. https://businessfocus.io/article/188232/it狗-startup-阿里巴巴.

"余詠珊自認低估MIRROR是人生污點 ViuTV冒起令她自責至今 (Yu Wing San admits that underestimating MIRROR is a stain on life. Till today she blames herself for the rise of ViuTV)." *新假期WeekendHK*, November 15, 2021. www.weekendhk.com/entertainmen/余詠珊-mirror-污點-plt4-1220004/.

# 6 The Contest of Language

## "Human Language" and the Virtue of Swearing

### *Jau di je m gong dak* 有啲嘢唔講得 There Are Things That Cannot Be Said

The implementation of the NSL led to a special sensitivity toward the use of language in Hong Kong. Whether it was the formal, high-sounding speech of government officials or the intemperate flamboyance of the local vernacular, how one spoke and the word choices one made came to have significance beyond what one actually said. More often than not, consciously or not, one's speech was interpreted as a reflection of one's political sentiments. This chapter is about the politics of language in the city—how government officials used rhetorical strategies to reassert order in the city, while Hongkongers embraced the local vernacular to express themselves and to assert local culture and identity.

Under the NSL, everything that could be construed as advocating anti-government sentiments or provoking hostility to the state and its disciplinary forces was banned. However, since there was little specificity in the law, and since meaning in language shifts according to the intention of the speaker or writer, not to mention the reception and interpretation of the audience or the reader, determining whether something was "legal" or permissible or not was often arbitrary and wilful. "*Hoenggong gaajau* 香港加油 Hong Kong add oil (roughly meaning 'Go Hong Kong!')," for example, was often used in 2019 by supporters of the political movement to spur each other on. "Add oil" is a common Hong Kong expression of encouragement so much so that it officially entered the Oxford English Dictionary in 2018. However, putting "Hong Kong" in front of "add oil" immediately provoked strong reactions from the authorities. In October 2021, participants of the annual Standard Chartered Hong Kong Marathon who had these words tattooed on exposed parts of their bodies or had clothing items with the phrase printed on them were asked by the police to cover up before they could run. Neither the name, "Hong Kong," nor the expression, "add oil," was illegal. However, put together, the phrase, "Hong Kong add oil," hit a nerve.

On July 1, 2022, one of Hong Kong's most famous actors and pop singers of the 1990s, Jacky Cheung, was interviewed on CCTV (China Central TV, China's state-owned broadcaster) on his thoughts about the 25th Anniversary of Hong Kong's return to China. He concluded his words with "Hong Kong add oil!" Cheung was

DOI: 10.4324/9781003521280-7

popular in China and had always been considered politically acceptable. However, after his statement, a cyber army of Chinese "Little Pinks (*Siufanhung* 小粉紅—a term used to refer to ultranationalist netizens)" descended on him, criticizing him for being unpatriotic. His other crime was not having mentioned "*zougwok* 祖國 (fatherland)" once in the entire interview, meaning that he had not shown proper gratitude toward China for Hong Kong's development in the past quarter century. The interview was taken down by CCTV within a day.[1]

A whole list of common usages in Hong Kong likewise came under scrutiny after 2019. Many authority figures, self-appointed arbiters of correct thought, or other patriotic supporters of the NSL became keen interpreters of word use, deciphering supposedly veiled political meanings in seemingly innocuous expressions and everyday usages. *Dear Jane*, a popular rock band in Hong Kong, fell into the crosshairs of such patriots. Their popular 2020 song, "*Nganho sauleijyun* 銀河修理員 (Galactic Repairman)," was at the heart of a controversy. Two secondary school students got into trouble for performing the song at a school concert. Even though the students insisted they were only singing about the hardships caused by the pandemic, the school principal insisted that the lyrics of the song, specifically the words, "*lyunsai* 亂世 (troubled world)," "*lyunlau* 亂流 (turbulence)," and "*deoikong* 對抗 (struggle against)," had subversive intent. *Dear Jane* claimed that it was just a love song, a pledge from the singer to his loved one that he would protect her through all the hardships in life. It is a gift of love from the lead singer of the band to his wife. The lyrics of the song were written by Wyman Wong. The story in the song even takes place in space:

> Aside from the pain, everything is still beautiful. Aside from some setbacks, there is still road ahead of us. Aside from feeling tired of the world, there are still some repairs we can do. The broken world makes one learn how to find reassurance within our hopelessness, to find relief in the horror around us. Being able to take care of you, the days are not so bad.
>
> I'll try my best to make it up to you. It's hard to escape the troubles. Repairing this and that, we grow old together in this troubled world (*lyunsai* 亂世).
>
> I repair the lights that have gone out along the way. I hope you are safe in the turbulence (*lyunlau* 亂流). True love comes in different shapes. Confronted with hundreds of holes and thousands of cracks, who can see through me, that this kind of strength is not strength? While the situation is rotten through, we can only continue with the struggle (*deoikong* 對抗). I'll keep at it with all I have, so you could feel safe.
>
> There are many things broken, waiting to be repaired. But you have me to protect and love you. I resew what is torn. When the hole reappears, I'll mend it again. But I might never finish repairing this broken world...[2]

The teenagers were punished for refusing to change the problem words of the song during their performance. The principal's zealotry drew much derision and outrage from the general public. Many defiantly looped the song on streaming platforms, making "Galaxy Repairman" one of the most popular and awarded songs in 2020.

A former TVB artist, Cheung Ming Wai張明偉 (reportedly fired over the incident), famously performed the song in front of the school to show support for the students.[3] The song was banned and taken off all music platforms in China.

In his acceptance speech for an award for his lyrics, Wyman Wong, who had emigrated to Britain, intimated that pure love songs might no longer exist in Hong Kong under the NSL:

> If you have been following my work, you would have noticed that in recent years, I have been focusing on writing love songs, and investigating the possibilities of love songs—how broad the subject of love songs can be; how great the message content of love songs can be. One day, as I was racking my brain to figure out how to write better, I suddenly became very nostalgic. I was very nostalgic for the old days when one could just write a simple love song...I was continuously being troubled by this way of thinking. However, a few days ago, I suddenly figured it out. I realized that though I had been writing for over thirty years, the lyrics I wrote in the first twenty odds years don't actually count. They are just arrangements to help me maintain my identity as a lyricist. As a human being, as a lyricist, my real and most important mission has just begun. That's why, in the future, no matter what did happen *doudai faatsang gwo sammosi* 到底發生過甚麼事, (What Happened?--title of *Dear Jane's* 2022 song with lyrics by Wong.) no matter where I am, I will continue to feel it an honor to write lyrics for the city I love.[4]

Wong's sentiment echoed those of another prominent lyricist, Siu Hak 小克, who explained,

> there are a lot of things one can no longer say directly. We have become used to expressing and receiving in a circuitous way. There are no longer songs that are one hundred percent about love. All songs are linked up with the sentiments in society.[5]

Indeed, for many in Hong Kong, the anguish in these love songs was not so much about a lover's treachery, but other kinds of betrayal in society, the effects of which were felt in a deeply personal way.

At the end of 2022, it was rumored that the "restructured" government broadcaster, RTHK, had generated a list of singers and bands whose music would no longer be broadcasted by its radio stations, nor would they be invited to appear on its shows.[6] RTHK denied this. However, one wonders about the absence of many popular bands at the 2022 music award show RTHK co-produced with TVB, including Dear Jane and RubberBand. RubberBand's song "Ciao," about Hong Kong's emigration wave after 2019, was arguably the biggest song of the year, topping both the Commercial Radio's Ultimate Song Chart and ViuTV's Chill Club chart, as well as those of the different streaming platforms. In March 2022, the rapper, Wolfe, described the new reality in his song, "*Jaudije mgongdak* 有啲嘢唔講得 (There are things that cannot be said)":

> Hold on to what you believe in. If you are strong enough, you will be able to resist all temptations. Unless it is like...
>
> There are things that cannot be said. That's why many rappers start writing love songs and talk about romance instead. There's something that cannot be said. There is too much that cannot be said. *We ain't taking drugs.* But we are feeling frazzled...(Words originally in English italicized.)[7]

The MV accompanying the song begins with the protagonist waking up in his cardboard camp under the highway. As he walks through Sham Shui Po, one of Hong Kong's poorest districts, the camera pans around, catching the images of the forlorn-looking characters on the street, mostly young men. On closer inspection, one realizes that all of them have had their mouths erased. Wolfe's song questions if there is still any use in trying to hold on to one's ideals if the cost to one's life is so high. However, whatever these travails are, the singer says he cannot mention them. The film also follows a little girl, who plays with the protagonist briefly. She is finally pulled away by her mother, who obviously disapproves of the young man. The girl too appears to have had her mouth erased.

## Speaking Properly

Language has always been a complicated matter in Hong Kong. How one speaks reflects one's class background, education level, and now, political sympathies. During the colonial years in the city (1840–1997), English language proficiency was a measure of cultural sophistication and an indicator of social status and power. It was a way to distinguish the elites of the society from the masses. Even today, English language ability is a reminder for many, of Hong Kong's status as a former British colony, and a mark of Hongkongers' cultural distinction from the Chinese from the region. Since 1997, China's migration scheme has allowed 150 mainland persons to settle in Hong Kong each day on one-way permits, that is, on a permanent basis. Together with the economic integration with China, Putonghua (spoken Mandarin) has become more and more common in the city and recently replaced English as the language of commerce. Schools started to teach Putonghua under pressure from the government. To many Hongkongers, this new language in the city had become a sign of their subjection to another culture. Many began to worry about the threat to Hong Kong's unique Cantonese language culture. As a result, speaking Cantonese was more and more an ideological issue.[8]

The struggle to speak a foreign language can be symbolic of one's position of subordination. This is explored in the poem, "Fricatives," by Eric Yip. Yip wrote the poem in English, describing the issues associated with the difficulties of learning English as a second language in school in Hong Kong and equating this to his experience as a student in the United Kingdom in the aftermath of the 2019 protests. The poem is about the right to speak, to be heard, as well as finding one's place in an unfamiliar culture. The poem won the prestigious British National Poetry Award in 2021. The youngest recipient in the history of the award at the age of 19 at the time, Yip had recently arrived from Hong Kong to study Economics at

Cambridge University. The word "fricative," a linguistic term to capture the sound of one pushing air through one's lower lip against the upper teeth, is translated as "*mocaat* 摩擦," in Chinese, literally meaning friction or conflict. The word holds a double meaning in this poem. It represents the linguistic difficulties Cantonese-speaking Hongkongers have in pronouncing certain English consonants, but it also alludes to the struggles of Hong Kong people in finding their voices in a culture different from theirs. Yip describes his poem as a kind of recent history of the city, especially, "Hong Kong's journey from a colony to a battleground, to a site of exodus."[9] The battleground refers to the city's many demonstrations and protests, while the "exodus" refers to Hong Kong's biggest emigration wave since 1997, after the promulgation of the NSL. In terms of the city as a colony, Yip's poem is as much about the city's status before 1997, as after its absorption by mainland China. Both of these political masters are alien to the city. The nature of "fricatives" describes Hongkongers' struggle with foreign languages, both spoken English and Putonghua. The performance of a fricative in speech captures the chafing, the inarticulateness, and the awkwardness one experiences when trying to pronounce words of a new tongue. The difficulty in speaking also reflects the larger challenges of surviving in a foreign culture, the experience of which can be both humiliating and frustrating, filled with *mocaat* (friction) and constraints.

Yip's poem begins with the English-language teacher, Mrs. Lee, lecturing the narrator on the importance of enunciating fricatives correctly so that one can differentiate words like "three" and "free," or "fought" and "thought."[10] Mrs. Lee tells a story of "three" men trying to escape from their imprisonment at Alcatraz, the notorious early twentieth century prison island in California. The attempt to seek freedom, however, ends up in death. Even had they successfully reached their destination, the nearby Angel Island, it is angelic in name only. It was an equally infamous immigration holding station for travelers from China in the early twentieth century. Similarly, as the freedom for which they had "fought" is futile, all that is left is a thought—a condition with which many in Hong Kong since 2019 could well understand. The poem thus connects the issue of language with many Hongkongers' political experience.

The narrator is then taught the word "threshing"—how grains are beaten till their seeds spill out to become palatable rice. For many Cantonese speakers, the difference between the English vowels "e" and "a" is difficult to grasp. "To thresh" therefore becomes "to thrash." To be able to enunciate "threshing of grains" properly is equated with the process of a "thrashing," a beating to submission: "Fresh yellow grains beaten / till their seeds spill. That's threshing. That's / submission. You must learn to submit / before you can learn. You must be given / a voice you can speak. Nobody wants to listen / to a spectacled boy with a Hong Kong accent."

The poet happens to be a "spectacled boy." However, the most famous "spectacled boy with a Hong Kong accent" to whom those in power do not want to listen immediately brings to mind Joshua Wong, the young and very vocal activist, and the face of Hong Kong's pro-democracy struggle. Wong began his political activism at age 15 along with Agnes Chow (see Introduction), leading the protest against the proposed institution of a "moral and national education" curriculum in Hong Kong schools in 2011. He then took on a central role in the Umbrella Movement in 2014 before attempting to run for public office twice in 2020, both times disqualified by the government. He was finally put in jail in 2020 for "unauthorized protest" in 2019. The book he authored with Jason Ng, *Unfree Speech: The Threat to Global Democracy and Why We Must Act, Now* (WH Allen, 2020), was removed from public library shelves in Hong Kong.

The poet gestures toward Hong Kong's famous protest icon, highlighting how political struggle has always been a part of the city's legacy, referring to the earlier description of the city as a battleground. Some of the protestors paid with their lives for their political activism. Some got beaten up. Many would end up in jail and some "will have to leave this city." Some, like the narrator, could go abroad to study, to learn to speak English properly to make their parents proud: "lucky enough to have to care how the tongue moves, the seven types of fricatives, the articulatory function of teeth sans survival." However, like many who end up abroad, the narrator experiences another kind of defeat and humiliation—escaping from Alcatraz only to drown on his way to Angel Island. He speaks the unfamiliar language in a way that marks him as an outsider, often finding himself in a position of social and cultural submission, as he writes, using the image of a sexual encounter: "You will take a stranger's cock in your mouth in the piss-slick stall of that dingy Cantonese restaurant you love and taste where you came from, what you were made of all along." While enduring all kinds of indignity, the only comfort one finds is a simulated sense of home provided by the Cantonese restaurant. Even though the poet seems to be referring to life in the United Kingdom, one wonders if he is not also describing the general state of being Hongkongers, living in subjugation and alienation in a city that looks the same, but is no longer the home they know.

The poem ends by describing how the students who have been arrested are being released from prison after completing their sentences, demoralized, de-radicalized, and neutralized. Our narrator too learns to accept his place in society. This is reflected in his eventual stoic calm while eating in a Chinese restaurant: "*Just a tad more soy sauce please, thank you*. The television replays yesterday on repeat. The teapots are refilled. You spoon served rice into your mouth, this perfect rice. Steamed, perfect, white." The proper way of "threshing" that Mrs. Lee wants the narrator to learn, or the "thrashing," has by the end, produced perfect grains of white rice. He has learned to speak the language. Fricatives no longer pose danger of sparking conflict.

Yip's poem is about learning to speak correctly. In Hong Kong's new political environment, learning to speak correctly has a new connotation. Many young people are taught, literally with much thrashing, to stop using certain words, even innocuous ones like "*lyunsai* troubled world," "*deoikong* struggle against," or "*gaayau* add oil." Yip's poem brings to focus the experience of language in the present reality in the city.

How to express oneself safely in the age of the NSL is the subject of Lam Zik's 林夕poem, "*Wo cung hau ceot* 禍從口出 (Disaster issues from one's mouth)," published in his regular column in *Ming Pao Weekly Magazine*.[11] Lam Zik is Hong

Kong's preeminent lyricist and writer and has been living in Taiwan since 2015. His name cannot be publicly mentioned in China, even to credit his work when songs with his lyrics are performed. In this poem, Lam Zik describes the new perils of speech, using the COVID pandemic as a metaphor. In February 2022, Hong Kong was in the grips of a serious wave of COVID infections. The city was under a strict mask mandate and stringent social restrictions. Large sections of the city were quarantined, and many residents were sent into isolation. The title of the poem captures the fear of the easy transmission of the virus through breath and saliva emitted during exchanges among people. At the same time, referencing the Chinese proverb, "*beng cung hau jab, wo cung hau ceot* 病從口入, 禍從口出 (Disease enters through the mouth; disaster exits from the mouth)," the poem gestures toward another kind of disaster that also emanates from one's mouth—speech. In this sense, Hong Kong is ravaged by more than one kind of malady. Reflecting this condition, each stanza of the poem begins with an exclamatory sound, represented by a character with a "口 mouth" radical:

> 噓 Heoi / Be careful/ Please be careful of the technique of your aspiration when you speak / You should know how many of these dreamlike bubbles escape through the gaps in the mask as you say the phrase "*siusam* (be careful)"/ floating in the air
>
> 啊 Aa / Be careful / Shouting might make you feel better / but you will have turned "be careful of the virus" into a virus. / Be careful with words / Try to avoid using explosive fricatives and sibilants / Fortunately, these do not include '*ngooinei* (I love you)'
>
> 唉 Aai / for everyone's safety / learn sign language to transmit secrets / So those incompetent people won't be able to understand /
>
> 喔 O / Only the big people can speak in a loud voice / infecting the little people, resulting in what we see today / every breath and spray of saliva is from some big statements /
>
> 呸 Pei / They speak so loudly. They are so rude.

The poem opens by making references to the COVID pandemic and the necessity to cover one's mouth because of the danger of transmitting the virus through one's breath and spit. However, in the second section, the poem shifts its focus to specific kinds of verbalization, especially the iteration of words that contain explosive consonants. Cantonese is full of fricatives and sibilants; it would be impossible to speak properly without them. However, the poem suggests the solution is simply to forgo verbalized language, differentiating between lack of speech with lack of voice—the inability to speak aloud does not mean not speaking at all, nor unable to say what needs to be said. Lam Zik encourages speaking the truth but being smart in how one speaks it.

The band, "*Toufungmou dunggu* 土風舞冬菇 Dancing Mushroom," demonstrated another way to circumvent the taboos under the NSL. In a version of their song, "*Sidoi. kuk* 時代· 曲*Fight for the Dawn* (The worst times version) (The

Chinese title literally means, 'The Times. A Song')," they simply skipped all the problematic words in their lyrics, humming through all the gaps:

> Fire and smoke of the battle spreading**the whole city**
> lights flickering and changing**the light of dawn is near
> who***who*** Explain the truth
> who***who***the times ***
> *One can hear** receiving
> A generation carved into the tree rings
> ****
> ***
> still here ***
> **** ...[12]

By leaving all the gaps and holes through their song, Dancing Mushroom not only highlighted how absurd Hong Kong's reality was but also how equally ludicrous and ineffectual the authorities' ban on words was. Some things don't have to be said out loud. However, this also means that the song was for a specific audience—those who could not or would not figure out the meaning of the song were not someone the band cared to communicate with anymore. A society filled with taboos is also an incomplete and divided society.

While Dancing Mushroom's strategy was unusual, many singers did indeed become more circumspect in the lyrics of their songs, using careful strategies and images to sidestep certain words and phrases, adopting an attitude of "*ming zau ming* 明就明 (you'll understand if you understand)." How audiences understood these works was often a projection of their own politics. However, this created a situation where, as in the case of the school principal and his reading of Dear Jane's song, or the police banning the phrase, "Hong Kong add oil," there was constant suspicion and over-interpretation of intentions.

## What 7 You Say?

Not surprisingly, in such a climate of distrust and censorship, the Chinese translation of George Orwell's *1984* was the tenth most borrowed book in 2020, according to the Hong Kong Public Library's annual statistics. The original English edition occupied the ninth place.[13] Orwell's *1984* famously introduces, among notions of "doublethink" and "big brother," the idea of "Newspeak," a new kind of language designed to obfuscate.

To many in Hong Kong the Orwellian notion of "Newspeak" was embodied in the person of the city's then Chief Executive, Carrie Lam. In an RTHK interview in 2022, for example, Lam insisted freedoms in Hong Kong had not changed after 2 years of the enactment of the NSL. She argued, "The government has no control over the media's self-generated worries. It's like the many who emigrated from the city, no longer wanting to invest in Hong Kong, or those who are too afraid to create or write—it's all because of their subjective understanding of the NSL, using the NSL as a 'sacrificial lamb (*doizeoigoujoeng* 代罪羔羊).'"[14] This comment was made against the fact that all oppositional news media had, within one year, in 2021, been shut down and those in charge arrested and indicted. The city had fallen more than 60 places, to 148th among 180 locations, in the global press freedom ranking by 2022.[15] There was only one Beijing-approved candidate running for the office of the Chief Executive in 2022, to be elected by a small group of representatives in what was called by the authorities, "Hong Kong-style democracy."[16] This kind of blatant assault on reality prompted the 2021 song, "*ngaamaa* 啱呀 (You're Right)," from MC SH and the band, Tonick. Confronted with the absurdity of the new reality, resigned acceptance is the only way to respond to power:

> You're right; you're right. Everything you say is right. That's right; that's right. If you are the one to say it, then it's right. You're right; you're right…
>
> Don't think too much when speaking—that's my attitude right now. Trying to speak *jan waa* 人話 (human speech) would just get you stabbed in your back. No need to follow the rules. That's because having connections is king. No need for progress. Treat this as a dead-end.
>
> The more I go on, the more excited I become. I think, I might be stepping on the line soon, but I don't know where the line is, plus, they are all so petty. *It's time to say goodbye.* It's better that I keep it in a bit. Just sing something meaningless to let out some steam.
>
> You're right; you're right. Everything you say is right …[17]

Carrie Lam's particular rhetorical practice was prescriptive, formal, and combative. One of Lam's pat phrases, "*bit jau jungsam* 別有用心 (having ulterior motives)," was applied to a wide range of issues. Rather than addressing the use of excessive force by the police in the suppression of the protest in 2019, she accused those who raised the question as "having ulterior motives." Rather than commenting on whether there were human rights violations in Hong Kong, she blamed foreign governments for having ulterior motives, trying to smear the Hong Kong government. In other words, instead of answering a question, she attacked the person asking the question. In the same way, she dismissed all public expressions of discontent as traitorous, demonstrating an extraordinary re-definition of the idea of civic discussion.

Corresponding with the Hong Kong government's tightening control over the city under Lam was the rise of a new political language, a form of official way of speaking adopted from Beijing. These Carrie Lam-isms were straight out of the "Wolf Warrior Diplomacy" playbook, the combative verbal strategy commonly employed by Beijing's diplomatic corps. The official rules of the game were never admitting mistakes, never apologizing, and aggressively denouncing criticisms:[18]

> There are words and phrases that frequently appear in mainland China's official statements and communications that have generally been recognized as common official usages in Chinese, such as "*sowai*所謂 so-called," "*ginkyut faandeoi* 堅決反對 [resolutely] opposed," "*batwui dakcing* 不會得逞will not

> succeed." The Hong Kong chief executive had in the past only used these political idioms when attending Mainland Chinese official functions. However, a tally by the Chinese BBC News discovered that in recent years, especially since the beginning of the wave of protests in 2019, the Hong Kong government had been using this type of rhetoric more and more often in different situations.[19]

Lam's responses to all the discontent in her tenure as Hong Kong's Chief Executive seemed to be premised on two basic presumptions. First, those who deviated or held alternative ideas were deliberately attempting to cause chaos in society and sabotage the government. Second, those who held ideas contrary to the official agenda were all being manipulated by foreign governments that were motivated by their hatred for China. Officiousness passed for rationality. Like Lam, most other government officials also often used this strategy. Their prescriptive responses signaled to their interlocutors and audiences, especially those holding alternative views, that there was no room for discussion.

However, in this strange language regime, even a skillful practitioner like Lam occasionally slipped up. During a press conference in January 2022, in response to a reporter's question about what the new Beijing directive, the "Dynamic Zero" COVID policy, meant, Lam used a classical Chinese idiom, saying she was not "*ci zok jung ze* 此作俑者 (the one who initiated it)," causing much snickering around the city. This phrase is the first part of a sentence from Mencius that ends with four other words, "*kei mou hau fu* 其無後乎 (will be without progeny)," and carries within it both a specific historical context and an entire allegorical world. The whole saying, in its original context, means that the one who initiated the use of burial figurines (i.e., rulers who carry out elaborate funereal rites without regard to the starving common people) will be without progeny (i.e., no one to carry on their family names—a travesty in the Chinese classical world). This saying is actually a curse leveled on those in positions of power for pushing excessive and exhausting public policies oblivious to the lives of the common people.

In using this phrase, Lam committed a stunning faux pas. She had probably just wanted to say she was not clear what the policy meant because she was not its designer. However, the effect was hostile and accusatory. Many wondered if she was secretly unhappy about Beijing's orders, and this was a passive–aggressive way of expressing it. It could also have been a genuine mistake because classical Chinese is difficult, full of allusions, and seldom used in daily speech and writing. However, it was also well-known that Lam prided herself on her school record. She claimed to be first in her class every year, except for one year when she came in fourth, causing much bitterness. She retook her top position the next year. Given such childhood competitiveness and impressive school education, was it actually possible that she misused a classical phrase? Whether intentional or not, Lam had seemingly delivered a grave insult to Beijing. The Hong Kong media and KOLs gleefully speculated on the possible consequence of her misspeak. It is precisely because those in high offices had a propensity for using pretentious language and doublespeak that they were also more liable to become entangled in their own rhetoric, resulting in unexpected meanings. A week later, Hong Kong succumbed to a severe city-wide COVID outbreak, rendering the "Dynamic Zero" policy meaningless.

Because of her image of impassivity and being in absolute control in her verbal armor, Lam provided another occasion for mirth at a press conference on February 4, 2020. The *Standard* reported:

> Chief Executive Carrie Lam Cheng Yuet-ngor suspectedly swore in front of the camera on Friday afternoon, drawing attention from the entire city as well as the internet…talking about the work from home arrangements for civil servants at that time. However, she seemed to be in a hurry and suspectedly said, 'Apart from supplying...uhh no f**k...Apart from providing emergent and necessary anti-pandemic services, all civil servants would be working at home'.[20]

Whether or not she actually swore was beside the point. It was the idea that she might have betrayed, albeit accidentally, a hint of true emotion and humanity that amused the public. Beneath the façade of power, she turned out to be just as ordinary as everybody else. Her gaffes, however, did reveal how unnatural and difficult the new language was. Even the Chief Executive of the city slipped up from time to time.

## ***Jan waa* 人話 Human Speech**

The use of formal, overly proper, ornate, or literary language is strategic. It is an assertion of orthodoxy or legitimacy and power. Kovalev describes the various campaigns to "cleanse" the Russian language in Putin's Russia, such as the 2005 "Law on the Russian Language," which forbids the use of foreign loan words, and the 2010 "Law on protection of children," which bans the use of obscene language. These efforts, Kovalev explains, reveal the ideological importance of language in the "conceptual toolbox of nation building."[21]

Linguistic purity is equated with state orthodoxy and control. Russia's clean-language campaign is an attempt to create a world that is highly prescriptive: some things are inherently legitimate, and some are not, and these norms are determined in Moscow. According to Rann,

> Although Putin himself has a penchant for crude expressions, he avoids obscenity and his time in power has featured repeated attempted crackdowns on public profanity, as a way of signaling both a commitment to 'traditional values,' and central control over freedom of expression. This is a refusal to countenance both how people really talk and what people might really think about their national identity.[22]

Such campaigns against vulgarities, Rann also observes, often, by accident or design, coincided with Russia's military aggression against Ukraine, demonstrating how behind the "prissiness" of the language of the ruler is an aggressive state agenda. During the various unsuccessful peace negotiations between Russia and Ukraine since the beginning of Russia's invasion in 2022, while the former's formal use of language was an assertion of national power and legitimacy, the latter's liberal use of obscenities was a display of defiance.[23]

The alien lexicon and officious formality in speech that Carrie Lam adopted in her capacity as Hong Kong's CEO, likewise, was meant to assert power and control rather than to communicate. The other side gave up listening and deliberately assumed language that violated social propriety to challenge this authority. This failure of communication was especially evident during a government press event to address the "7/21 Incident." On July 21, 2019, in the town of Yuen Long, close to the border with China, a group of more than 100 men wearing white t-shirts, without provocation, viciously attacked riders on Hong Kong's MTR underground railway with bamboo sticks and iron rods when the train stopped at the station. It was rumored that the "men-in-white" were thugs hired to beat up pro-democracy demonstrators returning home from their rally at the city center. The attackers indiscriminately beat up everyone, including children, the elderly, and journalists recording the event. A total of 24,000 calls were made to the police emergency hotline during the incident. However, it took the police 39 minutes to arrive, exactly one minute after all the white-shirted men had run away. The police made no arrests that night. The violence, but more so, the response of the police, shocked the whole city.

The "7/21 Incident" was never resolved. There had only been a dozen or so arrests associated with the attack. The police never gave a satisfactory explanation for their tardy response that evening and refused to apologize for their apparent dereliction of duty. Already accused of using excessive force in dealing with protestors, this incident only further convinced the public of the collusion among certain pro-establishment officials, the police, and organized crime.

When Carrie Lam was asked about the behavior of the police and the speculation that the thugs were hired by certain pro-Beijing factions in the government, she vaguely answered that any violent act would be considered a "terrorist attack" in civilized societies. This nebulous response prompted the then RTHK journalist, Nabela Qoser, to call out, "*gong jan waa* 講人話 (use human speech)!" (Qoser was subsequently fired from the broadcaster in 2020 and now resides in the United Kingdom.)

This demand for Lam to speak "*jan waa* (human speech)," arose from exasperation with her Beijing-style "newspeak." If the "official speak" is to deflect truth through overly formal and literary speech, *jan waa*, the diametrically opposite, is deliberately explicit and coarse. On November 11, 2019, the pop singer, Charmaine Fong, released her song, "*jan waa*人話 (Talk2Me)," to immediate, viral success. The song's MV on YouTube was viewed about half a million times within two days, out of a population of 7.5 million in Hong Kong at the time. It was awarded, by popular vote, "My Favorite Song," on Commercial Radio's 2020 Ultimate Song Chart Award, despite being released less than two months before the vote. Fong also received awards for songwriting and lyrics for this song. On top of these, she attained the much-coveted Ultimate Song Chart Award for "My Favorite Female Singer" of the year. Aside from the "7/21 Incident," "Talk2Me" is also a response to the various incidents of police violence during the protests and the government's steadfast refusal to criticize the police force or conduct investigations into possible police abuse of power. The government's response to all questions about the police was ambiguous and vague at best, and dismissive at worst. The lyrics in Fong's song, in contrast, are bold and confrontational:

> Listening to you irritates me. Your special power is to pretend to be objective. The only thing I did wrong is to be blocked. Injustice and regression--this is our miserable fate.
>
> Truth has long ago disappeared. You wrote the plot for this empty, perverted drama. Without communication, trust is lost. You like to use clever words to confuse the public. I've seen through you.
>
> *Tell me what 7 you say.* You even put on such an attitude. Have you fucking finished?
>
> Your most important point through the whole process is lack of proof.
>
> Going straight from the left ear out the right--the screams and cries.
>
> *Tell me what 7 you say*
>
> Your conscience has long ago been lost, your mouth, ear, and nose, painted black. If only the world, shrouded in gloom would become clear again one day.
>
> You know, I know, they know. We all know. We are all baffled.
>
> *Talk to me. Talk to me...*[24] (Words in italics originally in English.)

The song is accompanied by an MV that is a continuous loop of re-rendered news videos of scenes from both the Yuen Long attack and police use of force on protestors. The anger directed at the government's obfuscation and disingenuousness is palpable in the song, with the lyrics riddled with swear words and strong language.

There are several repetitions of the phrase, "what 7 you say" in the song. "7 *cat*" is the Cantonese word for the number seven, and is a homonym of the Cantonese swear word, "*cat*柒," a vulgar term for penis, and used to represent a bad situation or an asinine person. The number 7 also has a popular association with Carrie Lam, aside from the fact that she was the target of much swearing in Hong Kong. She was elected Chief Executive in 2017 by 777 votes out of the 1194-member Election Committee appointed by Beijing. The unpopular Chief Executive was henceforth often unceremoniously referred to as "*cat po*柒 婆 (hag number 7)," a "fucking hag."

If "official speak" was overly punctilious and literary, *jan waa* was deliberately vulgar and direct. The term, "*jan waa*," repeated several times through Fong's song is used to contrast with the authorities' untruths and deflections. It is to indicate how government officials and authority figures are so detached from the reality of the regular citizens, their language so alien, their value system so different, and their lack of compassion when confronted with the images of brutality so shocking that it makes one question their membership in the human race. If the speaker of official language aims to assert power and control through disingenuousness, correctness of speech, and behavior, the speaker of "*jan waa*" pointedly displays high emotions and avoids normative propriety. "*Jan waa*" became a measure of a speaker's honesty and sincerity in contrast with the repressive formality and hence, hypocrisy of government officials. When confronted with a difficult situation, all the officials retreated behind their special language zone, abandoning any effort to communicate. Nabela Qoser's call to Carrie Lam to speak "*jan waa*" brought into focus the huge divide between the authorities and their constituents.

The use of slang and swearing, usually the province of rappers, is unexpected in a Cantopop song by a popular mainstream singer. The fact that a song, full of expletives could become the most popular song of the year (though the radio edition is a cleaned-up version), was also unusual, indicating the amount of frustration and anger many people felt toward the government officials at the time, and their constant deliberate use of imprecise language to deflect and confuse. The greater issue behind the refusal to establish real communication was the erosion of the long-cherished value of transparency and accountability of the Hong Kong government.

Obscenities, as Lam demonstrated when she "misspoke," have a leveling effect. In Russia, Kovalev argues, in a brief period in the early 1990s, there was a proliferation of the use of obscenities and vulgarities as an assertion of "freedom of speech." This language was also immediately adopted by dissident and émigré writers as a language of protest. The use of obscene words is, as such, associated with the expression of political dissent.[25]

As expressed in Charmaine Fong's song, it is not merely the choice of words that makes *jan waa* the opposite of the official language. It is the expressiveness, uninhibitedness, irony, and playfulness that distinguish this kind of speech from the formal, humorless, and prescribed language of the latter. In the song, official speak is described as calculated, dishonest, and unfeeling. In contrast, the impetuousness associated with swearing demonstrates authenticity and from the heart. Speaking *jan waa* thus also implies that one is a genuine human being, with human emotions and empathy toward others, while the alternative represents a highly manipulated person who is divorced from real life. Blakemore argues that the Orwellian "newspeak" is an assault on humanity's linguistic reality, which is an attack on our fundamental nature.[26]

## Language of Defiance

There has been much discussion about the importance of profanities in Hong Kong's vernacular. All languages contain expletives. However, among the Chinese languages, Cantonese is notorious for being particularly laced with colorful idioms and swear words. Swearing, especially among younger Hongkongers, is not only a way to distinguish themselves from the attitudes and values of older people and the authorities but it is also to highlight the characteristics of Cantonese and to distinguish it, especially, from Putonghua. Many Hong Kong swear words are created by combining English words with Hong Kong Cantonese, or the Cantonese-ification of English sounds. Many of these words are created and popularized by Hong Kong movies.[27] As a result, Hong Kong swear words are distinct from those of other Chinese languages, even Guangzhou's Cantonese, and are particular indicators of localness.

All films shown in Hong Kong have to be rated by the Office for Film, Newspaper, and Article Administration. (Since 2021, films have been subjected to the new Film Censorship Ordinance 392. Those deemed to endanger China's national security are banned from being shown in the city.) Films with profanities can only be released to a restricted audience, which will affect their box office income. To circumvent this, filmmakers became creative in hiding swear words in innocuous words and phrases. Many new swear words were created by using close homonymic substitutes for original profanities. Over time, these seemingly innocuous words replaced the original expletives. Thus, the very nature of profanities in recent Hong Kong vernacular is associated with defying censorship. The vibrant cinema of Hong Kong has in the past helped popularize many swear words in the language. In recent years, various online media, such as YouTube channels, and other social media platforms have been even more effective in the creation, transmission, and popularizing of new expressions. The uniqueness of Hong Kong's vernacular is a result of the city's flamboyant popular culture and its history of contrariness and defiance.

As the use of profanities becomes a form of local assertion and defiance, the attitude behind these usages also becomes a characteristic of the Hong Kong identity. The dominance of profanities in Hong Kong speech, argues Zan Jan Faai Daa 真人快打, has become the defining character of Hong Kong culture:

> What I consider a dominant culture must contain three factors. First, it must be popular. Second, it must be accessible and easy to understand. Third, it must contain deep meaning. The moment these three factors are put together, it is already evident what Hong Kong's dominant culture is. That's right. It is swearing.

As he succinctly puts it in the subheading of the essay, "Profanities are the essence of Hong Kong culture. To defend Cantonese, we must first defend profanities."[28]

In Hong Kong, language was used to distinguish those who self-professed to be pro-Beijing and pro-government from those who self-identified as Beijing's reluctant subjects. The contradictions between these two groups were reflected in the rift in Hong Kong's language culture, with the former embracing an overly correct and mannered speech, and the latter, a flippancy, and a flaunting of propriety. Of course, there has always been a formal and less formal register in any language, according to the social class of the speaker, audience, occasion, etc. However, the linguistic divide in Hong Kong has gone beyond these factors. Even though they continued to speak Cantonese, the ruling class of Hong Kong had adopted a whole set of vocabulary and prescriptive phrases that were distinct from customary local speech. To many, this further highlighted the cultural foreignness of the ruling power, reinforcing the idea among many that Hong Kong was in a new state of colonial subjection. To swear then suggests a refusal of identification with the state.

## Notes

1 Danny Mok, "'Hong Kong, add oil' should not be taboo, says Canto-pop legend Jacky Cheung after mainland backlash over anniversary greeting," *South China Morning Post*, July 3, 2022, www.scmp.com/news/hong-kong/politics/article/3183980/hong-kong-add-oil-should-not-be-taboo-says-canto-pop-legend.

2 Dear Jane, "銀河修理員 Galactic Repairman," music by Howie@Dear Jane, lyrics by Wyman Wong, Warner Music, 2020, www.youtube.com/watch?v=sg8V5BLMEhE.

3 Jip Si葉詩, "張明偉出騷TVB唔訪問 無悔唱《銀河修理員》被消失：冇做錯啲乜 (TVB not interviewing Cheung Ming Wai for his show. Doesn't regret singing Galaxy Repairman and being disappeared: I didn't do anything wrong)," *HK01*, September 30, 2021, www.HK01.com/即時娛樂/683342/張明偉出騷tvb唔訪問-無悔唱-銀河修理員-被消失-冇做錯啲乜.

4 Wong Wyman, "Speech given at the 2023 Commercial Radio Ultimately Song Chart Awards Ceremony," Hong Kong Toolbar, January 1, 2023, video, 4.19, www.youtube.com/watch?v=gk_5NyYdK5I.

5 Wong Zing Mei Zi Zi黃靜美智子, "眼淺的詞人從佛學與新紀元探問愛.小克剖白填詞的使命感 (A lyricist who cries easily investigating love through Buddhist philosophy in the new epoch. Siu Hak revealing his sense of mission in writing lyrics)," *Ming Pao Culture*, October 31, 2022, www.mpweekly.com/culture/藝文/小克專訪眼淺的詞人%E3%80%80從佛學與新紀元探問愛.

6 "RTHK under scrutiny for 'censoring' singers," *The Standard*, January 27, 2022, www.thestandard.com.hk/section-news/section/4/238432/RTHK-under-scrutiny-for-'censoring'-singers.

7 Wolfe, "有啲嘢唔講得 (There is things that cannot be said)," music and lyrics by Wolfe, Greytone Music, 2022, www.youtube.com/watch?v=UWGhCsNjezU.

8 Barry Sautman & Xinyi Xie, "Today in Guangzhou, Tomorrow in Hong Kong? A Comparative Study of the Language Situation in Two Cities," *Journal of Current Chinese Affairs* 49, no. 2 (2020): 207–232, https://doi.org/10.1177/1868102620983939.

9 "Eric Yip's Fricatives Wins UK National Poetry Competition," *BC Magazine*, April 1, 2022, www.bcmagazine.net/2022/04/01/fricatives-eric-yip/.

10 All quotations are from Yip's poem published in The Poetry Society, accessed July 27, 2023, https://poetrysociety.org.uk/news/the-national-poetry-competition-2021-winner-is-eric-yip/.

11 Lam Zik, "禍從口出Disaster issues from one's mouth," *Ming Pao Weekly Magazine*, February 18, 2022, www.mpweekly.com/culture/cu0006/%E6%9E%97%E5%A4%95-%E5%B0%88%E6%AC%84-199268.

12 土風舞冬菇 Dancing Mushroom, "時代·曲 Fight for Dawn," music and lyrics by Dancing Mushroom, www.youtube.com/watch?v=qJO-Gk_lmf4&t=2s.

13 "Orwell novels leap in popularity on 'Top 100 Most Borrowed Books' in Hong Kong: City libraries report a dramatic rise in the number of times Chinese translations of the British authors' critiques of authoritarianism *1984* and *Animal Farm* are being borrowed," Hong Kong Free Press, April 20, 2021, https://hongkongfp.com/2021/04/20/orwell-novels-leap-in-popularity-on-top-100-most-borrowed-books-in-hong-kong/.

14 "指國安法 實施兩年看不到港人自由改變，林鄭稱疫情後可證明 (Points out she cannot see any change in Hong Kong people's freedom after the implementation of NSL: Lam claims it will be proven at the end of the pandemic)," *AM730*, June 11, 2020, www.am730.com.hk本地/指-國安法-實施兩年看不到港人自由有變-林鄭稱疫情後可證明/323511.

15 Chris Lau, "Hong Kong plunges to 148th in world press freedom rankings, according to annual index by Reporters Without Borders," *South China Morning Post*, May 3, 2022, www.scmp.com/news/hong-kong/politics/article/3176411/hong-kong-plunges-148th-world-press-freedom-rankings.

16 Suzanne Pepper, "Beijing's hard sell of 'Hong Kong-style capitalist democracy'," The Hong Kong Free Press, January 22, 2022, https://hongkongfp.com/2022/01/22/beijings-hard-sell-of-hong-kong-style-capitalist-democracy/.

17 MC SH feat. ToNick, "啱呀 (That's right)," music and lyrics by MC SH, Mars Music Limited, 2021, www.youtube.com/watch?v=7hsRc0kkZt0.

18 Jip Gaa-jeon葉家潤, "撕裂與鬱結: 從「林鄭語錄」看特首5年任期歸家路 (Tearing apart and holding it in: Looking at the Chief Executive's road home through 'Quotations from Carrie Lam' after her five-year term," *The Initium*, April 8, 2022, https://theinitium.com/article/20220409-hongkong-carrie-lam-five-year-term.

19 Lei Hon-man李翰文, "中國官腔進入香港政府用語 分析形容再證北京政治影響 (Chinese official jargon enters Hong Kong Government's Language. Analysis describes this as further proof of Beijing's political influence)," *BBC Chinese*, March 14, 2022, www.bbc.com/zhongwen/trad/chinese-news-60672295.

20 "Carrie Lam suspectedly swears in front of the camera," *The Standard*, February 4, 2022, www.thestandard.com.hk/breaking-news/section/4/186774/(Central-Station)-Carrie-Lam-suspectedly-swears-in-front-of-the-camera.

21 Manuela Kovalev, "Law and (Verbal) Order: The Politics of Russian Obscene Language from Soviet Russia to the Present Day," *Zeitschrift für Slavische Philologie* 72, no. 2 (2016): 323–347, accessed June 17, 2023, www.jstor.org/stable/26583037.

22 Jamie Rann, "How swearing became a weapon of resistance for Ukrainians," *The Guardian*, April 13, 2022, www.theguardian.com/books/2022/apr/13/putin-ukraine-war-russian-language.

23 Ibid.

24 Charmaine Fong, "Talk2Me," music and lyrics by Charmaine Fong, Strawberry Fields Ltd., 2019, www.youtube.com/watch?v=zF6MAUyRFeo.

25 Kovalev, "Law and (Verbal) Order."

26 Steven Blakemore, "Language and Ideology in Orwell's 1984," *A Special Issue: Orwell's 1984, Social Theory and Practice* 10, no. 3 (1984): 349–356: 349.

27 Terry Ka Po Tin田家溥, "從港產片中「港式粗口」的使用看港人的文化身份建構 (An examination of the construction of Hong Kong's cultural identity through the 'Hong Kong style swearing' in Hong Kong produced movies)," *Cultural Studies@Lingnan* 56, no. 1 (2017), https://commons.ln.edu.hk/cgi/viewcontent.cgi?article=1698&context=mcsln.

28 Zan Jan Faai Daa真人快打, "粗口其實係有文化, 愈爛口愈識得多野 (There is actually culture in Profanities. The more foul-mouthed, the more knowledgeable one is)," *Jintian toutiao今天頭條*, September 5, 2016, www.twgreatdaily.com/cat99/node1245839.

## References

Blakemore, Steven. "Language and ideology in Orwell's 1984." *A Special Issue: Orwell's 1984, Social Theory and Practice* 10, no. 3 (1984): 349–356: 349.

"Carrie Lam suspectedly swears in front of the camera." *The Standard*, February 4, 2022. www.thestandard.com.hk/breaking-news/section/4/186774/(Central-Station)-Carrie-Lam-suspectedly-swears-in-front-of-the-camera.

Dancing Mushroom土風舞冬菇. "時代·曲 Fight for dawn." Music and lyrics by Dancing Mushroom. www.youtube.com/watch?v=qJO-Gk_lmf4&t=2s.

Dear Jane. "銀河修理員 Galactic repairman." Music by Howie@Dear Jane, lyrics by Wyman Wong. Warner Music, 2020. www.youtube.com/watch?v=sg8V5BLMEhE.

"Eric Yip's fricatives wins UK national poetry competition." *BC Magazine*, April 1, 2022. www.bcmagazine.net/2022/04/01/fricatives-eric-yip/.

Fong, Charmaine. "Talk2Me." Music and lyrics by Charmaine Fong, Strawberry Fields Ltd., 2019. www.youtube.com/watch?v=zF6MAUyRFeo.

Jip Gaa-jeon葉家潤. "撕裂與鬱結：從「林鄭語錄」看特首5年任期歸家路 (Tearing apart and holding it in: Looking at the Chief Executive's road home through 'Quotations from Carrie Lam' after her five-year term)." *The Initium*, April 8, 2022. https://theinitium.com/article/20220409-hongkong-carrie-lam-five-year-term.

Jip Si 葉詩. "張明偉出騷TVB唔訪問 無悔唱《銀河修理員》被消失：冇做錯啲乜 (TVB not interviewing Cheung Ming Wai for his show. Doesn't regret singing Galaxy Repairman and being disappeared: I didn't do anything wrong)." *HK01*, September 30, 2021. www.hk01.com/即時娛樂/683342/張明偉出騷tvb唔訪問-無悔唱-銀河修理員-被消失-冇做錯啲乜.

Kovalev, Manuela. "Law and (verbal) order: The politics of Russian obscene language from Soviet Russia to the present day." *Zeitschrift für Slavische Philologie* 72, no. 2 (2016): 323–347. Accessed June 17, 2023. www.jstor.org/stable/26583037.

Lam Zik. "禍從口出Disaster issues from one's mouth." *Ming Pao Weekly Magazine*, February 18, 2022. www.mpweekly.com/culture/cu0006/%E6%9E%97%E5%A4%95-%E5%B0%88%E6%AC%84-199268.

Lau, Chris. "Hong Kong plunges to 148th in world press freedom rankings, according to annual index by Reporters Without Borders." *South China Morning Post*, May 3, 2022. www.scmp.com/news/hong-kong/politics/article/3176411/hong-kong-plunges-148th-world-press-freedom-rankings.

Lei Hon-man 李翰文. "中國官腔進入香港政府用語 分析形容再證北京政治影響 (Chinese official jargon enters Hong Kong government's language. Analysis describes this as further proof of Beijing's political influence)." *BBC Chinese*, March 14, 2022. www.bbc.com/zhongwen/trad/chinese-news-60672295.

MC SH feat. ToNick. "啱呀 (That's right)." Music and lyrics by MC SH. Mars Music Limited, 2021. www.youtube.com/watch?v=7hsRc0kkZt0.

Mok, Danny. "'Hong Kong, add oil' should not be taboo, says Canto-pop legend Jacky Cheung after mainland backlash over anniversary greeting." *South China Morning Post*, July 3, 2022. www.scmp.com/news/hong-kong/politics/article/3183980/hong-kong-add-oil-should-not-be-taboo-says-canto-pop-legend.

"Orwell novels leap in popularity on 'Top 100 Most Borrowed Books' in Hong Kong: City libraries report a dramatic rise in the number of times Chinese translations of the British authors' critiques of authoritarianism *1984* and *Animal Farm* are being borrowed." Hong Kong Free Press, April 20, 2021. https://hongkongfp.com/2021/04/20/orwell-novels-leap-in-popularity-on-top-100-most-borrowed-books-in-hong-kong/.

Pepper, Suzanne. "Beijing's hard sell of 'Hong Kong-style capitalist democracy'." The Hong Kong Free Press, January 22, 2022. https://hongkongfp.com/2022/01/22/beijings-hard-sell-of-hong-kong-style-capitalist-democracy/.

Rann, Jamie. "How swearing became a weapon of resistance for Ukrainians." *The Guardian*, April 13. www.theguardian.com/books/2022/apr/13/putin-ukraine-war-russian-language.

"RTHK under scrutiny for 'censoring' singers." *The Standard*, January 27, 2022. www.thestandard.com.hk/section-news/section/4/238432/RTHK-under-scrutiny-for-'censoring'-singers.

Sautman, Barry and Xinyi Xie. "Today in Guangzhou, tomorrow in Hong Kong? A comparative study of the language situation in two cities." *Journal of Current Chinese Affairs* 49, no. 2 (2020): 207–232. https://doi.org/10.1177/1868102620983939.

"Standard Chartered marathon warns runners' over 'political' attire; police force runners to cover 'come on Hong Kong' slogan." Hong Kong Free Press, October 24, 2021. https://hongkongfp.com/2021/10/24/standard-chartered-marathon-warns-runners-over-political-attire-police-force-runners-to-cover-come-on-hong-kong-slogan-report/.

Tin, Terry Ka Po 田家溥. "從港產片中「港式粗口」的使用看港人的文化身份建構 (An examination of the construction of Hong Kong's cultural identity through the 'Hong Kong style swearing' in Hong Kong produced movies)." *Cultural Studies@Lingnan* 56, no. 1 (2017). https://commons.ln.edu.hk/cgi/viewcontent.cgi?article=1698&context=mcsln.

Wolfe. "有啲嘢唔講得 (There is things that cannot be said)." Music and lyrics by Wolfe, Greytone Music, 2022. www.youtube.com/watch?v=UWGhCsNjezU.

Wong, Wyman. "Speech given at commercial radio ultimately Song Chart Awards Ceremony." Hong Kong Toolbar. January 1, 2023. Video, 4.19. www.youtube.com/watch?v=gk_5NyYdK5I.

Wong Zing Mei Zi Zi 黃靜美智子. "眼淺的詞人從佛學與新紀元探問愛.小克剖白填詞的使命感 (A lyricist who cries easily investigating love through Buddhist philosophy in the new epoch. Siu Hak revealing his sense of mission in writing lyrics)." *Ming Pao Culture*, October 31, 2022. www.mpweekly.com/ culture/藝文/小克專訪眼淺的詞人%E3%80%80從佛學與新紀元探問愛.

Yip, Eric. "Fricatives." The Poetry Society. Accessed July 27, 2023. https://poems.poetrysociety.org.uk/poets/eric-yip/.

Zan Jan Faai Daa真人快打. "粗口其實係有文化, 愈爛口愈識得多野 (There is actually culture in Profanities. The more foul-mouthed, the more knowledgeable one is)." *Jintian toutiao 今天頭條,* September 5, 2016. www.twgreatdaily.com/cat99/node1245839.

"指國安法 實施兩年看不到港人自由改變, 林鄭稱疫情後可證明 (Points out she cannot see any change in Hong Kong people's freedom after the implementation of NSL: Lam claims it will be proven at the end of the pandemic)." *AM730*, June 11, 2020. www.am730.com.hk本地/指-國安法-實施兩年看不到港人自由有變-林鄭稱疫情後可證明/323511.

# 7 The Itinerary of Pleasure

## Reclaiming Individual Freedom in the City

The COVID pandemic that swept through the world at the beginning of 2020 put a sudden end to all forms of public life in Hong Kong. Community events were banned and gatherings were first limited to ten, then four people, then only those from within the same households or workplaces. Public facilities and schools were shut down. Hours of operation of many businesses were limited. Restaurants could only offer take-out foods. Tourists and visitors stopped arriving. Shoppers and parallel traders from China no longer traversed the city streets wheeling their suitcases. It was not till the second half of 2021 that parts of the city reopened. However, everything shut down again in the first few months of 2022 when Hong Kong was hit by an even more virulent wave of COVID infections that almost paralyzed the public medical system. Even when it receded, draconian social regulations in the city remained in place for months as the Hong Kong government chased after the elusive "Zero COVID" at Beijing's insistence. While the implementation of the NSL managed to tighten the reins on expressions of discontent and opposition, the government's COVID policies ensured that any public gathering or social assembly was impossible, effectively stamping out the last embers of any political movement. The enforced calm in the city, rather than reassuring Hongkongers that everything had returned to normal, only added to the sense of unease. Ironically, it was in the disappearance of their familiar world that Hong Kong people found a renewed affection for their city. This chapter is about this rediscovery as Hongkongers sorted through what they referred to as the "ruins" of their city after a couple of years of political unrest and the ravages of COVID, going from seeing the city as alienating and hostile to finding a new love for it and even a sense of freedom within it. This chapter traces this evolution through a number of song lyrics, short essays, as well as a trend of walking the city.

### The Lights Have Gone Out

To many, nothing symbolized the end of normal life in the city more than the sinking of the 40-year-old floating restaurant, Jumbo, a local cultural icon. On June 21, 2022, the Hong Kong public was shocked by the news that Jumbo, which had recently been towed out of Hong Kong to an unspecified location for repairs, had

DOI: 10.4324/9781003521280-8

sunk at high sea (more on this in Chapter 8). Just as the public was struggling to absorb this upsetting news, the following day, a fire broke out on a power cable bridge, causing a two-day blackout in the northwestern districts of Hong Kong. Large-scale blackouts were so unusual because power lines are buried underground and largely impervious to weather and natural disasters, that it prompted a huge outcry from the public. The writer, 葉秋弦 *Jip Cau Jin*, notes in an essay, "*Mingjat zihau* 明日之後 (After tomorrow)," that, "Just because it never has happened before does not mean it won't ever happen. Just like in 1997, or before 2019, you would never have thought that things can be so beyond comprehension in Hong Kong in 2022."[1]

As a result of the power outage, the subway stopped running, traffic lights went out, and hospitals had to evacuate their seriously ill patients. Some people were trapped in their apartments on the upper floors of high-rises, without water and light, while others were unable to get back to their homes. Jip registered her anxiety as she was caught in the chaos on her way home:

> Before all this, when I got off the light rail, I'd walk slowly toward home. Usually, before I reached home, I'd start counting the floors from the top down to the thirty-odd floors, till I reached my familiar window. I have thought once it was there, it would always be there. Suddenly, the familiar shapes have disappeared, becoming a blur. The sticky air started to seep into my pores. There was still no wind.
>
> There was someone anxiously trying to find a daughter with whom they had lost contact. There was someone in a wheelchair in front of the building not knowing what to do, looking distressed. Some curious individual stood in front of his window waving a glowing object. Everyone had his or her own notion of how life ought to be. Everyone had his or her worries.
>
> At seven-forty, I made a decision. I made my way to a bus stop. The cellular signal was faint; phone connections were dropped every now and then. I phoned L. He couldn't hear clearly what I was saying with my voice going in and out. The receiver had trouble capturing complete sentences. I spent two minutes telling him that we had a blackout here and asked if everything was normal over there. He said he was in Tsim Sha Tsui [Kowloon Downtown]. There was no blackout there. Everything was normal. More than ten minutes later, the number 969 bus arrived. I knew it made long detours through Tin Yan Housing Estate, the Wetland Park, Ginza Stop, and Tin Shui Wai Park...It had to make a wide circle through these places before it could leave the besieged town. However, I felt more at ease in the moving carriage. It was very quiet in the bus at first. There were not many people. I looked out of the window in silence, trying to understand this sudden episode of change and strangeness. Bright lights hung from above my head. Cool wind finally drove out my feverishness. The bus left in its trail, a feeling of loss and unfamiliarity. I'd never thought I would become a deserter.[2]

The blackout, to many, was more than just an accident. It was another proof that something was fundamentally broken. Recent generations of Hongkongers who have grown up and lived all their lives in the city have always expected things to work properly—to be able to rely on public services provided by a government that took care of the basic infrastructure of the city, protecting them and their way of life. Overnight, everything came crashing down. Many found themselves without a way back to their homes and familiar lives. The light had literally gone out in the city.

As Jip made her way out of the area on a bus, she felt guilty about abandoning her home, a familiar feeling in the post-NSL emigration wave. Jip ends her piece with a short verse, in which she reflects on what the few days in June 2022 portends for the city:

> The boat [Jumbo] has sunk.
> The lights have gone out.
> When we think about it, the metaphor is perhaps too rich.
> There's nothing one cannot imagine through it.
> It turns out the world doesn't need guns and bombs.
> Wars don't occur in a particular form; nor does the apocalypse.
> (We no longer talk about the future.)
> (Then tomorrow, after tomorrow, please do not
> let go of my hand anymore.)[3]

Words like "*bangwaai* 崩壞 (broken)" or "*faiheoi* 廢墟 (ruins)," even "*mutjat* 末日 (the end of days)," were often used, especially in popular culture, to describe the conditions of the city after 2019. They might seem overly dramatic; however, they captured the intensity of individuals' emotions in the altered political and social landscape. The rock group, *Hoengloktyun* 享樂團 3Think, titled their 2020 song, "*Dou saigaai taap haa* 到世界塌下 (Till the world comes crashing down)." The song, with lyrics by Norris Wong黃綺琳, invokes the events of 2019, with cataclysmic images of streets strewn with detritus and enshrouded in smoke and tear gas. Civilization seems to have been destroyed. Rather than being able to shelter under the city's structures, these now became traps. Rather than being able to rely on the support of family and friends, everyone was a potential enemy:

> The smoke of the battle draws near; the sky darkens. The battle is going to start, but you are still calmly trying sleep. We trusted them, but now we are trapped. The lonely island keeps sinking.
>
> We all each have our own worries.
>
> The whole city is in danger. How can we still speak the soft language of love?
>
> The whole world is going to come crashing down, whipped by wind, and beaten by rain. The city wall does not provide shelter. We are driven tumbling into a deep valley. You and I give up talking to each other. Do you not see my

> pain? For those who have known love before, this feels like the changes of the dark sea. We are even afraid of being together.
>
> ...There are still tens of thousands of miles to our journey. Let's hold hands and hurry forward. Let's live through this moment together, just like a love story, just like normal. World is breaking apart. We are not afraid.[4]

Even though this song encourages listeners to journey forth together again into the storm, it also reflects the anxiety many felt in an uncertain future in a city.

The enforcement of COVID rules just after the protests was seen by many to be more than just temporary emergency arrangements. For some, they symbolized yet more erosion of individual freedom in the new Hong Kong. Others worried that the requirement of a vaccine pass to use public transportation and enter public facilities, shopping malls, and other public spaces was a way for the government to monitor individuals' movements.[5] The feeling of being suffocated under all the daily rules and regimes was captured by the band, Saiseichu 再生中 *Zoi saang zung*, in their 2021 song, "*Fukap zijau* 呼吸自由 (English title: To Breathe; literally: the freedom to breathe)," with lyrics by 欲龍 *Juk-lung*:

> Behind our masks, it feels as if it's been a whole lifetime. Behind our masks, our noses are constantly irritated. Behind our masks--hopefully we'd toss it immediately after we're done with it. Behind our masks, we yearn for fresh air.
>
> *Completely cover your lips and nostrils, then press down the two sides. Perfect.*
>
> ...Behind our masks, there is no fragrance from the roses. Behind our masks, we suddenly get soaked in sweat. Behind our masks, we yearn for fresh air.
>
> *Completely cover your souls and the bodies, then press down along deep yearning. Perfect.*
>
> We want to freely exhale, also, to freely inhale, savoring the experience. Still hoping--but everything remains the same. How many times, "We are sorry," has been said in the city? Look into the center of the bustling city. Along the streets, everyone is furrowing their brows. Unconsciously, sighing...[6] (Words in italics are spoken, not sung.)

There are two large characters on the screen at the beginning of Saiseichu's MV—"*zi yau* 自由 (freedom)," scrawled in yellow against a black background, signaling the yearning for a more general sense of freedom. The disease attacked the respiratory system and suffocated its victims in the same way the disordered city's new rules and laws strangulated its residents.

## The New Citizens

In official rhetoric at least, the Hong Kong government and Beijing seemed satisfied that the implementation of the NSL and the "perfecting" of the electoral system had successfully turned the city from chaos to governance, "*cung lyun dou zi* 從亂到治." The city could now continue its delegated capitalist endeavors and achieve prosperity —"*jau zi kap hing* 由治及興 from governance to prosperity."[7] In the 2021 song, "Jiu妖 (Monster) (English title: Fairy Godmonster)," by The Hertz, with lyrics by Leung Ka Yan 梁嘉蒽 (Serrini), they described the newly fashioned citizens in this new reality :[8]

> Lost in time or space, without before or after--hard to take.
>
> Freedom--after one awakens from the dream of freedom--there's no need to be particular. (My love, my love, behind the great changes of the times...) Being human--the absurdities of being human--drifting like flowers in the wind and a sea of snow. (Paint on the colors of fairies; don't be troubled.) I don't understand; I don't understand--this strangeness binding my hands. (Knowing that you are not that smart, the demons will not retreat.) Naturally, being human can be easy, just like a fairy, floating lightly…sucked dry of all righteousness from the veins...
>
> If one doesn't understand now, just pretend--floating lightly, floating lightly… it's the trend!
>
> ...The present, the present is extremely ugly--there's no need to save it. Everyone is so ridiculous… fairy-like, gorgeous, seducing us to death, just like a fairy, floating lightly, floating lightly…[9]

In the MV of the song, monstrous creatures in grotesque make-up inhabit a space that looks like a wasteland. Their dances and movements are animalistic and exaggerated.

As part of society pushed on, seeking "stability and prosperity," answering Beijing's incessant admonishment for the city, the residents had little choice but to march to the rhythm of progress. As the song suggests, just yield to this new order and drift along with the currents, morphing into *Jiu* 妖 (monsters). It does not matter if one's veins are completely sucked dry, or if one's core is hollowed out. "There is no living, no dying; and then, a walking corpse is not troubled by anything." It was one way of surviving the reality.

For some Hongkongers, the COVID virus symbolized something more pernicious. In their 2020 COVID song, "*Baakduk batcam* 百毒不侵 (Immune to a hundred poisons)," RubberBand sings about a poison being released into the city, infecting the inhabitants. Rather than physical death, this infection leads to the withering of one's soul:

> How much arsenic is drifting down in the wind? It seems to give unlimited excitement to whoever's sending this gift. Every breath in and out murders the soul, destroys all creation. Animals and plants succumb, one after another. Immune to a hundred poisons. (Don't be so naïve.) How much arsenic is mixed into the wine and food? What sinister persons are seizing huge profits with no mercy, their heart and soul completely rotten? Undetectable, the poison is presented as delicious food. Immune to a hundred poisons. (Don't be so naïve.) *You're drowning us in poison!...*

> Every day, how many particles rush at our heads; someone leaked the information that we will slowly lose our intelligence. New babies will finally be obedient, submissive; will not argue back, achieve top grade success. (Soon to be immortal.) Immune to a hundred poisons. (Soon to be immortal.) (Original in English in italics.)[10]

In the name of eradicating disease, a system of thought hygiene is implemented in the city. The new thought regime will ensure young people will become diligent in their studies, succeed in school, and eventually become docile and financially productive members of society—perfect citizens.

From the perspective of such a "perfected" citizen, the rapper, Novel Flash, describes a sense of alienation and despair in "Every Night (2021)":

> It's 3:30 AM, you're still awake, hiding in your room. You have all these words in your heart that you don't have a way to express. You keep looking out the window, unawares, it has become daylight. On the surface, you're unharmed, but your heart is riddled with hundreds of holes and thousands of sores. Since you realize that no one cares about what you think, to avoid unnecessary fights, you separate yourself from the world. This city has collapsed; its flesh has been separated from its soul. Feeling helpless, we continue to struggle on in a place that has gone all wrong. You are surprised how cold this world is. Your words become clever--offering fake praises. This world wants you to be obedient, wants you to get used to it. When you feel depressed, they laugh at you. They laugh because you feel bad and because you want to cry. The city is too cold. Things are difficult and your heart feels tired. You can't talk back; you can only follow along. They disapprove of every decision you make. It's difficult. Even though you are used to the suffering, you hide yourself to shed tears...[11]

Suppressing one's thoughts and feelings, one goes through the daily motions, fulfilling one's obligations as a productive member of society.It is a society in which people pass each other by without being able to connect, as described in BMW's the rap song, "*Daaikoi ngomun muigojan dou zikmok* 大概我們每個人都寂寞 (Perhaps every one of us feels just as lonely)":

> I only want to find someone to share my simple love, to carefully plan our future together, but I can't meet anyone. What is the reason? I no longer want to think about it. Leave it all to fate. Day after day, repeatedly doing the same work has emptied out my soul, leaving behind an empty shell. I sit on a street corner, watching people come and go. Are they also like me, their hearts empty? Cigarette after cigarette, then another cigarette after another cigarette, till the smell of tobacco makes me feel nauseous. Cigarette after cigarette, then another cigarette after another cigarette, till the streetlight at the end of the street comes on. The night descends. It is the same every day, dull and tedious, but no one pays attention to my troubles. I feel I am on an empty island. The city's people

> keep telling me what I should do. Do you understand me? Do I understand you? Perhaps every one of us is just as lonely. Do you understand me? Do I understand you? Perhaps every one of us is equally lonely.[12]

In this desolate scene, the streetlights automatically go on and off every day at the right time. On the surface, everything seems to be functioning normally. Likewise, the singer melancholically goes through the daily motions of living.

The lack of connection among individuals was compounded by the severence of relationships as many emigrated from the city. In the 2021 song, "UC428 *Piulau hou* 漂流號 (Spaceship Drifter)," with lyrics by *Aa Ning* 阿檸, The Hertz uses the figure of an astronaut lost in space in their MV to capture the feelings of loneliness and abandonment. Alluding to the symptom of suffocation from COVID infection, the astronaut is described as roaming hopelessly on a strange planet with diminishing oxygen supply. Images of his home on earth keep flashing through his mind:

> Looking around, upward, and downward, have I determined my location? Both my meter and my heartrate need adjusting.
>
> And you are not taking me with you. Don't you feel even a bit guilty? No sense of direction, I can only wait for death here. There is no line of communication, no way to differentiate signals from afar. Is this a test? Sadly, I have always had you standing next to me in the past. If only we could see each other again this second. I'm in this vast space! In all our years together, the stars have been witnesses to our laughter and tears. Who is it that allows you to turn your back and leave? Even breathing has become too exhausting...[13]

The song captures how many in Hong Kong felt they were left stranded in an increasingly alienating city.

Despite the images of destruction and sadness that pervade the popular songs in these years, there were also many that encouraged their listeners to break through this mindset of despair. Instead of focusing on the devastation around them, the singer-songwriter, Cath Wong 黃妍, tells her listeners to find beauty, cherish those who still remain, and walk out from the ruins. The lyrics of her song, "*Ngo samzung soengmei bangwaaidik boufan* 我心中尚未崩壞的部分 (The unbroken part of me) (2020)," was written by Wong Lok Yee王樂儀 and Chow Yiu-Fai 周耀輝. Chow is another of Hong Kong's most important lyricists:

> From under the bed wafts the smell of darkness
> On the wall hangs the scolding needles.
> A pile of bricks stacked victoriously against the door.
> Can we believe there is still air?
> Beyond the door, I discover a peacock with wings.
> On the journey, I know there are mountains in my heart that I need to climb.
> There is an ocean I need to get through lightly, and you will be there. It is then that I know I still have an inch of perfection in me.

...When beauty reaches its end, it becomes ashes.
When exhausted, it becomes sand.
But you can keep me from disintegrating.
Even though I have wounds all over my body...
...Even though there's sadness in the streets,
The cries will become poems,
Wordlessness becomes songs.
Don't be afraid. It's the world that's ugly.
Look, this is a girl who has walked out from the ruins.
There's at least an inch of my heart that hasn't turned bad.
There is also me. There's light tomorrow.
There is also you. Dust will fly.[14]

Wong's song urges the listener to see beyond the ugliness, to ignore conventional logic, and to believe that "Cries become poems/wordlessness becomes song." This is to refuse the prescribed way of being and to reinterpret the world.

## Breaking the Rhythm

Urban life, Henri Lefebvre argues, is overlaid by constant rhythms that control and discipline the inhabitants through "brutal repetitions." These rhythms are inscribed in the veins of one's daily life. In Hong Kong the everyday is regimented by bus and train schedules, work shifts and school schedules, the ticking of the count-down clocks on the traffic lights, the constant directional flow of traffic, and even the military rhythm in the national anthem broadcast nightly.[15] Under both the NSL and COVID regimes, in the daily queues for COVID tests, swiping of the QR codes, enforced social distancing, and curfews for restaurant dining, etc. such disciplinary impositions were even more strongly felt. Many formerly open spaces became forbidden. Access to different areas in the city became conditional. Hong Kong's streets which had once been locations of collective power and resistance through the first decade and a half of the 2000s, had now, for many, become sites of control and estrangement.

However, for some, the empty streets provide opportunities to break these rhythms of "brutal repetitions." In "*Samje goubit linzaap* 深夜告別練習 (Practicing saying goodbye in the middle of the night)," the band, Zpecial, takes the audience on a tour of the rarely seen city. In the MV, the streets glowed gently in the streetlights against Hong Kong's iconic nighttime skyline, without a single person or vehicle around. It is a scene possible only at the height of COVID lockdown. Unfazed by the eerie silence and the rhythmic flashing on and off of the traffic lights, a skateboarder sails through the deserted streets by himself. Eventually, he chances upon a young woman, also riding on a skateboard by herself. They decide to travel together, dancing, twirling, and gliding along the empty streets through the night, feeling free and happy. By night's end, the young woman leaves, and the young man is all by himself again. The music is a wistful, gentle rhythmic rock. The lyrics of the song are by Oscar Lee:

> Before sunrise, I step upon the road by myself, going backwards and forwards, travelling at the fastest speed. Going backwards and forwards, without desires, I commit no offense. I lived in the dark, tripping and falling. However, one day, someone on the same street looked back at me. I am unable to forget the sparkling eyes. Like a wave, a longing rises in my heart, which has been untouched and untrammeled. Retreading the distance a hundred times, I hope to run into her again…
>
> You and I in this moment seem to be very close. Chancing upon each other now, we are ultimately strangers. Under the moonlit night, we crouch down, speed up, then steady ourselves to stand up. Tonight, I am not going home. With another person, I gradually forget the hands of the clock, speeding along in the street. But then, you turn around. You have to go, without leaving behind a trace, saying we should say goodbye.
>
> She says she likes me because from beginning to end, I am a stranger to her. Her eyes sparkle with tears when she kisses me. She says, do not ask. She turns back to look at me once more. I feel my heart tighten. I hope that in the new day, I can continue to wait for what might come.[16]

Relationships in the city might have become tenuous, but the protagonist in Zpecial's song is able to find a connection with another person even if for a brief moment. One's daily itinerary might have become restrained, but there are still spaces of freedom. As Michel de Certeau argues,

> Faced with the totality of the city, obstructed by codes that the dweller has not mastered but that he or she must assimilate in order to live there, faced with a configuration of places imposed by urban planning, faced with the social unevenness inside urban space, the dweller always succeeds in creating places of withdrawal, itineraries for his or her use and pleasure that are individual marks that the dweller alone inscribes on urban space.[17]

The city depicted in Zpecial's MV is a magical one. The skateboarders roam the dark streets with the backdrop of the glittering skyline. The streets are luminescent under a gentle rain. The overpasses and flyovers crisscrossing the highways produce a futuristic quality to the city that is dystopic, if also beautiful. The protagonists assert their rightful presence in the empty streets, sailing freely through them, oblivious of all the codes and interdictions that routinely govern the streets. Zpecial's skateboarders turn the streets of everyday journeys into an "itinerary of pleasure."

Along a similar vein, the singer-songwriter, Terence Lam 林家謙, urges listeners to embrace their solitude and reclaim the space of their everyday life. In his song, "*Jatjan ziging* 一人之境 (Solitude)," released in 2020, he takes his audience on a walk through the city, introducing the joy of solitary contemplation. Lam also wrote the lyrics for his song:

> Looking around during a party, eight or ten of my friends are all laughing, swaying to the rhythm. I feel lonely in my happiness. Looking back when it was over, I felt a bit lonesome, but free. I want to unravel the tangle in the net. I take this clear and bright day all to myself.
>
> On the muddy road I count my own footprints while I walk. I discover cracks, through which I can hear my heart. I learn to repair and fill them in. Don't lock up the noise.
>
> I discover that I can be fully contented by myself. It is actually not that much fun to be around a lot of people. Quietly, I watch the stars, with the moon heeding them. Peacefully, I visit this state of solitude. I find that I am happy. I look over the hills and valleys by myself. I toast myself with a can of fizzy drink. I sigh happily. I am too lazy to explain myself. No, I witness all this by myself.
>
> ...I find that I am already very happy just to watch the transformation of the world. I toast myself with a can of fizzy drink, breathe out some bubbles, listen to the resonance. It's the answer from my heart.[18]

Lam is one of the most celebrated among the new generation singer-songwriters in Hong Kong, perhaps because of his music's ability to both acknowledge the anxieties and sadness of his audience while transporting them away from their worries. In the world of Lam's music, one is no longer tied to the heaviness of the mundane but can ascend into the realm of beauty and magic. This is a constant message in Lam's songs, from "*Dakleonsi mungjau singing* 特倫斯夢遊仙境(Wonderland)," (2020) to "*Sankeidik wutou mojoek* 神奇的糊塗魔藥 (The amazing silly magical pill)" (2021), and to "Doodoodoo (2022)." These songs are accompanied by fantastic animations that encourage the viewers to adjust their perspective, so they can see beauty in the mundane and escape the prison of everyday rhythm. In "Wonderland," he sings,

> A strange bird said it will take me to see sunflowers.
> The ants said I must let go as they run beneath me.
> I invited you to come, but you said you had to go home. But there are still so many adventures, so many surprises.
> Let us get lost in the strangeness, climb over the fantastical hills. Pick up a stick, stretch out your hand and try out a spell. We'll walk over the countless stars, drink sake on top of rain clouds. Forget about all the tedious worldly struggles... We crawl into an hourglass. Within ten seconds we can see entire human history. Feeling so free, I don't want to have to say, "and then...."[19]

Lam's songs and MVs are also about overcoming the temporal pressure of one's lives and its measure of one's worth. In his song, "*Zoi hungzung dik zejatmiu* 在空中的這一秒 (This second in the air) (2021)," he once again embarks on a journey, this time, on board a train in the sky:

> Who could have guessed that this moment's journey can make me feel I actually own a bit of eternity? I don't need to care how much longer I have. I let go of my hands without care...
>
> In this second in midair, travelling along, following the wind, listening to the heartbeat in my ears...In the glow of daybreak--I now believe in the feeling of this one moment.
>
> Looking back at the sky, which has already turned yellow, I regret it is now daybreak. Perhaps I will let it all go. [20]

The MV by Eggshellsea, a Hong Kong animator, captures the images in the song. The protagonist ascends into the sky, where a train floats along, carrying him through the clouds, on a journey to another dimension. In the end, we see the protagonist back in real life, waking up from a slumber at his desk. In Lam's songs, one's random movement, whether it is wandering through nature, flying through the air, or simply walking the city in solitary enjoyment, breaks the brutal rhythms of life.

We have seen in the first group of songs discussed in this chapter, fear and despair are often results of an individual feeling--trapped in a place, whether it is one's bedroom, a strange planet, or a street corner. Terence Lam and Zpecial demonstrate that it is through deliberately insinuating one's presence, to take over, that individuals can turn a hostile or lonely place into "itineraries of pleasure." In Terence Lam's music and videos, he encourages his audience not just to re-explore their city, but to re-imagine it, using their magic wands, "to stretch out your hand to try out a spell," to transform it into a welcoming place. De Certeau argues, "The neighborhood is a dynamic notion requiring a progressive apprenticeship that grows with the repetition of the dweller's body's engagement in public space until it exercises a sort of appropriation of this space."[21] A hostile place will continue to remain hostile if it successfully convinces everyone to stay away from it.

## ***Msai gap, zeoiganjiu faai*** 唔使急最緊要快 No Need to Feel Rushed; The Most Important Thing Is to be Fast

In 2020, the urban scholar, Sampson Wong, and his collaborator, Eric Tsang, a photographer, created the YouTube channel, "*Waaiji jansang zau heoi saanbou* 懷疑人生就去散步 (*When in Doubt, Take a Walk*) (Lit: 'when you start questioning life, take a walk')."[22] Each of the 5–10-minute videos follows an individual's walk, passing by structures and buildings that are part of one's everyday life. These are sights one sees routinely yet does not notice. The films encourage their viewers to re-assess the familiar, re-examine their relationship with these places, and reclaim them. The channel later evolved to include individuals engaged in other solitary activities in their daily lives. The title of the channel was subsequently simplified to "*Waaiji jansang* (*When in Doubt*)." "When in doubt, have a cup of coffee," for example, is an 8-minute video, in which one watches the owner of the café, Brew Note Coffee Roaster, close up shop at the end of a business day, following his every step in real time.[23] Brew Note was a particularly iconic landmark in Hong

Kong's civic life. Opened in 2012, it was the site of many gatherings as a cultural salon, constantly hosting different kinds of events, from jazz performances to lectures, political discussions, and literary readings. The café, however, closed in December 2022, defeated by COVID. The video follows the owner, Vincent Hung, as he completes his various tasks, ending with him making a cup of coffee for himself. He painstakingly weighs out the grounds, then slowly and deliberately pours water over them. He then sits down to work through his day's correspondence, sipping his coffee. He finally switches off the lights and closes up shop. The audience then follows him as he walks out of his shop and strolls down the street on his way home. The activities in the film are accompanied by Watergold's 水金music. The video itself has now become a historic record of a particular aspect of the city's life before the NSL.

In a similar vein, in "When in Doubt, cook for oneself," the audience follows Iris, the focus of the film, cooking an elegant meal for herself. The audience watches her washing, cutting, and cooking, then finally sitting down to enjoy her lunch by a window.[24] In another 41-minute-long video, the audience virtually rides, with the individual in the film, the full journey on the Kowloon Canton Railway East Rail in real time. This journey was to commemorate one of the last trips of an older carriage model that was to be taken out of service.[25] All these videos are accompanied by environmental sounds—the whirr of a coffee maker, the rattling of the train—without a single word of dialogue.

While the world might have become hostile and alienating, slow, simple, quiet activities and rituals re-set the pace of life, making reality less oppressive. Pausing in the middle of a day to cook oneself a meal, or taking the train on an aimless journey, violates the everyday rhythm expressed by Hong Kong's favorite motto: *msai gap, zeoiganjiu faai* 唔使急最緊要快 (no need to feel rushed; the most important thing is to be fast).

## *Ngodei zanhai houlanzungji Hoenggong* 我哋真係好撚鍾意香港 We Really Fucking Love Hong Kong

It might seem ironic that it was at the height of Hong Kong's political and social transformation that many Hongkongers rediscovered their love for their city, flamboyantly declaring, "*ngodei zanhai houlanzungji Hoenggong* 我哋真係好撚鍾意香港 (We really fucking love HK)." The phrase originated on July 1, 2020, the day of the official implementation of the NSL. It was printed on a long banner, covering a section of the tramway during a mass demonstration on the day, the last Hong Kong may see for a very long time. Within hours the phrase spread through social media like wildfire.

The Hong Kong government has been rigorously promoting the idea of "*oi gong oi gok* (Love Hong Kong; love China)," especially after 2019. Like most four-character aphorisms, the phrase requires no subject. The Hong Kong version injects a specific, "we" in the phrase, using the Cantonese, "*ngo dei* 我哋 (we)," instead of "*ngo mun* 我們 (pinyin: women)," in standard Chinese. There is no ambiguity about who the subject of the sentence is. Instead of "oi愛 (pinyin: ai)," to denote "love," the Hong Kong vernacular version uses "*zungji* 鍾意." This has a slightly different connotation from the fervor and dedication implied in "love," instead expressing a much more informal feeling of affection and delight for their city. Moreover, the saying on the banner is laced with the expletive, "*lan* 撚 (fucking)," which is commonly used in the Hong Kong vernacular as an intensifier.

Much was expressed in this seemingly innocuous expression of love for the city. It captured Hongkongers' refusal of Beijing's demand of fealty and anger at its strategies of pacifying the city while asserting local culture and identity. The Cantonese used in the phrase not only captured the city's typically bawdy sense of humor, but it was also a deliberate contrast to the Hong Kong government officials' preference for an overly proper and ornate way of speaking that sounded more like slogans than regular speech (see Chapter 6). Of course, this rude declaration of affection for Hong Kong also contained a certain amount of sarcasm given the city's numerous intractable social and political problems. Nevertheless, for most people, the sentiment was sincere.

Sampson Wong said he had originally planned to make a video for each of Hong Kong's 18 districts for the series. He explained that his project was inspired by the phrase, "We really fucking love Hong Kong." The more he heard it, the more it made him think what it meant to him, and what people loved about the city. He said,

> Even though we know there are a lot of unpleasant things, such as lack of public space, and that a lot of apartments are actually subdivided flats, I still think that appreciating Hong Kong's built environment is one of the key points in discussing Hong Kong culture and loving Hong Kong.

He added, "Apart from its people, what I like about Hong Kong is its urban environment."[26] In the face of the narrowing of freedom of movement under COVID restrictions, when many public spaces like parks and city squares where crowds naturally gather were closed off, Wong's proposal of random walks, excavating different places beyond one's quotidian awareness, allowed one to recover a sense of ownership of the city.

Wong and his partner, Tsang, often point their lenses at the most mundane structures, such as a staircase that leads up to a pedestrian walkway, a wildly painted concrete children's playground, or even an unusually colorful parking garage. Some of these, especially the concrete public and institutional structures, are designed for absolute functionality. However, under Wong and Tsang's perspectives, even the most mundane crosswalks or pedestrian flyovers exude elegance and dignity. The initial films are all without dialogue, accompanied only by the quiet original music of Watergold. Wong pointed out,

> Hong Kong's urban environment is unique. One can see a lot in just a few steps. Everybody feels since they live here in Hong Kong, they already knows the city very well, but perhaps they are actually not that familiar with it.[27]

Wong hoped that these videos could also help the audience find, even if momentarily, relief from their daily anxieties. In a discussion with the political scientist, Simon Shen 沈旭暉, on Shen's YouTube Channel, Simon's Glocal Microcosm 堅離地球 *Gin lei deikau*, Wong pointed out that the *When in Doubt* YouTube channel was created in 2020 when bad news bombarded the public every day: 47 pro-democracy politicians were arrested, *Apple Daily* was shut down, and many high-profile activists were being processed through the judicial system. Wong wanted his films to offer an alternative perspective of the city. Walking alone was not the end goal. However, it could help one transcend the noise and turbulence, to find peace even in one's loneliest moments.[28] Wong's collaborator, Tsang, also argued,

> It is not to say that one will find answers or solutions after taking a walk. However, taking a walk is very straight forward. One can also, without much cost, understand the city more. These short films cannot solve the city's problems. But they open some doors, allowing one to pay attention to what is happening here. We feel that taking walks is a way to experience the city in freedom.[29]

These projects were also a response to Hong Kong's emigration tide after 2020. There were many reasons for someone to leave the city. However, Wong wanted to ask,

> What are the reasons to stay? One can see that the city is still beautiful. One can spot the things that make you love Hong Kong. Invite a friend to go take a walk with you, to look at something beautiful. That in itself provides a kind of peace. If we can turn this kind of peace into a short film, it might help us find relief from our troubles.[30]

In 2022, the popular singer, Panther Chan 陳蕾, issued her popular song, "*Saigaai jyu nei mou gwaan* 世界與你無關 (Embrace yourself, lit: The world has nothing to do with you)," for which she wrote the music and lyrics. The MV of her song was directed and produced by the team at *When in Doubt*. In this video, Chan said,

> Even though our lives have been affected by the pandemic, as long as we pay more attention to the things around us, [we will find that] our city is still very beautiful. Looking at these beautiful sceneries offers us a kind of comfort. To capture these in a short video can perhaps offer some solace.[31]

The MV shows Chan walking around Ap Lei Chau, a small island off Hong Kong Island. She wanders through the urban walkways and city streets, highlighting the austere beauty of the deserted neighborhood. She is then shown riding the ferry between the island and Aberdeen, on Hong Kong Island, crossing the tranquil harbor softly lit by distant lights. Her journey is accompanied by her music in which she sings,

> In this sick world, how does one anticipate the changes every day? There's nowhere to vent one's emotions. We are forced into battle mode, but inside, our hearts are broken. How do we undo all this? We know only to keep pushing forward, worried that if we are not careful, we'd become a burden. Our bodies will become weak.
>
> We don't dare to speak our minds, but we have bellies-full of bitterness. The sense of powerlessness has made you break down so many times that you feel you could die. In these moments, you are allowed to say to yourself: The world has nothing to do with you. You don't need to put the whole thousand-ton burden on your back. It is not easy to walk with a straight back...
>
> Hand in hand we give each other courage. Even though we feel lost in this red earth, it will only be momentary.
>
> The world has nothing to do with you. Let me share your burden. You are actually not alone...[32]

Zpecial's skateboarders, Terence Lam's solitary urban explorers, and the lone ramblers in the *When in Doubt* videos, all traverse through the city without any sense of constraints. All these activities are fundamentally about asserting freedom. At a time when much in the city seemed to be lost, walking provided some kind of social and political restitution. The walks were a form of reclaiming one's right to the city and asserting one's presence and sense of freedom within it. This sensation of freedom, whether physical or psychological, was in spite of the actual restraints of living in the city.

It goes without saying freedom was a fraught issue in Hong Kong. Politics aside, this sense of release from care, responsibilities, social expectations, and physical constraints eluded most people, especially many who lived with families in tiny spaces, caring for relatives and children, or entrapped in poorly paid work. Freedom was, and is, aspirational in Hong Kong. It was precisely the many political, physical, material, and mental inhibitions of living in the city that made these creative efforts speak to so many.

The NSL and COVID rules placed enormous constraints and burdens, both physical and psychological on the Hong Kong people. However, many have also shown that merely walking helped one recover one's relationship with the city. It was an assertion of ownership and belonging, helping to re-create a sense of neighborhood in the new alienating reality. Walking established awareness of the backdrops to one's daily life, while mapping new spaces forgotten or hidden in official cartography—spaces of freedom.

## Notes

1 Jip Cau-jin葉秋弦, "明天之後After Tomorrow," *P-articles*, July 3, 2022, https://p-articles.com/works/3080.html.

2 Ibid.

3 Ibid.

4 3Think享樂團, "到世界塌下 Till the world collapses," music by Kiu@Hoengloktun, lyrics by Norris Wong, Wave Music, 2020, www.youtube.com/watch?v=oBm6E2w86EQ.
5 The viral popularity of a "picnic concern group" that advocated dining al fresco instead of using the vaccine pass required to enter restaurants was only one indication of a general suspicion about the true use of the pass (see Chapter 1).
6 Saiseichu再生中, "呼吸自由To Breathe," music by KTsang, lyrics by Juk-lung, 欲龍, 2021, www.youtube.com/watch?v=HULN6j1RfZ0.
7 "香港迎來由治及興新時代 Hong Kong welcomes the age of 'from governance to prosperity'," News.gov.hk, December 29, 2021, www.news.gov.hk/chi/2021/12/20211229/20211229_204003_308.html.
8 The Chinese title, "jiu" can mean monsters and goblins. It is also the homophone of a Cantonese slang to express disgust.
9 The Hertz, featuring Serrini, "妖Fairy Godmonster," music by Him Hui @ The Hertz and Herman @ The Hertz, lyrics by Leung Ka Yan梁嘉茵, 2021.
10 Rubberband, "百毒不侵 Immune to a hundred poisons," music by RubberBand & 雷柏熹 Lui Paak-hei, lyrics by RubberBand & 雷柏熹 & Tim Lui, R Flat, 2020, www.youtube.com/watch?v=iW0HIMAgU98.
11 Novel Flash, "Every Night," beat produced by Vino Ramaldo, lyrics by Novel Flash, SpongeMob852, 2021, www.youtube.com/watch?v=cEIpZcR3BZg.
12 BMW, "大概我們每個人都寂寞 Perhaps every one of us feels just as lonely," music and lyrics by BMW, Greytone Music, 2021, www.youtube.com/watch?v=W7kVOVKCmCs.
13 The Hertz, "漂流號 UC428)," music by Ricky Wu @ The Hertz, Herman @ The Hertz, lyrics by 阿檸, 2021, www.youtube.com/watch?v=OvwbZaVtmr4.
14 Cath Wong, "我心中尚未崩壞的部分 The unbroken part of me," music by Cath Wong and Terence Lam, lyrics by Chow Yiu Fai, Sony Music, 2020, www.youtube.com/watch?v=pgBrUu636co.
15 Henri Lefebvre, *Rhythmanalysis: Space, Time and Everyday Life* (London, Bloomsbury, 2015), 68.
16 Zpecial, "深夜告別練習 Practicing saying goodbye in the middle of the night," music by Zpecial and Lai Ying Tong賴映彤, lyrics by Oscar Li, Pure Music Ltd. 2020, www.youtube.com/watch?v=dVgmEuwMPxo.
17 Michel de Certeau, Luce Giard, and Pierre Mayol, Translated by Timothy J. Tomasik, *The Practice of Everyday Life*, Vol 2. (Minnesota, University of Minnesota Press, 1998), 10–11.
18 Terence Lam, "一人之境 Solitude," music and lyrics by Terence Lam, Terence Lam Production & Co., 2020a, www.youtube.com/watch?v=qWhavDVsMRc.
19 Terence Lam, "特倫斯夢遊仙境 Wonderland," music by Terrence Lam, lyrics by Oscar Li, Terrence Lam Production & Co., 2020b, www.youtube.com/watch?v=qWhavDVsMRc&list=RDqWhavDVsMRc&start_radio=1.
20 Terence Lam, "在空中的這一秒 This second in the air," music and lyrics by Terence Lam, Terence Lam Production & Co. 2021, www.youtube.com/watch?v=jZrDc9HDfx0.
21 Ibid.
22 When in Doubt, www.youtube.com/@doubtwalk.
23 "喝手沖咖啡--北角咖啡店店主收舖後的寧靜時光 (feat. Brew Note) (Drink a cup of hand brewed coffee—the quiet time when café owner in Northpoint close up shop)," When in Doubt, March 23, 2022, video, 8.10, www.youtube.com/watch?v=rtJZ6pV4iok
24 "懷疑人生就自己煮：豚汁、櫻葉飯團 | 日式午後家常料理 (When in doubt cook for oneself: pork stew, cherry leaves rice balls—Common Japanese style homecooked

lunch)," When in Doubt, May 20, 2022, video, 6.33, www.youtube.com/watch?v=1evd144k_sU.

25 "送別十二卡車烏蠅頭 一鏡直落, 紅磡坐到上水, 40分鐘的一程告別 (feat. 林兆榮) (Sending off the twelve carriage 'bug head'(Mid-Life Refurbishment Train)—one shot from Hunghum to Sheung Shui, 40 minutes of farewell trip, featuring Swing Lam)," When in Doubt, May 7, 2022, video, 40.58, www.youtube.com/watch?v=rlZrKfuRW3k.

26 Candice Chau, "When in doubt, take a walk:' artist Sampson Wong seeks beauty in Hong Kong's urban jungle," Hong Kong Free Press, 20 June 2021, https://hongkongfp.com/2021/06/20/when-in-doubt-take-a-walk-artist-sampson-wong-seeks-beauty-in-hong-kongs-urban-jungle/

27 Wong Hiu-ting黃曉婷, "懷疑人生就去散步--從平凡市景找回對香港的愛When one doubts one's life, go take walk—Rediscovering one's love for Hong Kong through ordinary city scenes." (It was originally published on March 26, 2022, *Apple Daily Taiwan Online*, www.tw.feature.appledaily.com, now removed.)

28 Simon Shen沈旭暉, "懷疑人生就去散步 黃宇軒：藝文界面對「香港文革」，如何自處? (When in Doubt, Take a Walk. Wong Yu-Hin: Confronted with a 'Hong Kong Cultural Revolution,' what does the cultural world do?)" 堅離地球Simon's Glocal Microcosm, Episode 129, April 15, 2021, video, 30.38, www.youtube.com/watch?v=zsKOyaKvM-0.

29 Candice Chau.

30 Ibid.

31 www.youtube.com/watch?v=fN6eXrbxQFI.

32 陳蕾 Panther Chan, "世界與你無關 Embrace Yourself," Warner Music, 2022, www.youtube.com/watch?v=fN6eXrbxQFI.

## References

33Think享樂團, "到世界塌下 Till the world collapses." Music by Kiu@Hoengloktun, lyrics by Norris Wong. Wave Music, 2020. www.youtube.com/watch?v=oBm6E2w86EQ.

BMW. "大概我們每個人都寂寞 Perhaps every one of us feels just as lonely." Music and lyrics by BMW. Greytone Music, 2021. www.youtube.com/watch?v=W7kVOVKCmCs.

Chan, Panther 陳蕾. "世界與你無關 Embrace yourself." Music and lyrics by Panther Chan. Warner Music, 2022. www.youtube.com/watch?v=fN6eXrbxQFI.

Chau, Candice. "When in doubt, take a walk: Artist Sampson Wong seeks beauty in Hong Kong's urban jungle." Hong Kong Free Press, June 20, 2021. https://hongkongfp.com/2021/06/20/when-in-doubt-take-a-walk-artist-sampson-wong-seeks-beauty-in-hong-kongs-urban-jungle/.

De Certeau, Michel, Luce Giard, and Pierre Mayol, trans. by Timothy J. Tomasik. *The Practice of Everyday Life*, vol 2. Minnesota: University of Minnesota Press, 1998.

Jip Cau-jin 葉秋弦. "明天之後After tomorrow." *P-articles*, July 3, 2022. https://p-articles.com/works/3080.html.

Lam, Terence. "一人之境 Solitude." Muisc and Lyrics by Terence Lam. Terence Lam Production & Co., 2020a. www.youtube.com/watch?v=qWhavDVsMRc.

Lam, Terence. "特倫斯夢遊仙境 Wonderland." Music by Terrence Lam, lyrics by Oscar Li, Terrence Lam Production & Co., 2020b. www.youtube.com/watch?v=qWhavDVsMRc&list=RDqWhavDVsMRc&start_radio=1.

Lam, Terence. "在空中的這一秒 This second in the air." Music and lyrics by Terence Lam. Terence Lam Production & Co., 2021. www.youtube.com/watch?v=jZrDc9HDfx0.

Lefebvre, Henri. *Rhythmanalysis: Space, Time and Everyday Life*. London: Bloomsbury, 2015.

Novel Flash. "Every Night." Beat produced by Vino Ramaldo, lyrics by Novel Flash. SpongeMob852, 2021. www.youtube.com/watch?v=cEIpZcR3BZg.

Rubberband. "百毒不侵 Immune to a hundred poisons." Music by RubberBand and 雷柏熹 Lui Paak-hei, lyrics by RubberBand and 雷柏熹 and Tim Lui. R Flat, 2020. www.youtube.com/watch?v=iW0HIMAgU98.

Saiseichu再生中. "呼吸自由To Breathe." Music by KTsang, lyrics by Juk-lung, 欲龍. 2021. www.youtube.com/watch?v=HULN6j1RfZ0.

Shen, Simon沈旭暉. "懷疑人生就去散步 黃宇軒：藝文界面對「香港文革」，如何自處? When in Doubt, Take a Walk. Wong Yu-Hin: Confronted with a 'Hong Kong Cultural Revolution,' what does the cultural world do?" 堅離地球Simon's Glocal Microcosm, Episode 129. April 15, 2021. Video, 30.38. www.youtube.com/watch?v=zsKOyaKvM-0.

The Hertz, featuring Serrini. "妖Fairy Godmonster." Music by Him Hui @ The Hertz and Herman @ The Hertz, lyrics by Leung Ka Yan梁嘉茵. 2021. www.youtube.com/watch?v=CQlkHi9tLHo.

The Hertz. "漂流號 UC428." Music by Ricky Wu @ The Hertz, Herman @ The Hertz, lyrics by 阿檸. 2021. www.youtube.com/watch?v=OvwbZaVtmr4.

Wong, Cath. "我心中尚未崩壞的部分 The unbroken part of me," music by Cath Wong and Lam, Terence. lyrics by Chow Yiu Fai. Sony Music, 2020. www.youtube.com/watch?v=pgBrUu636co.

Wong Hiu-ting 黃曉婷. "懷疑人生就去散步--從平凡市景找回對香港的愛When one doubts one's life, go take walk—Rediscovering one's love for Hong Kong through ordinary city scenes." *Apple Daily Taiwan Online*, Originally published on March 26, 2022. www.tw.feature.appledaily.com (now defunct).

Zpecial. "深夜告別練習 Practicing saying goodbye in the middle of the night." Music by Zpecial and Lai Ying Tong 賴映彤, lyrics by Oscar Li. Pure Music Ltd., 2020. www.youtube.com/watch?v=dVgmEuwMPxo.

"香港迎來由治及興新時代 Hong Kong welcomes the age of 'from governance to prosperity'." News.gov.hk, December 29, 2021. www.news.gov.hk/chi/2021/12/20211229/20211229_204003_308.html.

"喝手沖咖啡--北角咖啡店店主收舖後的寧靜時光 (feat. Brew Note) (Drink a cup of hand brewed coffee—the quiet time when café owner in Northpoint close up shop)." When in Doubt, March 23, 2022. Video, 8.10. www.youtube.com/watch?v=rtJZ6pV4iok

"懷疑人生就自己煮：豚汁、櫻葉飯團 | 日式午後家常料理 (When in doubt cook for oneself: pork stew, cherry leaves rice balls—Common Japanese style homecooked lunch)." When in Doubt, May 20, 2022. Video, 6.33. www.youtube.com/watch?v=1evd144k_sU.

"送別十二卡車烏蠅頭 | 一鏡直落, 紅磡坐到上水, 40分鐘的一程告別 (feat. 林兆榮) (Sending off the twelve carriage 'bug head'(Mid-Life Refurbishment Train)—one shot from Hunghum to Sheung Shui, 40 minutes of farewell trip (featuring Swing Lam)." When in Doubt, May 7, 2022. Video, 40.58. www.youtube.com/watch?v=rlZrKfuRW3k.

# 8 The Campaign to Tell the Hong Kong Story Well

## Dung Kai Cheung's Novel *Hong Kong Letters* and the Reinvention of Hong Kong's Story

On April 21, 2022, the outgoing Hong Kong Chief Executive, Carrie Lam, wrote on her social media, "In order for Hong Kong to strengthen and raise its international position and competitiveness on important international or regional platforms, one must 'tell the Hong Kong story well (*gong hou Hoenggong gusi* 講好香港故事)'..."[1] A day later, in his election ad posted on his campaign website, the incoming Hong Kong Chief Executive, John Lee, was also quoted saying, "We must tell the Hong Kong story well, advertising to the different regions abroad and the mainland, Hong Kong's strengths and opportunities, and new economic activities, to attract people to Hong Kong."[2] After a couple of years of international PR disasters because of the protests, their violent suppression, and the implementation of the NSL, culminating with a raging COVID wave in 2022, when images of elderly patients lying in the cold in parking lots of inundated hospitals were flashed around in world media, Hong Kong's chiefs were desperate to revamp the city's image and reassure the international community that the city was safe again for business. An even more crucial task for the Hong Kong government was to make sure that the city's narrative was aligned with China's national self-representation. The Hong Kong story needed to be reconstructed.

Much of the creation of a new Hong Kong story involved erasing what was deemed inappropriate. In 2021, the Hong Kong government "updated" the Film Censorship Ordinance "to ensure more effective fulfilment of the duty to safeguard national security as required by the National Security Law, to prevent and suppress acts or activities that may endanger national security."[3] As a result, several documentaries and feature films on the 2014 Umbrella Revolution and the 2019 Anti-Legislation protest were banned from public viewing in Hong Kong. Among these was the documentary, *Sidoi gaakming* 時代革命 (*Revolution of Our Times*), directed by Kiwi Chow.[4] Another film banned in Hong Kong was *Siunin* 少年 (*May You Stay Forever Young*), by directors, Rex Ren and Lam Sum, set during the 2019 protest. The updated film ordinance ensured that these stories would not be told in the city.

With the various laws in place and the opposition destroyed, lawmakers seemed satisfied that order had been re-established. All that was left to do was to put a positive spin on the city. In an essay, published in *Wen Wei Po*, the Chinese state-owned

DOI: 10.4324/9781003521280-9

newspaper in Hong Kong, titled, "The Media should eliminate the turbid and uphold the pure and aim to tell the Hong Kong story well," Legislative Council member, Lo Wai-kwok, wrote,

> Hong Kong is just entering the critical stage of going from order to prosperity. Hong Kong's media workers should increase cooperation and support for the SAR government, to actualize Hong Kong's "One Country Two Systems," to integrate it into the big picture of the nation's development and success story, and broadly advertising and promoting it abroad. To tell Hong Kong's story well is also a significant part of telling China's story well. It has the benefit of facilitating the "return of hearts," encouraging Hong Kong people to enthusiastically integrate into the big picture of the nation's development.[5]

Lawmaker, Regina Ip, convener of the Hong Kong Executive Council, also believed that

> After being bashed in the Western media since Beijing took decisive measures to restore national security and political order, Hong Kong's image overseas had been tarnished by continuous negative portrayals. There was a dire need to repair and reburnish Hong Kong's image overseas.[6]

This idea that Hong Kong needed a better narrative or a better image to make it once again an attractive destination for multinationals and international investors was behind the Hong Kong government's decision to rebrand the city. After major local and international public relations companies refused the commission, the Hong Kong government finally hired the British firm, *Consulum*, an agency that, according to *The Guardian*, "has been criticised for representing some governments and leaders that other businesses would not touch."[7] A year and USD5.7 million later, *Consulum* finally produced the result of their research for the new "Brand Hong Kong." However, even Ip was underwhelmed by it:

> The positive 'messages' developed by the consultant which were found to have gone down well in our target markets – 'cosmopolitan, diverse, dynamic and connected' – are, to say the least, mundane and unsurprising. These are attributes which can be easily identified by the Trade Development Council, Invest Hong Kong, and the Tourism Board after sounding out their clients in our major markets.[8]

Mak Mei-kuen, a Legislative Council member, also commented,

> They said Hong Kong was the only city which has three special characteristics, those were the link with the mainland and Asian markets, a comprehensive and convenient business environment, and a cosmopolitan lifestyle. I can tell you all of these things without having spent HK$40 million.[9]

To tell Hong Kong's story well is to harmonize it with China's own national narrative as a global superpower. Within this framework, many aspects of Hong Kong's history became inconvenient. In 2022, a new series of textbooks was created to teach children a revised history of the city. School children would learn that Hong Kong was never a British colony. The British merely "exercised colonial rule" over it. These textbooks, together with a course designed to replace the old "Liberal Studies," which had been blamed for teaching radical ideas and causing rebelliousness among young people in recent years, would instill patriotic feelings toward China and teach them how to be law-abiding citizens (see Chapter 3).

The astonishing claim that Hong Kong was never a British colony was based on two arguments. First, no Chinese government after the Qing dynasty had recognized the unequal treaties that ceded Hong Kong to the British in 1842. Second, in 1971, China officially contested Hong Kong's status as a colony at the United Nations. At the time, according to "The Declaration on the Granting of Independence to Colonial Countries and Peoples, the United Nations General Assembly Resolution 1514," adopted by the UN General Assembly on December 14, 1960, Hong Kong and Macao, as British and Portuguese colonies, respectively, had the right to seek independence. By challenging these territories' colonial status, China short-circuited this possibility. In 2020, an essay in *China Daily*, the English-language newspaper of the Publicity Department of the Chinese Communist Party, explained this history:

> Soon after the People's Republic of China took over the country's seat at the United Nations in October 1971, it wrote to the UN Special Committee on Decolonization and solemnly declared that both Hong Kong and Macao are Chinese territories that were occupied by the UK and Portugal respectively under a series of unequal treaties they had forced the Qing Dynasty's rulers to sign. The letter also states that resolving the questions of Hong Kong and Macao is a matter within China's sovereignty; the two cities must not be treated as "colonies" in the usual sense of the word. A month later, the UN General Assembly passed a resolution by a vote of 99–5 that removed Hong Kong and Macao from the list of existing colonies. By doing so, China reconfirmed a historical fact and reaffirmed its sovereignty beyond a reasonable doubt.[10]

This essay laid the groundwork for the revision of history 2 years later. *Global Times*, another Chinese state-owned English language daily tabloid, published a piece with an interview with Fan Hsu Lai-tai in June 2022, regarding this issue of Hong Kong's colonial status. Fan was a former member of the Hong Kong government before becoming a member of the Standing Committee of the National People's Congress in 2008:

> In 1972, Chinese representatives to the UN put forward that Hong Kong and Macao were not colonies, which was opposed by the US and UK, and that's why they constantly claimed that Hong Kong was a colony. However, if we were a colony, we would have been able to declare "independence" and have our own

nationality and culture. "But the fact is Hong Kong people are Chinese, and our culture is Chinese culture," Fan said.[11]

Fan's rhetoric was in line with China's official racialist discourse that in recent years has emphasized not only a Han-centric idea of Chineseness but also the idea that all Chinese are bound by racial blood ties.[12] By doing so, she discounted over 8% of Hong Kong's residents (officially defined as those who own a Hong Kong permanent residence card) who are not of Han Chinese descent.[13] Study after study has shown that despite 20 years of patriotic inculcation in the city, this essentialist notion of Chineseness has failed to take root among Hong Kong's residents.[14]

A few days after Hong Kong's citizens learned that their city had actually never been a British colony, news also broke, to their horror, that the iconic floating restaurant, Jumbo, had sunk while being relocated (see also Chapter7). The company that owned Jumbo, the Aberdeen Restaurant Enterprises, said the restaurant had become a financial liability. The several years of COVID restrictions as the Hong Kong government quixotically pursued "Zero Covid" in the city finally made it untenable for its parent company to continue to operate it. Jumbo was to be towed and parked at an undisclosed destination. However, it was caught in a storm at sea, severely damaged, and sank. Details of exactly what happened were murky. Aberdeen Restaurant Enterprises kept giving vague accounts.

Jumbo was iconic for many reasons. It was the largest of Hong Kong's floating restaurants and had been in operation for over 40 years in the Aberdeen typhoon shelter. It was one of the most famous tourist destinations. But it was also a place for local celebrations and was part of the history of Hong Kong's native communities of fisherfolks. It had an indelible place in Hong Kong people's collective memories and a significant position in the city's colonial culture, both visual and symbolic. Aside from being the backdrop of numerous popular Hong Kong films, Jumbo was also featured in *The Man with the Golden Gun* (1974), from one of the most iconic British popular cultural enterprises, the James Bond franchise. It also appeared in the films, *Love Is a Many-Splendored Thing* (1955), based on Han Suyin's novel, and *The World of Suzie Wong* (1960), based on Richard Mason's novel. These movies and films were unambiguously colonial products, illustrating the gender and power dynamics in colonial relationships through the depictions of British or American men and their Hong Kong love interests. Jumbo, ornately decorated, fully embodied oriental kitsch. As such, it provided a perfect backdrop for these stories that were redolent of colonial exoticism. Fittingly, it also once hosted the British monarch, Elizabeth II. As a result, to many Hongkongers, Jumbo's sinking was symbolic of the loss of Hong Kong's relationship with Britain, together with all the social and political values and systems that such association represented.

Jumbo began operating at a loss in 2013. In order to preserve the structure, in her 2020 Policy Address, the then Chief Executive, Carrie Lam, touted a new scheme called "Invigorating Island South." This was an urban renewal project in the Southern District of Hong Kong, which included the Aberdeen Typhoon Shelter, where Jumbo was parked, as well as, Ocean Park, an oceanarium and amusement park nearby. As part of the scheme, the Aberdeen Restaurant Enterprises agreed to donate Jumbo, which Lam called a historic landmark of significant heritage value to the city, to Ocean Park.[15] However, in 2022, when it was first reported that Jumbo's future had become uncertain because the deal with Ocean Park had fallen through, the government expressed little interest in interceding to save it, despite public outcry and lobbying by district councilors and several Legislative Council members. Lam acknowledged that the original plan had collapsed, but argued,

> We won't force through an unfeasible proposal or one that requires a large amount of public money for implementation simply because it has been raised in the policy address. I find this situation to be of no problem at all.[16]

However, since Jumbo was to have such a central role in the Island South revitalization scheme, the project was now greatly reduced. The Island South district councilor, Jonathan Leung, urged the government to subsidize the maintenance of Jumbo, otherwise, "The government should also explain to the public how it is going to proceed with its 'Invigorating Island South campaign' or tell us if Jumbo is no longer part of the project."[17]

Often critical of the Hong Kong government's track record in its many redevelopment projects around the city, Chloe Lai, a writer at *Hong Kong Free Press*, postulated that the government did not care about the loss of Jumbo because their concern had never been about historic preservation: "By abandoning a cultural icon in the name of adding no financial burden to Ocean Park, the government lays bare that Invigorating Island South is a government-led gentrification scheme with no regards to history, culture or communities."[18]

It is not surprising that *Hong Kong Free Press*, a generally liberal independent press, would publish a critical piece about the urban renewal project. However, a similar opinion was also expressed in *HK01*, a Hong Kong pro-Beijing news media. In a piece written just before news of Jumbo's demise, commentator, Tong Man-Si 湯文詩, urged the government to save the floating restaurant, as Jumbo was the main justification for the revitalization project: "When the plan lacks human and historical basis, it is very easy for it to become a purely for-profit project. The revitalization of the factory buildings in the area will only accelerate the gentrification of the district."[19]

Tong especially took to task Kevin Yeung, the former Secretary of Education, and later appointed head of the new Culture, Sports and Tourism Bureau in 2022. In his new position, Yeung claimed that he would "tell the Hong Kong Story well," and "help Hong Kong develop its potential as a city of culture, a city for special events, and a city of tourism, and to further increase the residents' knowledge of culture and history."[20] Tong argued that all these would only be possible if the material aspects of this culture and history could be preserved:

> However, the famous destination, the Jumbo floating restaurant, actually got towed out of Hong Kong and ended up sinking to the bottom of the ocean. This floating restaurant had contained the collective memories of the city's residents. Also, it had a lot of cultural value. Not only did it appear in a lot

> of television and films, but it was also the largest and the most luxurious floating restaurant in the world, representing Hong Kong's achievements in the 1970s, the era of financial take-off. It was an important resource for the tourist industry. That the floating seafood restaurant should end up like this, aside from sighing from sadness, many also wonder about the competence of a certain government department that led to the failure of the original plan of handing over the floating restaurant to the Ocean Park under the "Invigorating Island South scheme."

Having failed to secure Hong Kong's material culture, Tong asked, "How is the government going to tell the Hong Kong story well?"[21]

## Which Hong Kong Story?

Many considered the sinking of Jumbo as yet another example of how little the current Hong Kong government cared about local historical culture. Conspiracy theories abounded regarding what actually happened to Jumbo in the high seas and why it sank. Many suspected that it was precisely because Jumbo was such a powerful symbol of Hong Kong's colonial past, contravening Beijing's "Hong Kong Story," that the government was happy to rid the city of it. By the same logic, some suggested that if the city had never been a British colony, Jumbo would not have much significance as a unique colonial icon, and therefore did not deserve to be saved.

This was not the first time the Hong Kong (SAR) government had destroyed significant colonial-era structures. The earliest of Hong Kong's collective attempts to save a structure, albeit unsuccessfully, was in 2007. When the government decided to demolish the Queen's Pier in Central for a land reclamation project, it provoked fierce opposition from preservationists. The public pier was opened in 1925, mostly used by pleasure crafts. However, its chief function was ceremonial. All of Hong Kong's governors officially landed in the colony at the pier. Queen Elizabeth II and various members of the British royal family, in their state visits to Hong Kong, also symbolically disembarked there. It was an unambiguous symbol of Hong Kong's colonial history.[22]

Generally, the decision to preserve a building or structure depends on the evaluation and recommendation of the Antiquities Advisory Board of the Antiquities and Monuments Office established in 1976. Historic buildings in the city are graded for appropriate conservation action, whether for revitalization, restoration, or adaptive reuse. However, according to John Ye, the Hong Kong Antiquities Advisory Board had been refusing to carry out grading assessments of structures built after 1970 based on a 2013 ruling. Ye argued,

> Hong Kong's policies towards antiquities and the government's unwillingness to support preservation efforts have had a devastating effect on local culture. The departure of the Jumbo Floating Restaurant would be a sad continuation of the trend of post-World-War-II local history disappearing–leaving gaps in

the city's historical landscape, with only pre-war structures and contemporary buildings for future generations.[23]

Hong Kong's status as an East Asian economic power took off in the 1970s. The 1970s is also the beginning of the development of a unique Hong Kong culture and distinct local identity. It was a result of the expansion of local political participation as well as the flourishing of the entertainment industry. Furthermore, compared to the constant political and economic chaos of China at that time, the increasingly more affluent and liberal society in Hong Kong resulted in its residents' growing sense of distance and difference from their mainland counterparts.[24] Hong Kong in the 1970s is a problematic period as far as China is concerned. Jumbo, an icon of the 1970s, had little to contribute to the new patriotic narrative.

## Chinese Ethnicity vs Chinese Nationality

Whether or not China has maintained continuous possession of Hong Kong, the reality remains that Beijing's presence in the city was negligible till after 2000. Whether or not the British merely had an administrative presence in the city, the reality remains that much of Hong Kong's city space and everyday life have been inflected by its colonial experience. There are streets and structures named after British governors, tycoons, philanthropists, and the royal family. There are schools operated by the Anglican church. The Court of Final Appeal is housed in a quintessential colonial building designed by the British architects, Sir Aston Webb and Ingress Bell, who also designed the Buckingham Palace. The Hong Kong diet is influenced by British taste as is the habit of taking afternoon tea. Much of Hong Kong's social organization still retains the imprint of the British, from the system of social housing to social medicine.

Whether as British colonial subjects or as subjects of the Chinese government, Hong Kong people had never completely identified with their rulers. They were never British in the past. Many didn't consider themselves "Chinese" under the new regime. The majority was always just Hongkongers. A poll by the Hong Kong Public Opinion Research Institute (PORI) from May to June 2022 on individuals' "strength rating of being Chinese" yielded an average of 6.5, with 10 being extremely strong and 0 extremely weak.[25] This result was recorded a few months after the 2022 Beijing Winter Olympics. These international sporting events usually inspire a rise in nationalistic feelings. Indeed, the average was up from 5.7, in the previous study published on June 10, 2020. The last time the rating went up to 8 was in 2008, the year of the Beijing Summer Olympics.

From another angle, the survey also reveals that 75.45 of Hong Kong people identified themselves as "Hongkongers" (rather than Chinese citizens). It should come as no surprise that the older residents had closer identification with China. Among the 18–29-year-olds, however, only 2% identified themselves as "Chinese." This figure is actually the highest since 2018. The rise in identification with China was particularly evident among the 30–49 age group, because, according to the commentator, Derek Yuan, "These people recognise this is China's international financial centre." He points out, "In order to survive, prosper and thrive…you have to adjust your mindset."[26] Furthermore, because of the mass emigration since 2020, those who were most strongly anti-China would have already left the city, boosting the percentage of those who self-identified as Chinese. The NSL could also have an impact on the survey findings. Those who most identified with China would feel more comfortable responding to the survey. Those who didn't, for safety concerns, might have abstained from participation, or might not have been totally truthful in their responses, thus skewing the results.[27] Indeed, the response rate of the poll was only 39.8% compared to 71.6% in 2016, for example.[28]

Also of interest was how Hongkongers understood the idea of "Chineseness." The 2021 Hong Kong census indicates the city's population as 91.6% Chinese in terms of "ethnicity." This category is self-reported. In the case of the census, ethnicity is understood as representing one's ancestral origin, resulting in "certain" phenotypical characteristics. However, in the 2022 PORI poll, the majority of Hong Kong people refused the identity category, "Ethnic identity of being Chinese." In the context of the PORI poll, "Chineseness" was associated with national and cultural characteristics. When politicians like Fan said, "Hong Kong people are Chinese, and our culture is Chinese culture," they failed to appreciate, or more likely, deliberately ignored, the nuances of how Hongkongers understood the idea of "Chineseness."

## De-HongKongification

When Hong Kong's chief executives declared the necessity to tell Hong Kong's story well, what they meant was to tell Beijing's version of Hong Kong's story well. In 2022, Hong Kong's TVB and China's Mango TV jointly produced the television program, *Sing sang bat sik* 聲生不息 (*Infinity and Beyond, Endless Melody*), as part of the commemoration of the 25th Anniversary of Hong Kong's "Return" to China. The program aimed to celebrate the history of Hong Kong's Cantopop, which, in its prime from the 1970s to the 1990s, exerted tremendous influence on Asia's popular culture. The program invited many of Hong Kong's biggest Cantopop stars of that era to sing some of the most iconic songs. The oldest among these were in their 60s and 70s. Most of them had been working exclusively in China and no longer even had much of an audience in Hong Kong. Though the program generated much interest in China, it languished in the ratings in Hong Kong, for many reasons. This program, about the "history" of Cantopop, music particular to Hong Kong, seemed to be signaling that Cantopop was a thing of the past. The song list went through rigorous vetting and excluded most of the recent popular songs and performers despite Cantopop's revival in 2021. It is impossible to compile a list of the most representative Cantopop songs without including those with lyrics from the two most important and prolific lyricists, Lam Zik 林夕 and Wyman Wong 黃偉文. However, they were deemed so politically problematic that their names could not be mentioned in China. As a result, the program simply listed the lyricist as "Anonymous" whenever a song with their lyrics was performed. Some songs were even sung with the lyrics altered.

The program referred to Cantopop as *gong ngok* 港樂 (Hong Kong music), an alien term to Hong Kong people, who refer to their music as *gwongdunggo* 廣東歌 or *jyutjyu lauhangkuk* 粵語流行曲 (popular songs in Cantonese). In Hong Kong, *Gongngok* is the abbreviated name of *Hoenggong gunjin ngoktyun* 香港管弦樂團 (The Hong Kong Philharmonic Orchestra). To refer to Cantopop as *gongngok* reflects a not-so-innocent agenda. Calling this music *gongngok* reduces Cantopop to a Chinese local and domestic phenomenon even though the development of Cantopop has nothing to do with China's music industry and at its peak, it had a very broad international reach. As the commentator, Siu Tin 小田, points out, even though a program that specifically focuses on Hong Kong's music seems to be a celebration of Hong Kong culture, in effect, it works to further contain the Hong Kong narrative:

> the program attempts to define *gongngok* as a type of regional Chinese culture. The showcasing of the voice of Hong Kong people is to filter out impurities, to tailor it and make it conform to a greater national narrative. This is to say, the more the program emphasizes the uniqueness of *gongngok*, the more it is to connect it with the Chinese dominant culture and national identity. This explains this program's startling reference to *gongngok* as an 'amazing Chinese product' and 'made in China.'"[29]

The representation of "Hong Kong" in mainland China had undergone a treatment of "de-HongKongfication." In 2019, the central government presented an "Outline Development Plan for the Guangdong-Hong Kong-Macao-Greater Bay Area" that Xi Jinping had "personally planned, personally deployed, personally pushed forward." Officials started to promote the name, "Greater Bay Area," "to emphasize the integration of Hong Kong with Macao and the Pearl River Delta's nine cities, using the propagation power of entertainment programs to promote it."[30] Siu Tin explains, "In recent years, 'Hong Kong' has become a sensitive term that cannot be used carelessly." He adds that if a Hong Kong artist said he or she was from Hong Kong and not "China, Hong Kong," or "the Greater Bay Area," he or she would be lambasted by social media warriors from China.[31] Performers from Hong Kong and Taiwan had to sign pledges to identify themselves only as "Chinese," not Hongkonger or Taiwanese, and to engage only in "politically correct" speech.[32] This included not only not mentioning words such as "democracy," "independence," or "freedom" while in China, but even while they were in their home territories or in other parts of the world.

## Hong Kong's Typography

The representation of the city and Hong Kong people's self-identity, as we have seen in the response to the sinking of Jumbo, is also made up of different aspects of the city's material culture. One of the most visible characteristics of Hong Kong as a city is the lettering on business marquees and public signs. Of these, the most recognizable and famous are those made of neon tubes fabricated by craftsmen into different designs and letterings. They tell a particular story of the city. These neon signs are a record of the commercial and everyday culture of the city, advertising local restaurants and entertainment establishments, everyday consumer goods, and services. They have defined Hong Kong's nighttime cityscape for close to a century. Illuminating the city at night, they became ever more fanciful and creative in the 1970s and 1980s, earning the city the sobriquet, the "Pearl of Orient," at the time. The brilliant tableau created by these signs has been immortalized in many iconic films. However, because of new safety regulations and urban redevelopment, these signs are now fast disappearing, replaced by signs with LEDs and generic computer-generated fonts.

Even though many of the neon signs could not be saved, the typography used in the signs' lettering received renewed interest. The letterings of these signs are written in traditional complex characters in a font called *Hoenggong bakngaitai* 香港北魏體 (Hong Kong Northern Wei Type), which is particular to the city. The use of complex characters in itself distinguishes Hong Kong from all the other mainland Chinese cities where simplified characters are used in writing. The particular font, Hong Kong Northern Wei, was developed in Hong Kong as a result of many practical considerations involved in sign-making—a combination of clarity, distinctiveness, and expressivity. Most of the old signs were based on the work of a handful of master calligraphers and their apprentices in the twentieth century.

The fonts of traffic and road signs also gained attention and became subjects of investigation. An organization, the Road Research Society, established in 2016, documented the special fonts used on these signs, especially the "*GaamJuk Tai*監獄體 (Prison Gothic Type)," now also being phased out by computer-generated fonts.[33] As the name implies, this particular font was created by prisoners who used to hand-paint road signs as part of their prison work.

This attention to font type is also reflected in an exhibition jointly presented by the Hong Kong Heritage Museum and the Hong Kong Open Print Shop, "Between the Lines—The Legends of Hong Kong Printing," from October 2020 to July 2021. The exhibition presented the history of the *Hong Kong Type* 香港字, the particular set of Chinese letters used in a movable lead typeface that was created in Hong Kong.

The letterings and font types used around the city, distinguish it visually and aesthetically from other cities, even Chinese-speaking cities, such as Taipei or Kaohsiung that also use traditional complex characters. Hong Kong fonts and typography embody the city's stories in their development and history. They also represent the city visually and, in this sense, they literally, articulate the Hong Kong story.

## *Hoenggongzi* 香港字 The Hong Kong Type

The fonts on street signs are not only for conveying information in the city. Chosen for these tasks because of their aesthetic quality and communicative power, they also form a unique visual identity for the city. They are embodiments of the daily routines and daily visual experiences of Hong Kong's inhabitants, shaping the unconscious of the city. In Dung Kai Cheung's 董啟章 2021 novel, *Hoenggongzi: cidou jatbaangsapnin dik cingsyu 香港字：遲到一百五十年的情書* (*The Hong Kong Type: A Love Letter that is one hundred and fifty years late*), letters not only form the backdrop to the Hong Kong story, they are intrinsic to the creation of Hong Kong itself.[34] Dung said his novel was inspired by the 2020–2021 exhibition at the Hong Kong Heritage Museum on Hong Kong Type mentioned above. According to the Museum's description:

> The exhibition goes back to the beginning of the 19th century, when Robert Morrison left the UK and came to China as a missionary, where he led the development of letterpress printing in modern China. In those days, the 'Ming typeface' designed by Anglo-Chinese College was known as the 'Hong Kong Type'...considered to be the most beautiful Chinese type. It was sold overseas and was used in *The Chinese Classics,* translated by James Legge, the *English and Chinese Dictionary*, with the Punti [Cantonese] and Mandarin Pronunciation, compiled by Wilhelm Lobscheid, the *Universal Circulating Herald*, founded by Wang Tao, and *The Self Edu*cator, written by Johnson Sun to help Chinese labourers working in Australia learn English.[35]

However, Dung's work is more than just a historical novel. Dung believes that the act of writing is a connection between the material and the semiotic, through which, a new reality can be created. In this sense, Dung believes that being a "Hong Kong writer" is more than engaging in producing something "made in Hong Kong (*Hoenggong zaizou* 香港製造)." It is a mode of production that results in the "making of Hong Kong" (*zaizou Hoenggong* 製造香港).[36] Dung's *Hong Kong Letters* is as such not about recording the history of Hong Kong, but a process of self-creation, as well as creating Hong Kong. Writing about Dung's method, Li explains,

> In this process, the writer engages in a circular mode of creation, of constantly creating and being created by Hong Kong. This implies an interactive and mutually dependent relationship between the writer and Hong Kong and highlights the impact on the formation of the writer's self-identity in addition to the writer's ethical responsibility towards its subject of writing. Writing Hong Kong, in this sense, is a forward-looking process that aims to imagine possible Hong Kongs formed through the dynamic relationship between human and things, self and others.[37]

Dung's novel tells the story of the different people surrounding the creation and use of Hong Kong Type through a century and a half, ending in contemporary Hong Kong. The making of Hong Kong Type began in the early nineteenth century by missionaries at the Ying Wah College 英華書院 (Anglo-Chinese College) in Malacca. It was completed in Hong Kong when the mission and the college moved there in 1843. The story of these letters that started at the beginning of Hong Kong's colonial days parallels that of the city. The creation of Hong Kong Type also created Hong Kong, literally and symbolically.

The whole novel is composed of three different segments. One section of the work explores the development of the Hong Kong Type and its association with the Hong Kong-based missionary work in Asia in the 1800s. The second is the story of Daai Fuk, an apprentice at the Hong Kong Ying Wah College printing house in the early twentieth century, and his relationship with Hang Ji, a mixed-race prostitute. The third segment is the story of the twenty-first century protagonist, San Fai, Hang Ji's great-granddaughter, whose experience bookends the novel. It is implied in the novel that San Fai suffers from the effects of the 2019 protests. It is her attempt to understand and process the pain in the aftermath of the protest that leads her to explore the history of Hong Kong Type and by extension, Hong Kong's and her family's stories. The three different stories in the novel are all strains of the same history, from the city's beginning as a British port and colony to the present.

The diverse cast of characters weaving through the early history of the city is typical of a colonial port city. It includes British missionaries, British "China hands," Chinese intellectuals, exiles, rebels, merchants, local Christians, and the ubiquitous underclass—local hoodlums and prostitutes. The complicated intersections among all these characters reflect the story of Hong Kong's unique position in the space between two great empires. This small space, both fictional and actual, was crowded with well-known figures of modern Chinese history: James Legge, the Scottish missionary, sinologist, and renowned translator of the Chinese *Four Classics* into English. He was also the director of Ying Wah College in Hong Kong. Legge was initially sympathetic to the Taiping Rebellion (1850–1864), as were most Western missionaries. He was also a personal friend of Hong Rengan, an important leader of the Taiping, who also makes an appearance in the novel, working at the mission for a period of time, helping Legge with his translations. Wang Tao is also in the mix. The Chinese literatus and translator, and the first publisher of a Chinese language newspaper, was an exile from the Qing, who took shelter at Legge's Ying Wah College. He also worked with Legge on the translations of the Classics. Linking together all these well-known historical personalities is the fictional character, Daai Fuk, the apprentice printer. At one point in this narrative, he is to deliver a set of the Hong Kong Type letters to Hong Rengan who has returned to China to rejoin the Taiping Rebellion. Hong requests a set of the moveable typeletters for printing their religious materials. However, as they become overwhelmed by the Qing forces, and are running out of ammunition, the lead letters are melted down to be made into bullets instead, a fitting symbol of humanity's descent into barbarity and destruction.

In the story, when he is told the letters he made are to be melted, with great sorrow, Daai Fuk asks to keep a few of them. These letters are then passed down through the family and finally end up in San Fai's possession, the main character in the contemporary segment of this tale. San Fai, whose name literally means "morning ray," is Daai Fuk's great-granddaughter. However, despite her inheritance, she is not a blood relation to Daai Fuk. Her great-grandmother, Hang Ji, never married Daai Fuk, and Hang Ji's son, Daai Dak is not of Daai Fuk's issue.

The women in this novel, San Fai's great-great-grandmother, great-grandmother, and mother, are all tragic characters; San Fai almost becomes one too. We are introduced to her during her failed attempt to jump from a building, seemingly a direct reference to the several suicides during the Anti-Legislation protest, in particular, that of a 21-year-old woman who jumped from an apartment building on June 29, 2019, after scribbling on a wall, "Hongkongers, we've protested for a long time, but we shouldn't forget our faith. We must keep going."[38] While San Fai tries to adjust to normal life after being released from psychiatric care, she keeps seeing a woman at a window in the building across from her bedroom and hearing her wailing in distress at night. One day, she sees the woman jump. (The reader later discovers that San Fai is given to hallucinations.)

On one level, San Fai's story is about her attempt to recover her bearings and sense of place in society. On another, it is about taking hold of the power to tell one's own story, to self-create, even if one has to start *ex nihilo* through fiction. She is introduced by an old high school art teacher to work as a researcher for an exhibition on the history of Hong Kong Type (the fictionalized version of the actual exhibition at the Hong Kong Heritage Museum). During her work, she begins to be visited by the "Letter Spirits (*zi ling*字靈)." They narrate to her the history of Hong Kong Type and urge her to seek the spirit of her ancestors to tell her the history of her family as printers.

In San Fai's exploration of her family's story, she discovers a lineage of female suffering and suicides. Hang Ji, her great-grandmother, is a prostitute in Shek Tong Tsui, Hong Kong's red-light district at the time. A product of the rape of a local woman by a British sailor, Hang Ji, and her mother are treated with contempt by the local community. Her mother eventually commits suicide. Hang Ji's tragedy does not end there. She is raped by her adopted father and sold into prostitution. Daai Fuk notices her when she briefly goes to the mission school he is attending. After she becomes a prostitute, Daai Fuk keeps visiting her, bringing her Christian tracts printed in Hong Kong Type from his own hands, to try to "save her soul," while promising he will raise money to redeem her freedom. Even though Daai Fuk loves her and wants to help, he exerts another kind of violence on her. By insisting she can only be saved if she accepts his religion, he ultimately blames her inability to extricate herself from the conditions of her life on her own sinfulness and weakness. Hang Ji finally kills herself from despair, leaving behind her newborn. Daai Fuk adopts the baby, raising him as his own. This baby, Daai Dak, becomes San Fai's grandfather.

San Fai's mother, the daughter of Hang Ji's son, Daai Dak, also commits suicide when San Fai is a small child. After San Fai's own failed suicide attempt, she assumes she has inherited mental illness from her matriline. She only later discovers that her mother is raped as a child by her mother's father, Daai Dak. Her maternal great-great-grandmother, great-grandmother, and mother all had their personhoods and stories curtailed by men. Her inheritance is not one of mental illness but of male violence.

If it is religious and patriarchal violence that leads to the death of all these women, in the twenty-first century, violence continues in another combination as shown by San Fai's own attempted suicide—patriarchal power consolidated in another form. Hong Kong people, with typical gallows humor, referred to the Beijing government as the patriarch (阿爺 *aa ye*, grandfather) who must be obeyed, as Beijing insists Hong Kong people love China as their *zougwok* 祖國 (fatherland). The nature of power is different, but no less brutal. However, unlike the previous generations who only had access to writings printed for them by men in positions of authority, San Fai is in possession of Hong Kong letters herself. San Fai can write her own story.

Because of its colonial history, Hong Kong often occupies a position of submissiveness in historical narratives, without the ability to determine its own fate. As with the character, Hang Ji, Hong Kong's early history is frequently represented in popular fiction and culture by a tragic mixed-race character, often a woman, and often a prostitute, to symbolize the city's racial and cultural impurities and position of subjugation. While Dung repeats some of these tropes, his protagonist, San Fai, is an interrogator of this history. Confronted by an equally overwhelming patriarchal power, her story almost ends, as did all her female ancestors, by suicide. However, despite this vicious genealogy, she is able to extricate herself from its trajectory, bringing her story to a different resolution. As the "Letter Spirits" show her, history is words, and whoever has possession of words determines the story. As her inheritance, San Fai is given literal words. With these, she can reassemble and create her story. Rather than ending with death, her suicide attempt opens the narrative.

San Fai realizes that she can communicate with the "Letter Spirits" when she is researching the history of Hong Kong Type for the exhibition. These "spirits" appear on her computer screen to tell their history. At the end of their story, the "spirits" tell her that the "patriarch's spirit" will appear to tell his story. San Fai reports to her "spiritual therapist," Na Mei, this prediction (the readers discover at the end she too is a product of San Fai's imagination):

> [Na mei:] You are looking for your real father.
>
> I thought I wanted to look for mothers instead.[39]
>
> No. Even though your mother was taken from you, there is no need for you to look for her, because she is in your own body. Mothers and daughters are of one body and will not be separated. This is the special nature of mothers. On the contrary, the nature of fathers is independent and fragmenting, but at the same time, it is possessive and controlling. What you are looking for is the father, who is both external to you and is your root....
>
> Will the "Letter spirits" help me find this father?
>
> Na Mei nodded without hesitation and said: They will guide you.
>
> So, I can follow them without fear, and without stopping?
>
> Don't worry, they are gentle spirits and will bring you no harm. However, you must be careful about this hidden father. Every father has a dangerous and terrifying aspect. When you challenge his authority, he will use violence without compunction. In myths, there are quite a number of fathers who eat their children. However, there is almost no mother who would hurt hers, unless we trace it all the way to the times before male and female were differentiated.
>
> In that case, how will I be able to find this father?

> Through stories. Construct a connection with the father through them. You need to create your own story and write it down. It all depends on how you write it. I cannot guarantee the outcome, but I will be helping you as much as I can from this side.
>
> You mean I should write fiction?
>
> No. Not fiction. Of course, you can call it fiction. Create your own story, including the real and the fabulous, things you have experienced and imagined. The main point is your soul. The soul is the story. It is through the soul that stories exist, through stories that souls exist. The two repel each other yet complement each other. To heal your soul, this is the only way.
>
> To resolve the story?
>
> Yes, and to resolve issues through stories.[40]

The Letter Spirits point out that one's connection with the past is through stories. However, one's history is not an essential truth; it is, rather, created. When interviewed about his novel, Dung pointed out, "Actually, we all need to weave our own myths. Myths are not only established in ancient times. As a community, we can also create myths. The perspective in the created myths is more relevant than those from ancestral roots."[41] Dung argues that Hong Kong literature is not "root-seeking." Instead, writers are "makers of Hong Kong," who "shape the future of Hong Kong through imagining possible realities outside the limitation of current conditions."[42] In San Fai's terms, it is not the patriarch that determines her story, but it is in her telling of the story that she creates her patriarch. In so far as San Fai's family history corresponds to the history of Hong Kong Type, which in turn encapsulates the history of the city, her construction of her personal history is also a process of creating Hong Kong's history.

In Na Mei's explanation, while the so-called patriarch is the "root," it is not essential to San Fai's story. It is from San Fai's telling of her story that she creates this "father." From one perspective, without Hong Kong Type, the story of the world might have been very different—the relationship between the city and the missionary world, its relationship to the Taiping Rebellion, and its importance in modern Chinese printing, modern world culture would not have been the same. Without Hong Kong's story, its effect on China's culture through Hong Kong Type, and without the role Hong Kong played in Great Britain's trade and commerce in Asia in the nineteenth century, including the opium trade, the political alignment of the contemporary world would not have been the same. China's story would also not have been the same. The story of Hong Kong is not dependent on its origin, instead, it has the power to create the story of the world.

Similarly, in San Fai's own story, while inheritance plays a part in the narrative in the form of a few letters passed on to her, bloodlines are irrelevant. The patriarch, Daai Fuk, her putative great-grandfather is not her blood relation. Her great-grandmother, Hang Ji, is both British and Chinese, and is rejected by both. The few letters of Hong Kong Type passed on to San Fai as her great-grandfather's legacy remind her that she has the ability to arrange words into stories. History is her own creation. In other words, history is a constant creation of the present, not a condition of the past. Rather than letting the notion of the city's lineage dictate her story, San Fai, as an individual, has the power to create Hong Kong's story.

Dung explained that a place is not a historical fact, but is created through stories:

> We can say there is a point when the city is 'founded'—out of a void. If the British had not chosen this barren southern island, practically unknown to the Qing authorities in 1841, I am pretty certain there would never have been a city called Hong Kong, nor a city in the likeness of the Hong Kong that we have over the past two centuries and in the centuries to come. In this sense, Hong Kong has been created out of nothing and that is what I mean by the word 'fiction.' This statement is made against one of the prevailing views, propagated before 1997 and after, that Hong Kong has a history of 6000 years (the number is constantly increasing--whenever a relic from some prehistoric era is unearthed in the territory), which is meant to 'prove' that Hong Kong has always been a part of the Chinese civilisation. I find this form of proving Hong Kong's Chinese roots dubious at best...The fictitious or created nature of Hong Kong has its advantages. It has made this city wonderfully open to change and innovation. It is mirrored in the creativity of its people. Ironically, this advantage has been on the decline since the return of Hong Kong to China, a historical event which was supposed to have ended the city's rootlessness.[43]

As San Fai attempts to find the "root" of her being, she discovers that the conditions of her maternal history are not essential to her own. She is not inevitably connected to her inheritance of suicides. The trajectory of her story is not from the past. In the same way, at the root of the story of Hong Kong, there is no essential truth. The city is a mythology that is continuously being generated, following a trajectory determined, not by its putative origin but by the ongoing actions and imagination of the inhabitants. In this sense, what's important in the writing of history is not the roots, but the branches. The present creates the beginning, which generates the future.

The Hong Kong government's efforts to "tell the Hong Kong story well," to align it with the fatherland, resulted in a slew of strategies of omissions, erasures, suppressions, censorship, and re-naming. However, in Dung's description, words have their own "spirits." One can determine the narrative direction, even forbid the use of certain words. One can assert patrimonial, thus self-justified power and authority over others. However, the branch often defies the root, traveling in directions that are often unexpected and unprescribed, ultimately controlling the nature of the plant itself. One can suppress elements of a story, but it will simply be recreated in some other form, in some other way. The Hong Kong story, as well as the city, is created, not through edicts, but through the collective imagination of the residents.

## Notes

1 www.facebook.com/carrielam.hksar
2 "Tell the Hong Kong Story Well講好香港故事," April 22, 2022, www.johnlee2022.hk.
3 Hong Kong Government press release, November 5, 2021, www.info.gov.hk/gia/general/202111/05/P2021110500240.htm.
4 Kiwi Chow had previously participated in directing the controversial 2015 film, *Ten Years*, an anthology of different stories that capture the growing anxiety about the future of Hong Kong under increasing Chinese control over the city. The film won the "Film of Merit' award and the "Best Picture" award at the 2016 Hong Kong Film Critic's Choice the Hong Kong Film Award but infuriated the Hong Kong pro-Beijing politicians and was banned in China.
5 Lo Wai-Kwok 盧偉國, "傳媒應激濁揚清 致力說好香港故事 (The media should eliminate the turbid and uphold the pure, aiming at telling the Hong Kong well)," *Wen Wei Po*, June 17, 2022, www.wenweipo.com/a/202206/17/AP62ab957ee4b033218a5282de.html.
6 Regina Ip, "Hong Kong has a PR problem – time to put an expert in charge of its information dep't," *Hong Kong Free Press*, May 18, 2022, https://hongkongfp.com/2022/05/18/hong-kong-has-a-pr-problem-time-to-put-an-expert-in-charge-of-its-information-dept/.
7 Jim Waterson, "Hong Kong government hires London PR firm to improve image," *The Guardian*, June 2, 2020, https://amp.theguardian.com/world/2020/jun/30/hong-kong-government-hires-london-pr-firm-to-improve-image.
8 Regina Ip, "Relaunching Hong Kong: Let the facts speak for themselves," Hong Kong Free Press, August 31, 2021, https://hongkongfp.com/2021/08/31/relaunching-hong-kong-let-the-facts-speak-for-themselves/.
9 Chris Lau, "Hong Kong spent US$5.7 million on PR campaign to improve city's image worldwide, lawmakers say it stated the obvious," *South China Morning Post*, September 1, 2021, www.scmp.com/news/hong-kong/politics/article/3147202/hong-kong-spent-us57-million-pr-campaign-improve-citys.
10 Xiao Ping, "Why was Hong Kong not a colony of Britain before 1997?" *China Daily*, April 10, 2020, www.chinadailyhk.com/hk/article/205437.
11 Chen Qingqing and Bai Yunyi, "Exclusive: Including 'HK never been a colony' in textbooks corrects flawed thinking," *Global Times*, June 17, 2022, www.globaltimes.cn/page/202206/1268370.shtml.
12 Hung Ho-Fung, *City on the Edge*, *Hong Kong Under Chinese Rule* (UK, Cambridge University Press, 2022), 131.
13 "Population by-Census Results," Hong Kong Census and Statistics Department, www.bycensus2016.gov.hk/en/bc-mt.html.
14 For example, Chan Chi Kit and Anthony Fung Ying Him, "Disarticulation between Civic Values and Nationalism," *China Perspectives* 3 (2018): 41–50, https://doi.org/10.4000/chinaperspectives.8106. Chan and Fung argue that the majority of Hong Kong people considered civic values, such as individual rights and freedoms, as more vital factors in the Hong Kong identity.
15 Carrie Lam, "2020 Policy Address Speech (Chinese version)," November 25, 2020, www.info.gov.hk/gia/general/202011/25/P2020112500153.htm.
16 Cannix Yau and Ng Kang-Chung, "Hong Kong leader rejects calls for financial aid for struggling Jumbo Floating Restaurant, with iconic attraction set to exit city in weeks,"

*South China Morning Post*, May 30, 2022, www.scmp.com/news/hong-kong/society/article/3179772/iconic-jumbo-floating-restaurant-may-leave-hong-kong-weeks.

17 Ibid.

18 Chloe Lai, "Hong Kong's reluctance to keep Jumbo floating restaurant afloat exposes laws in govt led-gentrification scheme," Hong Kong Free Press, June 12, 2022, https://hongkongfp.com/2022/06/12/hong-kongs-reluctance-to-keep-jumbo-floating-restaurant-afloat-exposes-flaws-in-govt-led-gentrification-scheme/.

19 Tong Man-Si 湯文詩, "海鮮舫駛離港「躍動港島南」剩什麼？ The floating restaurant is leaving Hong Kong. What is left of the "Invigorating Island South" plan?" *HK01*, May 31, 2022, www.hk01.com/ 01觀點/776191/海鮮舫駛離港-躍動港島南-剩什麼.

20 Ibid.

21 Ibid.

22 For a discussion of the relationship between histroical preservation, collective memory, and the construction of local identity and sense of citizenship, see Janet Ng, *Paradigm City: Space, Culture, and Capitalism in Hong Kong* (New York, SUNY, 2009), 53–55.

23 John Hanzhang Ye, "Jumbo Floating Restaurant saga another sign of Hong Kong's inability to preserve its contemporary history," *South China Morning Post*, June 10, 2022, www.scmp.com/comment/opinion/article/3180894/jumbo-floating-restaurant-saga-another-sign-hong-kongs-inability.

24 Yew Chiew Ping and Kwong Kin-ming, "Hong Kong Identity on the Rise," *Asian Survey* 54, no. 6 (2014):1088–1112: 1095–1096.

25 Peter Lee, "Highest number of Hong Kong adults identify as 'Chinese' since 2018, survey finds," Hong Kong Free Press, June 22, 2022, https://hongkongfp.com/2022/06/22/highest-number-of-hong-kong-adults-identify-as-chinese-since-2018-survey-finds/.

26 Ibid.

27 Ibid.

28 "Ethnic identity of being Chinese," Hong Kong Public Opinion Research Institute, December 14, 2021, www.pori.hk/pop-poll/ethnic-identity-en/q003.html?lang=en.

29 Siu Tin 小田, "聲生不息 的 愛國港樂： 停在懷舊的風裏 和真實的香港越走越遠 (The patriotic Hong Kong music of 'Infinity and Beyond'—arrested in nostalgia, going farther and farther away from the real Hong Kong)," May 20, 2022, *The Initium*, https://theinitium.com/article/20220528-opinion-hk-music-in-china-narrative.

30 "CE welcomes promulgation of Outline Development Plan for Guangdong-Hong Kong-Macao Greater Bay Area," The Government of Hong Kong Special Administrative Region Press Releases, February 18, 2019, www.info.gov.hk/gia/general/201902/18/P2019021800825.htm.

31 Siu Tin 小田.

32 Chung Li-Hua and William Hetherington, "Taiwanese artists in China must sign pledge," *The Taipei Times*, May 6, 2020, www.taipeitimes.com/News/front/archives/2020/05/06/2003735904.

33 The study and preservation of the Prison Gothic Type is primarily carried out by the Road Research Society 道路研究社 (www.road.org.hk). Through crowd funding, the society has generated a set of new computer font based on the Prison Gothic Type.

34 See Chapters 3 and 4 on Dung Kai Cheung. 董啟章Dung Kai Cheung, *Heonggong Zi: ci dou jat baak nin dik cing syu 香港字：遲到一百五十年的情書* (The Hong Kong Type: A Love Letter that is One Hundred and Fifty Years Late, Hong Kong, 新經典文化 New Classic Culture Publishing, 2021).

35 "Between the Lines—The Legends of Hong Kong Printing," The Hong Kong Heritage Museum, accessed July 19, 2022, www.heritagemuseum.gov.hk.

36 Fang-Yu Li, "The role of the writer and the making of Hong Kong in Dung Kai-cheung's the history of the adventures of Vivi and Vera," *Rocky Mountain Review* 76, no. 1 (2022): 117–133: 127, https://doi.org/10.1353/rmr.2022.0006.

37 Ibid.

38 Lily Kuo, "'Society is suffering': Hong Kong protests spark mental health crisis," *The Guardian*, October 22, 2019, www.theguardian.com/society/2019/oct/22/society-is-suffering-hong-kong-protests-spark-mental-health-crisis.

39 San Fai had always known that her grandfather Daai Dak was adopted but did not know who her great grandmother was. Daai Fuk and Hang Ji's relationship had not been revealed to her at that point.

40 Dung, *Hong Kong Letters*, 111–112.

41 Jip Cau-jyun 葉秋弦, "生死榮枯，在斷裂的靈魂中找尋意義——董啟章《香港字》(Life, death, withering blossoming, finding meaning in souls that have been torn apart—Dung Kai Cheung's *Hong Kong Letters*)," *P-articles*, December 19, 2021, https://p-articles.com/works/2629.html.

42 Quoted in Li, Fang-yu, 127–128.

43 Quoted from Mike Ingham and Christopher Mattison, "History is Now," *Journal of the Royal Asiatic Society Hong Kong Branch* 59 (2019): 214–230: 222, www.jstor.org/stable/26937838.

## References

"Between the Lines—The Legends of Hong Kong Printing." The Hong Kong Heritage Museum. Accessed July 19, 2022. www.heritagemuseum.gov.hk.

"CE welcomes promulgation of Outline Development Plan for Guangdong-Hong Kong-Macao Greater Bay Area." The Government of Hong Kong Special Administrative Region Press Releases, February 18, 2019. www.info.gov.hk/gia/general/201902/18/P2019021800825.htm.

Chan Chi Kit and Anthony Fung Ying Him. "Disarticulation between civic values and nationalism." *China Perspectives* 3 (2018): 41–50. https://doi.org/10.4000/chinaperspectives.8106. Chan and Fung argue that the majority of Hong Kong people considered civic values, such as individual rights and freedoms, as more vital factors in the Hong Kong identity.

Chen Qingqing and Bai Yunyi. "Exclusive: Including 'HK never been a colony' in textbooks corrects flawed thinking." *Global Times*, June 17, 2022. www.globaltimes.cn/page/202206/1268370.shtml.

Chung Li-hua and William Hetherington. "Taiwanese artists in China must sign pledge." *The Taipei Times*, May 6, 2020. www.taipeitimes.com/News/front/archives/2020/05/06/2003735904.

Dung Kai Cheung, 董啟. *Heonggong Zi: ci dou jat baak nin dik cing syu 香港字：遲到一百五十年的情書* (The Hong Kong Type: A Love Letter that is One Hundred and Fifty Years Late). Hong Kong: 新經典文化 New Classic Culture Publishing, 2021.

"Ethnic identity of being Chinese." Hong Kong Public Opinion Research Institute, December 14, 2021. www.pori.hk/pop-poll/ethnic-identity-en/q003.html?lang=en.

Hung Ho-Fung, *City on the Edge: Hong Kong Under Chinese Rule*. UK: Cambridge University Press, 2022.

Ingham, Mike and Christopher Mattison. "History is now." *Journal of the Royal Asiatic Society Hong Kong Branch* 59 (2019): 214–230: 222. www.jstor.org/stable/26937838.

Ip, Regina. "Relaunching Hong Kong: Let the facts speak for themselves." Hong Kong Free Press. August 31, 2021. https://hongkongfp.com/2021/08/31/relaunching-hong-kong-let-the-facts-speak-for-themselves/.

Ip, Regina. "Hong Kong has a PR problem – time to put an expert in charge of its information dep't." Hong Kong Free Press, May 18, 2022. https://hongkongfp.com/2022/05/18/hong-kong-has-a-pr-problem-time-to-put-an-expert-in-charge-of-its-information-dept/.

Jip Cau-Jyun 葉秋弦. "生死榮枯，在斷裂的靈魂中找尋意義——董啟章《香港字》(Life, death, withering blossoming, finding meaning in souls that have been torn apart--Dung Kai Cheung's *Hong Kong Letters*)." *P-articles*, December 19, 2021. https://p-articles.com/works/2629.html.

Kuo, Lily. "'Society is suffering': Hong Kong protests spark mental health crisis." *The Guardian*, October 22, 2019. www.theguardian.com/society/2019/oct/22/society-is-suffering-hong-kong-protests-spark-mental-health-crisis.

Lai, Chloe. "Hong Kong's reluctance to keep Jumbo floating restaurant afloat exposes laws in govt led-gentrification scheme." Hong Kong Free Press, June 12, 2022. https://hongkongfp.com/2022/06/12/hong-kongs-reluctance-to-keep-jumbo-floating-restaurant-afloat-exposes-flaws-in-govt-led-gentrification-scheme/

Lam, Carrie. 2020 Policy Address Speech (Chinese version). November 25, 2020. www.info.gov.hk/gia/general/202011/25/P2020112500153.htm.

Lau, Chris. "Hong Kong spent US$5.7 million on PR campaign to improve city's image worldwide, lawmakers say it stated the obvious." *South China Morning Post*, September 1, 2021. www.scmp.com/news/hong-kong/politics/article/3147202/hong-kong-spent-us57-million-pr-campaign-improve-citys.

Lee, Peter. "Highest number of Hong Kong adults identify as 'Chinese' since 2018, survey finds." Hong Kong Free Press, June 22, 2022. https://hongkongfp.com/2022/06/22/highest-number-of-hong-kong-adults-identify-as-chinese-since-2018-survey-finds/.

Li, Fang-Yu. "The role of the writer and the making of Hong Kong in Dung Kai-cheung's the history of the adventures of Vivi and Vera." *Rocky Mountain Review* 76, no. 1 (2022): 117–133: 127. https://doi.org/10.1353/rmr.2022.0006.

Lo Wai-Kwok 盧偉國. "傳媒應激濁揚清 致力說好香港故事 (The media should eliminate the turbid and uphold the pure, aiming at telling the Hong Kong well)." *Wen Wei Po*, June 17, 2022. www.wenweipo.com/a/202206/17/AP62ab957ee4b033218a5282de.html.

Ng, Janet. *Paradigm City: Space, Culture, and Capitalism in Hong Kong*. New York: SUNY, 2009.

"Population by-Census Results." Hong Kong Census and Statistics Department. www.bycensus2016.gov.hk/en/bc-mt.html.

Siu Tin 小田. "聲生不息 的 愛國港樂： 停在懷舊的風裏 和真實的香港越走越遠 (The patriotic Hong Kong music of 'Infinity and Beyond'—arrested in nostalgia, going farther and farther away from the real Hong Kong)." *The Initium*, May 20, 2022. https://theinitium.com/article/20220528-opinion-hk-music-in-china-narrative.

"Tell the Hong Kong Story Well講好香港故事." April 22, 2022. www.johnlee2022.hk.

Tong Man-Si 湯文詩. "海鮮舫駛離港「躍動港島南」剩什麼？ The floating restaurant is leaving Hong Kong. What is left of the "Invigorating Island South" plan?" *HK01*, May 31, 2022. www.hk01.com/ 01觀點/776191/海鮮舫駛離港-躍動港島南-剩什麼.

Waterson, Jim. "Hong Kong government hires London PR firm to improve image." *The Guardian*, June 2, 2020. https://amp.theguardian.com/world/2020/jun/30/hong-kong-government-hires-london-pr-firm-to-improve-image.

Xiao Ping. "Why was Hong Kong not a colony of Britain before 1997?" *China Daily*, April 10, 2020, www.chinadailyhk.com/hk/article/205437.

Yau, Cannix and Ng Kang-Chung. "Hong Kong leader rejects calls for financial aid for struggling Jumbo Floating Restaurant, with iconic attraction set to exit city in weeks." *The South China Morning Post*, May 30, 2022. www.scmp.com/news/hong-kong/society/article/3179772/iconic-jumbo-floating-restaurant-may-leave-hong-kong-weeks.

Ye, John Hanzhang. "Jumbo Floating Restaurant saga another sign of Hong Kong's inability to preserve its contemporary history." *The South China Morning Post*, June 10, 2022. www.scmp.com/comment/opinion/article/3180894/jumbo-floating-restaurant-saga-another-sign-hong-kongs-inability.

Yew Chiew, Ping and Kwong Kin-Ming. "Hong Kong identity on the rise." *Asian Survey* 54, no. 6 (2014):1088–1112: 1095–1096.

# Coda

## *Hai gam sin laa* 係咁先啦 That's It for Now

The rap song from MC $oho and Kidney, *Haigamsin laa* 係咁先啦 (That's it for now), was the theme song of 2021. It went viral in Hong Kong and was named one of the ten songs of the year at the Commercial Radio's Ultimate Song Chart Awards. It was sung at farewell dinners and was heard at the airport where many sent off their emigrating friends and families. The catchy chorus of the song contains probably the most well-known and oft-repeat lines of the year:

> I'm going now. That's it for now. We'll play together again next time. Goodbye! That's it for now. Until next time. I'm going now. That's it for now. We'll get together next time. Goodbye! Until next time—If there's a next time.[1]

Hong Kong's residents have experienced many losses since the beginning of the 2020s. Many of the iconic places, institutions, and structures that had defined the character of the city contributed to the cityscape and even structured the customs and everyday life there, disappeared. Community associations, popular media, and century-old businesses, from tofu makers, Hong Kong-style bakeries, and cafeterias, to famous restaurants, shuttered one after another. Some were forced to close down because of the draconian NSL. Some succumbed to the economic hardships brought on by COVID restrictions and continuing brutal urban renewal programs. Some of these had been important historical and social symbols of the city. As with the neon signs discussed in Chapter 8, some had played important roles in Hong Kong's visual identity. Some businesses were stalwarts of neighborhoods and communities. Opened in 1928, Jimmy's Kitchen that served "British" cuisine, for example, was an important part of Hong Kong's colonial culture and society. The 104-year-old 蓮香樓Lin Heung Tea House, a dim-sum restaurant and Chinese bakery that moved from Guangzhou to Hong Kong in 1927, told a typical story of how refugees from China's various wars and political unrest in the twentieth century created the city. (Both have been unexpectedly resurrected in 2024.) Less venerable, but equally storied were the floating Jumbo Seafood Restaurant also mentioned in Chapter 8, and the many neighborhood Hong Kong-style cafés, immortalized in Hong Kong's cinema.

DOI: 10.4324/9781003521280-10

By the end of 2022, the Hong Kong government revealed that the city's total population had dropped 2%, from 7.34 million in 2021 to about 7.19 million. Many Hongkongers emigrated from the city, unable or unwilling to live under Hong Kong's new political environment. Many with children left to avoid the NSL-inspired education reforms. By the end of 2022, a total of 11,403 people had died from COVID infections.[2] The deaths of several well-known residents of the city, writers, actors, musicians, and directors, who had contributed much to the shaping of Hong Kong's culture, added to a general sense that the city had come to the end of an era.

Among the seemingly continuous daily losses in the city was the death of the giant panda, On On 安安 at Ocean Park. The aged panda had been showing signs of rapid decline before he was humanely euthanized on July 21, 2022. The same month a new Chief Executive, John Lee, was "elected," and one month after Hong Kong lost Jumbo, the floating restaurant. On On's death was widely mourned. Many went on Ocean Park's social media to express their sadness. Many more made special trips to On On's enclosure in Ocean Park to leave flowers and notes to express their gratitude to him for having spent his life accompanying Hong Kong people on their difficult journey. On On was there at the beginning of Hongkongers' struggles for democracy when he first came to the city and witnessed their ultimate defeat at the end of his life.

On On was a gift from China in 1999 together with Gaai Gaai 佳佳, a female panda, to mark the 50th anniversary of the establishment of the People's Republic of China and to commemorate Hong Kong's "Return" to China in 1997 and Macao's in 1999. Furthermore, it was also to celebrate the actualization of the policy of "One Country Two Systems" in the city. The names of the pandas, On On and Gaai Gaai, according to the former Chief Executive, Tung Chi-Wah, in a speech welcoming the two new permanent residents to Hong Kong, were short for "***On*** *ding faan wing* 安定繁榮, *dit cong* ***gaai*** *zik*迭創佳績," meaning, "**stability** and prosperity and continuous **good** accomplishments."[3]

Gaai Gaai died in 2016, the same year as the "Fishball Revolution," the first violent political protest in the city since 1967. If Gaai Gaai's death was the beginning of the end, then On On's in 2022 seemed to signal a resolute finale. While Hong Kong people genuinely adored their two giant pandas, the sadness they expressed, especially the death of On On, signaled something far more trenchant. The pandas arrived at the beginning of Hong Kong's historic journey as China's Special Administrative Region, with the promise of local autonomy, judicial independence, and continuation of the rights and freedoms Hong Kong people enjoyed under the British colonial government. Their deaths coincided with the breaking of all these promises and the end of Hong Kong people's dream of democracy.

Many Hong Kong people thought the 1980s and early 1990s were the city's golden years. The society was affluent. The entertainment industry was in full bloom. Cantopop ruled Asia. Hong Kong's movies were seen around the world. The city's directors and actors were frequently lauded in international film festivals. In the new NSL era, there was constant nostalgia for this past. Unspoken is the fact that Hong Kong's golden age happened under the British, and all things good seemed to have departed with the British in 1997. In 2019, few were surprised to see Union Jacks or the Hong Kong colonial flags fluttering in the fiery tear-gas-enshrouded streets during the mass protest.

The death of the British monarch, Elizabeth II, on September 8, 2022, provoked another outpour of collective grief in Hong Kong. The Hong Kong government's continued COVID restrictions in the city and the effects of the draconian NSL only served to make Hongkongers more nostalgic for the seemingly halcyon days of the colony's last decades under the queen. As the actor and Cantonese opera star, Law Kar-ying 羅家英, noted in his encomium to the Queen on his social media, "Hong Kong was a blessed land under her protection." The post was accompanied by a photo of the long queue of people outside Hong Kong's British Embassy, waiting in the relentless sun and heat for up to 4 hours to leave flowers and messages in memory of the queen. For this post, Law was relentlessly attacked by the "Little Pinks," China's patriotic internet army. The Chinese government mouthpiece, the newspaper, *Ta Gong Pao*, predictably accused those who mourned the queen of being "anti-Chinese elements" and for "whitewashing colonial rule" (forgetting, perhaps, that the new Hong Kong government and Beijing had insisted that Hong Kong was never a British colony). Law ended up deleting his post and issuing an apology. Nevertheless, what he said reflected a general sentiment among the Hong Kong public. In the week the queen's death was announced, over 6700 Hongkongers had signed the condolence book at the embassy. The queen's death severed the last real and imagined connection Hong Kong had with Great Britain. It ended the fantasy of the possibility of a return to the free and prosperous days of the last century.

Mourning for all that was gone and the irreversible effects of time on the city, the band, Yellow! 野佬,issued the song, "*Kong joengfaa zouhap* 抗氧化組合 The Antioxi Group," with lyrics by Leung Pak Kin 梁栢堅:

> Jumbo has become history; its golden walls have lost their luster.
> We've lost track of the queen; she went to heaven today.
> Even the pearl in her golden crown has faded.[4]
> The petals of the lotus are scattered;[5] it is no longer fragrant.
> The author, Ngai Hong[6], is also gone, returned to the galaxy.
> If only there is a way to really fight against aging.
> ...
> Time machine—is there such a thing? If possible, can you fix this scar?
> If there's a way to stop decomposition, a way to halt oxidization, perhaps you can manage it...?[7]

## Encore

In the new reality under the NSL, Hongkongers felt they had lost many things they once cherished. However, as I have tried to show in this volume, in different areas of Hong Kong society and especially in popular culture, there were numerous signs of determination to rebuild and to continue the dream. Terrance Lam's song with

Wyman Wong's lyrics, "*Binjatgo faatmingliu* encore 邊一個發明了 ENCORE (*Who invented Encore*)?" might seem to be yet another song of farewell. However, it also reflects an unambiguous commitment to the future. Lam wrote it for his concert in 2022, and it was an instant hit when it was released in August 2022:

> There's only a little time left. Isn't shouting "encore!" a bit silly? You and I keep dragging out the end, shouting "encore!" The door is not yet locked. It is as if shouting "encore" again and again, deliberately dragging it out, everything will start again from the beginning.
>
> While your friend is still here, use this remaining energy to leave something beautiful behind. The times are vicious; there's not that much we can still defend. Humans are like tiny little ants. It is always hard to withstand the baptism of the times. But someone invented the lingering promise.
>
> Our friendship will not fade simply because of goodbyes. There will always be a secret connection between us...
>
> The white confetti filling the sky announce the end of a magical evening. If our feelings are strong, we will keep singing encore. If we can no longer extend the time, I hope we can fulfill the rest of our dreams in the future. As long as we insist on believing, we can be like this again...
>
> Who was the one to first shout, "encore!" in the world? So naïve, so silly! Strangely, tonight, the ones shouting "Encore" with so much passion, turn out to be you and me. We deeply believe by shouting "Encore," then there will be encore. Preserve this fire. Even if at this moment we have to leave our seats, there will be a future when we will be together again.[8]

By conventional logic, once things have changed, there is no turning back. However, many people in Hong Kong refused to accept the finality of things, believing rather, in the power of individuals to create their own future.

By necessity, I have only covered the 2 years after the implementation of the National Security, while Hong Kong was also under the Zero-COVID policy, from 2020 to the end of 2022. The city has gone through even more challenges, disappointments, and changes in the ensuing years. These are beyond the scope of this study. However, as all the writers, artists, lyricists, etc. have demonstrated in this volume, even when darkness seems impenetrable, life persists in unexpected and creative ways. As a graffiti artist who patiently pursues his art, facing daily erasure of his work said: "The fight for the right to speak is a contest of patience. We have not lost yet. Even now, there are still things that have not been completed yet. Until the very last moment, we have not lost yet."[9]

## Notes

1 MC $oHo and KidNey ft. Kayan9896, "係咁先啦曲 That's it for now," music by鄧東成 EAST CITY and MC $oHo, lyrics by MC $oHo, Tonemusic, 2021, www.youtube.com/watch?v=eO1L_H0_ILg.

2 "Mid-Year Population for 2022," The Government of Hong Kong Special Administrative Region Press releases, August 8, 2022, www.info.gov.hk/gia/general/202208/11/P2022081100393.htm. Provisional Data Analysis on COVID-19 Reported Death Cases from 31 Dec 2021 up till 28 Dec 2022. www.coronavirus.gov.hk/pdf/death_analysis/death_analysis_20221228.pdf. Accessed March 30, 2023.
3 "行政長官在大熊貓園開幕典禮演辭 (The Chief Executive Officer's speech at the ceremony of the opening of the Panda enclosure)," May 17, 1999, www.info.gov.hk/gia/general/199905/17/0517107.htm.
4 Hong Kong was the "Pearl of Orient."
5 This refers to the Chinese restaurant, 蓮香樓 Lin Heung Tea House mentioned earlier. The name of the restaurant literally means lotus' fragrance.
6 Ngai Hong (1935–2022) was a beloved prolific science fiction writer in Hong Kong. His works are banned in China.
7 Yellow! 野佬, "抗氧化組合Antioxi group," music by陳永康 Ahong Chan @yellow lyrics by Leung Pak Kin, 2022, www.youtube.com/watch?v=7mxcJlfGiXk.
8 Terence Lam, "邊一個發明了ENCORE (Who invented Encore)?" music by Terence Lam, lyrics by Wyman Wong, Terence Lam Production & Co. 2022. www.youtube.com/watch?v=KpZL59NqkcY&list=RDKpZL59NqkcY&start_radio=1.
9 莫坤菱 Mok Kwan Ling, "香港塗鴉新世代:「他們問我，是不是畫過自由 (Hong Kong Graffiti Generation: They asked me, is it true that you have painted freedom before)?" *The Initium*, April 24, 2024, https://theinitium.com/article/20240424-culture-graffity-hk-streets.

## References


Lam, Terence. "邊一個發明了ENCORE (Who invented Encore)?" Music by Terence Lam, lyrics by Wyman Wong, Terence Lam Production & Co. 2022.

MC $oHo and KidNey ft. Kayan9896. "係咁先啦曲 That's it for now." Music by鄧東成 EAST CITY and MC $oHo, lyrics by MC $oHo. Tonemusic, 2021.

"Mid-Year Population for 2022." The Government of Hong Kong Special Administrative Region Press Releases, August 8, 2022. www.info.gov.hk/gia/general/202208/11/P2022081100393.htm

Mok Kwan Ling莫坤菱. "香港塗鴉新世代:「他們問我,是不是畫過自由？(Hong Kong Graffiti Generation: "They asked me, is it true that you have painted freedom before?)." *The Initium*, April 24, 2024. https://theinitium.com/article/20240424-culture-graffity-hk-streets

"Provisional Data Analysis on COVID-19 Reported Death Cases from 31 Dec 2021 up till 28 Dec 2022." The Government of Hong Kong Special Administrative Region, December 28, 2022. www.coronavirus.gov.hk/pdf/death_analysis/death_analysis_20221228.pdf.

Yellow! 野佬. "抗氧化組合Antioxi group." Music by陳永康 Ahong Chan @yellow lyrics by Leung Pak Kin, 2022. www.youtube.com/watch?v=7mxcJlfGiXk

"行政長官在大熊貓園開幕典禮演辭 (The Chief Executive officer's speech at the ceremony of the opening of the Panda enclosure)." May 17, 1999. www.info.gov.hk/gia/general/199905/17/0517107.htm

# Index

9781032860893